D1582672

Th
be i
dat

Gl
Li
na

More Praise for

HOW TO CATCH A RUSSIAN SPY

'Every now and then, the safety and security of our country depends on an everyday young American doing the right thing. What sets Naveed apart is that he obviously had such a blast doing it. As amusing as it is to read this book and watch an admitted amateur get over on a Russian operative here in the United States to steal secrets, it's also sobering to contemplate how many bad actors there are waiting to take advantage of the fact that we live in an open society.'

—Frances Fragos Townsend, former Homeland Security adviser to President George W. Bush

'One early lesson I learned leading SEAL units is that it's not enough to begin with a good plan—an effective operator must adapt to fast-changing conditions and adjust the plan accordingly. Despite his lack of training, Naveed Jamali intuitively grasped that lesson, repeatedly calling on the main weapon in his amateur's arsenal—ingenuity—to deceive his opponent. In a time when our nation's enemies vigorously troll for information that will give them an edge, it's comforting to know that American resourcefulness can triumph even out of uniform.'

—Rorke Denver, *New York Times* bestselling author of *Damn Few*

'So celebrated in American pop culture are the tactics of espionage that even a motivated amateur—with a talent for improvisation and a taste for Hollywood flair—can take on a real-life Russian intelligence operative and best him at his own game. What's most charming about this page-turning account is Naveed's honesty about his missteps and the joy he takes in designing deceptions that actually work. Readers will smile right along with him.'

—Lindsay Moran, bestselling author of *Blowing My Cover: My Life as a CIA Spy*

HOW TO CATCH A RUSSIAN SPY

The True Story of an
American Civilian Turned Double Agent

NAVEED JAMALI
AND
ELLIS HENICAN

SIMON &
SCHUSTER

London · New York · Sydney · Toronto · New Delhi

A CBS COMPANY

Certain names and identifying characteristics have been changed.

All statements of fact, opinion, or analysis expressed are those of the author and do not reflect in any way the official positions or views of any U.S. Government agency. Nothing in the contents should be construed as asserting or implying U.S. Government authentication of information or endorsement of the author's views.

First published in Great Britain by Simon & Schuster UK Ltd, 2015
A CBS COMPANY

Copyright © 2015 by Naveed Jamali

This book is copyright under the Berne Convention.
No reproduction without permission.
All rights reserved.

The right of Naveed Jamali to be identified as the author
of this work has been asserted by him in accordance with sections
77 and 78 of the Copyright, Designs and Patents Act, 1988.

1 3 5 7 9 10 8 6 4 2

Simon & Schuster UK Ltd
1st Floor
222 Gray's Inn Road
London WC1X 8HB

www.simonandschuster.co.uk

Simon & Schuster Australia, Sydney
Simon & Schuster India, New Delhi

The author and publishers have made all reasonable
efforts to contact copyright-holders for permission, and apologise
for any omissions or errors in the form of credits given.
Corrections may be made to future printings.

A CIP catalogue record for this book
is available from the British Library

Hardback ISBN: 978-1-47114-088-4
TPB ISBN: 978-1-47114-089-1
Ebook ISBN: 978-1-47114-091-4

Interior design by Jill Putorti

Pri

Glasgow Life
Glasgow Libraries

SH

that is m: C 006161121   orest
Stewardsh   ation.
Our b   **Askews & Holts** | 20-Jan-2016   r.

327.1273092 /Pc | £16.99

For Casey, Toby, and Ava

CONTENTS

HOW TO
CATCH A
RUSSIAN SPY

INTRODUCTION

I gripped the wheel tightly and steered the Jeep toward the warehouse. My heart was thumping so hard I thought Oleg might be able to hear it in the passenger seat.

"You okay?" he asked in that flat, stiff English of his.

"Totally," I lied.

The air was chilly for early April, but the morning was unusually bright. The year was 2008, nearly two decades after the Berlin Wall tumbled and the Cold War was consigned to the history books. The Jeep was a black-on-black SRT8 6.1-liter Hemi V8 with 425 horsepower and all the subtlety of a cinder block through a giant plate of glass.

I'd been waiting for this day for almost two years. Ted and Terry, my FBI handlers, had been gaming it out with me for nearly six months. What would I say when Oleg asked how much money I wanted? What would I do if he pulled out a gun? Lately, things between us had grown unusually tense. The agents had done what they could to prepare me. But all along they kept telling me, "You have to be ready to think on your feet."

What the hell did that mean? Think about what?

As I eased the Jeep to a stop in front of the old brick building, Oleg was staring straight at me. I knew this was a big day for him as well. The documents I'd promised, cockpit manuals for two of the U.S. Navy's most important combat aircraft, weren't classified TOP SECRET. But you couldn't just buy them on Amazon or eBay. These were the technical operating procedures that American pilots relied on in Iraq and Afghanistan. These two fat, blue three-ring binders told you everything you needed to know in the pilot's seat.

A handoff like this one, I knew, would inspire Oleg's Russian imagination. But it would do more than that. It would help convince his bureaucratic superiors in Moscow that he had recruited a potentially valuable mole in New York, a well-placed American civilian capable of delivering U.S. military data. I was the kind of American asset the secret-hungry Russians searched for, someone with the motivation and the technical expertise to deliver the goods.

"We make an excellent team, you and me," Oleg said.

The binders were inside a large cardboard box in the trunk of my other car, a black Corvette Z06, which was parked inside this huge auto-storage warehouse on a quiet back street in suburban Westchester County, twenty miles north of New York City. The box was too heavy to drag into a restaurant or a coffee shop, which was where Oleg and I usually met. So he and I came up with an alternate plan. He would take the Metro-North train from Grand Central. I'd meet him at the station in Hastings-on-Hudson. The warehouse was down by the water, two blocks away.

"You could make a lot of money," Oleg said as I keyed my PIN into the security keypad outside the warehouse and the metal slats groaned up.

"What's a lot?" I asked him.

"That Corvette you are so proud of?"

"What about it?"

"You could buy ten."

I did love fast American cars.

As I pulled the Jeep inside, the warehouse was chilly and dark. But once I flipped my headlights on, I could see the rows and rows of parked vehicles. Expensive sports cars covered with monogrammed tarps. A Mustang, a Lotus, a Porsche, various Benzes and BMWs—the weekend cars of affluent city people. There was also a giant dump truck and a couple of vintage fire engines. Even in this light, I could tell the fire engines were gleaming red.

The warehouse was deathly quiet. As far as I could tell, Oleg and I were the only people around.

As I drove deeper inside, Oleg glanced left and right and then behind us. What was he expecting? A dozen FBI agents rushing the Jeep? A *spetsnaz* special-forces team from the Russian GRU? I understood why he might feel jumpy. I felt jumpy, too. "The Corvette is down this row and to the right," I said as calmly as I could. So much was on the line, for Oleg and for me, I couldn't afford to screw anything up.

Just then, a horrible squealing sound went off. I gasped, and Oleg froze. It took a second for me to realize where the alarm was coming from. For some reason, the Jeep's radar detector had gotten tripped.

I scrambled to quiet it, but the off button wasn't where I thought it should be. Damn, that thing was loud! The noise was designed to be heard over a roaring engine on the interstate with the windows open or the air conditioner on and the audio system blasting. In a closed-up Jeep at three miles an hour in a quiet suburban warehouse, that little sucker really screamed. After a couple of frantic seconds that felt like an hour and a half, I found the right button. "It's okay," I said to Oleg. "It's only my radar detector."

I wasn't sure what had made the device go crazy. Maybe my hidden recorder had set it off somehow. Maybe Oleg had something on him. I didn't know. I just didn't want anything spooking him.

"We're right up here," I said, relieved to be in silence again.

Getting my hands on the cockpit manuals wasn't nearly as difficult as I'd expected. All it took was a ride to Long Island and a couple of well-crafted lies. Ted and Terry drove me to the office of a major defense contractor and sent me inside alone. I told the friendly clerk I was a researcher with a small tech company preparing a digital database system, and I needed some test documents. The only question was what I wanted.

NATOPS, the blue binders said. *Naval Air Training and Operating Procedures Standardization.* "You wanna catch a spy, you gotta do a little spying," Terry said with a shrug as we drove back to the city that day.

Now I was about to hand them directly to Oleg, who was finally breathing steadily once more. I parked the Jeep behind the black Corvette, pulling in at a careful angle.

"Before we start," Oleg said, "can you turn off your phone, please?"

"My phone?" I answered. "Okay."

He'd never asked me to do that. I knew he was worried I was recording him with my cell phone. He was right that I was recording him, just wrong about how. So I didn't only turn the phone off. I opened my door. I quickly scanned the area, making sure no one was around. And I set the phone on the hood of a sleek black BMW M6 parked next to us.

"Better?" I asked Oleg.

"Thank you," he said.

I had passed that test.

"You wanna have a look?" I asked him. Oleg stepped out of the Jeep and stood next to me behind the Corvette. I opened the trunk. The cockpit manuals were just where I'd left them.

Oleg stared for a moment. Then he picked up the manuals, confirming that both of them were there. One was for the F-14 Tomcat fighter jet. The other was for the E-2 Hawkeye early-warning aircraft.

Oleg concentrated first on the F-14 binder. As he flipped through the pages, I glimpsed a sketch of the fighter jet's instrument panel.

I saw several schematic diagrams and other charts and graphs. There were drawings and blocks of dense gray type. Oleg stared intently, looking almost transfixed.

"You wanna sit in the Jeep and have a closer look?" I asked him.

He nodded.

I lifted the big cardboard box from the Corvette trunk and placed it on the concrete. Then I reached with my right hand to close the trunk.

I don't know what I was thinking. Obviously, I wasn't thinking at all. Or at least I wasn't paying attention to the precise location of Oleg's head.

"*Awwwww!*" he screamed.

Somehow I'd managed to slam the trunk on the back of Oleg's skull. I heard a horrible *clunk* as the metal hit bone, and then two more very loud screams. "*Owww! Eewwww!*"

It all happened so quickly, I didn't know what to think.

I knew I'd done something profoundly stupid. I had done it at the worst possible time. Just as Oleg and I were moving together from covert to operational. Just as the noose was settling around his neck. Just as I was convincing him that he could really trust me. Just as I was proving what a valuable asset I could be. We were taking this leap together into espionage—and I'd slammed the damn trunk on his head.

As I leaned over to check how badly I had hurt him, terrible thoughts were racing through my head.

I had just blown the whole operation. I had maimed a senior Russian diplomat. Certainly, he would think I was trying to kill him. It was all being recorded. Would Oleg be convinced he should never do business with the likes of me again?

For three nerve-wracking years, I spied on America for the Russians, trading thumb drives of sensitive technical data for envelopes of cash, selling out my own beloved country across noisy restaurant tables and in quiet parking lots.

Or so the Russians believed.

In fact, I was a secret double agent working closely with the FBI. The Cold War wasn't really over. It had just gone high-tech.

I had no previous experience as a counterespionage operative. Everything I knew about undercover work I'd learned from books, movies, school assignments, and *Magnum P.I.* episodes. *Ronin, Spy Game,* anything with *Bond* or *Bourne* in the title—I devoured that stuff. I was in my late twenties by then, a bright but aimless New York University graduate, working in a family business with my immigrant parents, trying to figure out what to do with my life. I had a nice apartment on the Upper West Side of Manhattan, a young wife freshly out of grad school, and a tendency to spend way too much time in front of computer screens. I'd read a bunch of books about the Cold War and the Soviet Union, and I'd seen almost every war movie ever made. But I didn't speak Russian. I never liked borscht. And the closest I'd gotten to Moscow or St. Petersburg was a medium-priced bottle of Stolichnaya from International Wine & Spirits on Broadway and 113th Street. I certainly didn't fit anyone's stereotype of a smooth double agent.

Jamali, Naveed Jamali? Don't make me laugh!

And yet there I was, at the center of a long-running counter-espionage operation that I cooked up mostly on my own (thanks to an unusual family connection), then convinced the FBI and the Russians to go along. It was proactive, not reactive—and I was the active one. Looking back, I can hardly believe I pulled it off. How I did it, why it worked, and what I learned about my country, my family, and myself—that's a story I want to tell.

By the time we were finished, we had cast a bright light on an active espionage campaign operating out of the Russian Mission to the United Nations in New York. We had suckered an experienced

Russian military-intelligence officer into trusting a young American amateur, embarrassing him and his nation. We had earned a solid American win in the escalating hostilities between Moscow and Washington. And we had helped to disprove, for those who had any doubt, the supposedly benign intentions of Russia's post–Cold War leaders, Vladimir Putin especially, who kept telling America how much they wanted to be our partners and our friends.

I apologized profusely to Oleg that day in the storage garage. "Oh my God," I said when he finally looked up. "I'm so sorry!"

He seemed dazed but alert. "Are you all right?" I asked, putting my hand on his shoulder.

"All right," he said. "I have a very hard head." Then he flashed a faint smile. "A hard head," he repeated.

It was a lame joke, in Russian or in English, but a welcome one. I was relieved that Oleg was conscious enough to deliver it. I knew right then that he and I had crossed a crucial line. Despite my squealing radar detector, my clumsy trunk slam, and my amateur's nerves, Oleg wanted me as much as much as I wanted him. Even more so. By the time we left the warehouse, I had an envelope of Oleg's cash inside my jacket pocket. I'd fed him a story he could validate from the outside. I had solidified his personal confidence.

The experienced Russian military man was convinced he could trust the young American amateur. He would not turn back. He did not want to. He was persuaded that I was for real. Oleg wasn't letting anything, including a trunk lid to his hard skull, divert the two of us from where we were headed next.

CHAPTER 1

NEW AMERICANS

I always thought of myself as a fairly typical modern American kid—tech-savvy, a bit of a smart-ass, and thoroughly multicultural. Take one look at my olive complexion. That's the future face of America, not the goofy grin of Beaver Cleaver or Richie Cunningham. I was born here, though my mom and dad were not. They arrived as immigrants from deeply chaotic places. They didn't come to New York to toil in sweatshops or stand by pushcarts on the Lower East Side, like generations of immigrants before them. They came for graduate school, my mother from France, my father from Pakistan. They met at a party near Columbia University in 1968, just as the administration building was being occupied by student protestors, including one young man in a very cool pair of sunglasses who plopped himself in President Grayson Kirk's leather chair and fired up an oversize cigar. There's a famous photograph of that. I totally get where that guy was coming from. He took something that started out serious and turned it into unexpected fun.

My ancestors always had a nose for action, wherever history

dropped them. The French Revolution, the partition of India, the march of science—if the world was tumbling into fresh upheaval, chances are I had relatives there. Notably, my great-great-great-grandfather on my mother's side, Jean-Antoine Chaptal, was a world-renowned chemist credited with coining the term *nitrogène* (look him up on Wikipedia). Just as important as the nitrogen—maybe more so to his wine-loving countrymen—he developed a process for adding sugar to unfermented wine, which miraculously boosted the alcohol content. French oenophiles turned up their noses. There were actual demonstrations in the streets. The purists complained that the extra kick would only encourage the peasants to get drunker on the cheap stuff. But the results proved highly popular in France's lesser wine regions. The process is still called *chaptalization,* after my *arrière-arrière-arrière-grand-père.*

À la vôtre!

Chaptal went on to found Paris Hospital. He reorganized the French loan system. Under the first emperor of France, Napoleon Bonaparte, Chaptal was treasurer of the French Senate. He died in Paris in 1832 and was buried with his wife, Rose, in Père Lachaise Cemetery, which most Americans had never heard of until the Doors singer Jim Morrison died of an overdose and joined him there. Today Jean-Antoine's name is inscribed on the steps of the Eiffel Tower. In light of such achievements, the rest of us were destined to seem like slackers for generations to come.

Bernard Chaptal, my mother's father, was quite an adventurer. He worked in Argentina as a gaucho, traveled the world, returned to France, and married a Russian Jewish girl named Alice Feldzer just in time for World War II. He joined the French army and fought the Nazis valiantly. When the German blitzkrieg outflanked the Maginot Line in the spring of 1940, my grandfather escaped to Switzerland, where he spent two years in a prisoner-of-war camp. His mother-in-law and her twin sister were killed in the Holocaust.

My mother's first name is Claude, which, in France, isn't just a boy's name. She was born in 1943. She, her brother, and two sisters adjusted as well as they could to the postwar shortages, though their mother was a legendarily awful cook. "She can hardly make toast, even when there is bread on the store shelves," her children liked to tease.

My mom was a bright, creative girl. Like her father, she had a strong independent streak. She was torn between her passion for the arts and her love for science. She graduated from the Faculté de Médecine in Paris, then moved to New York to pursue a post-baccalaureate art degree at Columbia. At a grad-student party on a rare night out, she met a doctoral student of philosophy, attending New York University on a Fulbright scholarship. He had a deadpan sense of humor. He was a year older than she was. His name was Naseem Zia Jamali. He was also new to New York.

The Jamali family went as far back into the history of India as the Chaptals did in France—probably farther, though the details were not so intricately recorded. My father's father, whose name was Zia, was a young Muslim physician in Delhi with a wife named Zora and seven little children. In 1947, when my father was five, the British divided India in two, carving out Pakistan for the Muslims and leaving the rest of the country to the majority Hindus. The young Jamali family left Delhi for Lahore and then the humid river city of Hyderabad.

The partition of India was a bloody and bitter affair, for most people, anyway. Ghost trains of massacred Muslims arrived each day in Karachi, Pakistan, as ghost trains of massacred Hindus arrived in Delhi and Bombay. When I asked my father one day how his family managed to survive the ghost trains, he answered with his usual ironic shrug. "We flew," he said. "It was lovely."

My father was educated the way affluent Pakistanis were—in a British-style private school where the students memorized long passages from the classics and wore neatly pressed uniforms. After graduating from college, he won the President of Pakistan merit scholarship to graduate school at the University of Edinburgh in Scotland.

He hated Scotland. It wasn't just the damp, chilly weather or the bland Scottish food. The whole place felt old and unwelcoming. When he tried to rent an apartment, he was told, "Sorry, it's already rented. I have nothing for you."

But soon my father's luck began to change. He won the Fulbright scholarship from the U.S. State Department and moved to New York. He entered the doctoral program at New York University, rented a tiny apartment in Greenwich Village, and began to inhale the openness and freedom and turbulence of the late 1960s. He experienced the pleasure of meeting other smart young people from around the world, including a dark-haired French woman named Claude.

Despite—or because of—the pair's very different backgrounds, sparks flew immediately, the good kind. He was the self-deprecating philosopher-intellectual. She was the art-school graduate discovering the firmer truths of science. Both of them felt like they'd finally arrived where they belonged. They moved in together, then married, but didn't rush to start a family. Their big-eyed, long-lashed son, Naveed Alexis Jamali, was born February 20, 1976, a post-Vietnam, post-Watergate, bicentennial baby arriving at a moment of relative cultural calm and patriotism. Naveed means "bearer of good wishes" in Arabic, the "ee" being the Pakistani spelling, not the Persian "i." My parents spoke English and French at home. I learned both as only a toddler can, weaving them together in totally haphazard ways. Other than a few simple words, I never learned to speak my father's Urdu. My mother swears my first word was *auto,* which is the same in all three languages and, I am convinced, was the earliest appearance of my lifelong passion for cars.

My mom had already decided that medical school wasn't for her. She was working as a researcher at Rockefeller University. My dad, with his fresh NYU PhD, was adjunct-teaching philosophy courses at NYU and Adelphi Universities, and traveled to NYPD stationhouses in all five boroughs to teach ethics and philosophy courses to police officers. The cops, he found, enjoyed what they thought of as the Sherlock Holmes side of police work. "Many of these guys," he liked to say of his students in blue, "if they hadn't become cops, you know they'd have ended up as criminals. They have a foot on either side of the law." My father never had much of a filter between his mouth and his brain.

I was a child of the city and a child of the world. Our two-bedroom apartment on West 112th Street was just down the block from Columbia and the Cathedral of St. John the Divine. My parents took me in my little stroller to the parks in the neighborhood, Central, Morningside, and Riverside. Each summer, we visited the relatives in France and Pakistan. At three, I attended the Columbia Greenhouse Nursery School on West 116th Street, one of the oldest in America, then went on to pre-K a few blocks south at the progressive Bank Street School for Children. I moved again for kindergarten, this time to the Calhoun School on West End Avenue. These were all top schools with excellent reputations. Like me, the other children came from educated families with roots around the world. My closest friend at Calhoun was a Japanese boy named Jason, whose father was a ballet instructor. Life was innocent and fun. "I like school," I remember saying to my mom midway through kindergarten. "I'm going back tomorrow."

But that was a tough time in New York. Crime was rising. Graffiti was everywhere. Crack cocaine hadn't hit our neighborhood yet, but heroin definitely had. Suddenly, the tiny apartments and crowded subways felt dangerous, confining, and cramped. Coincidentally, my mother had been studying that phenomenon in her Rockefeller University lab. When I went to see her at work one day, she described her research to me. They were studying brain development using rats. This was accomplished by injecting the rats with radioactive hormones and then examining their brains to see what paths the isotopes had traveled. When I asked what happened to the rats, I learned that the experiment was good for science but not so much for the rats. Then, so the research-ers could study their brains, the rats had their heads chopped off.

"You chop their heads off?" I asked my mother, excited at the drama of it but also slightly alarmed. I'd never seen a beheading on the 1 train, even in the gritty 110th Street station.

She assured me that the rules of science required it.

My parents got spooked when the super's son was found dead in front of our apartment building. That wasn't their idea of the Great American Dream. Abruptly, we exchanged city life for the sprawling lawns and strong public schools of New York's northern suburbs. Our new town, Hastings-on-Hudson, wasn't exactly a bedroom community for Wall Street. Hastings was a history-minded river town that attracted people like my parents, academic and professional types who had con-sidered themselves city people until the first or second child came along.

That corner of Westchester County felt right to my upwardly mobile, immigrant parents. But as the crickets chirped monoto-nously and the stars twinkled across the broad Westchester sky, all I could think was: *What kind of fun am I ever going to find up* here?

I was five years old.

We had a two-family house on leafy Cochrane Avenue. Shortly before my brother, Emmanuel, arrived, we traded up to a turn-of-the-century two-story expanded colonial on the same block. My parents yanked off the white aluminum siding, installed a deck, upgraded the landscaping, tore up the driveway, built a rock garden, and turned the detached garage into a furnished studio. Actually, my mother did all that work herself, including jackhammering the driveway and remov-ing the special garage extension installed by the previous owner to accommodate his 1962 Cadillac fins.

Moving to the suburbs was startling for me. I wasn't the one who found the city oppressive. To me, it was an all-you-can-eat buffet of discovery, diversion, and delight. I never had trouble sleeping amid the noise of grinding garbage trucks and honking taxi horns. The nights were too quiet in Hastings-on-Hudson—what kind of name was that, anyway?—and at first I felt out of place at Hillside Elementary School on Lefurgy Avenue. Most of the other kids had started together in kindergarten. I was a year late for the in crowd, and I didn't look like any of them. I promise you, there weren't too many French-Pakistani children in the lunchroom or the schoolyard. There was one black girl in my whole grade. She and I *were* the diversity. And she had the benefit of an easy-to-pronounce name. I had to repeat mine two or three times before the other children could get it right. I toyed with the idea of calling myself "N.J." or "Alex," shortening my middle name. But I couldn't get either of those to stick. I just knew that at the card-and-gift shop on Main Street, the novelty rack of mini–license plates went from Nancy straight to Norman, completely skipping Naveed.

Our first-grade teacher, Mrs. Wassenberg, was explaining to the class about Christopher Columbus and the people he met when he landed in America. She mentioned something about Indians. I raised my hand. "Like my father?" I asked.

"No," Mrs. Wassenberg shot back. "Your father is a *different* kind of Indian!" I didn't think she meant it as a compliment.

But as the school year rolled on, I gradually found my place in this strange new environment. Our school was small. We had fewer than one hundred children in each grade. One by one, we all got to know each other and found little places for ourselves.

It turned out I was funny, and funny was good. I liked to tell jokes. I knew how to make the other children laugh. I could mimic the teachers, and even some of the teachers seemed to get a kick out of that. I decided I was the official class clown. For me, making fun of myself became a survival skill. People went from laughing *at* me to laughing *with* me. I made easy friends, including some of the popular kids. By the middle of first grade, I realized how much I wanted to be part of the club. Being on the outside, I decided, really sucked.

Too bad my social prowess wasn't being matched academically. As adept as I was at making people like me, that was how poorly I performed on my homework assignments and tests. I began to depend on my humor for more than making playground friends. I realized that as long as I was making people laugh, they weren't getting mad at me. If they weren't getting mad at me, I could get away with stuff.

"So, Naveed," my teacher asked in class one day, "where's your homework?"

"I could tell you a lie," I answered, "but I have too much respect for you to do that."

I could see she wasn't angry, amused by my attempt at a grown-up excuse. "Go sit down! Bring it in tomorrow!"

To me, my youthful schmoozing seemed a whole lot easier than doing the work. I think the teachers also admired the fact that the French-Pakistani boy could use a Yiddish word like *schmooze*.

I always liked to read. From *Thomas the Tank Engine* to *Gulliver's Travels* to *Huckleberry Finn*, I loved stories of adventure in exotic locales. But when it came to studying, I had a difficult time buckling down. My teachers seemed to think I was bright enough. They'd met my parents and watched me work the room. But on a math assignment, I might do the first four equations, no problem at all, and then the fifth question would be a hard one, and I would tell myself, "I'll come back to that later." And I never would.

I'd forget to do my homework. Or I would do it—poorly—five minutes before class. Or I'd study hard and do awesome on one test, then wouldn't study at all and would bomb the next three. As much as I liked to read, I never learned to sit down and focus on my schoolwork. The whole concept of self-discipline was like the Urdu that my father could speak fluently but I never learned at home.

I just thought, *Why bother?* "You're so bright," my teachers often said. "Why don't you apply yourself?" They knew I wasn't trying. I was the kid in the back of the classroom, making stupid faces and passing folded-paper notes.

Given my parents' backgrounds, you'd think they would have been appalled, and I suppose they were. They were high academic achievers, upwardly mobile first-generation immigrants. They'd shown the drive and the focus to move halfway around the world and make successful lives for themselves. They both worked incredibly hard. I remember seeing them rush off at seven-thirty a.m. while I was chomping down my Wonder bread with Nutella and Sunkist soda and telling myself, "I don't really *have* to do that homework!"

But as driven as my parents were, they were also steeped in the attitudes of the era, the belief that children should be given the freedom to find their own paths. "He'll figure it out eventually—or he won't," my father said, sighing.

By then, my parents had gone into business for themselves. "Why work for other people when you can be your own boss?" my father said at dinner one night. He'd been teaching his college students and police recruits. My mom had been toiling away in the Rockefeller lab. It was anyone's guess how many rats she'd decapitated. There was no denying that they always worked hard. But they both, I think, felt a little stuck where they were.

Books & Research, their new company was called. It wasn't that big a leap from their lives in academia. Both my parents were excellent at researching obscure topics. What is graduate school if not a training ground for that? Now, instead of assembling data for their professors and exam committees, they were doing it for paying customers. They were Google for a pre-Google age, delivering articles, reports, and technical data to businesses and government agencies in the United States.

and abroad. The Internal Revenue Service might need a thousand training manuals. The state of Arizona would call for sample environmental regs. Or it might be the research librarian at an army base in Florida, asking about a journal article no one could seem to find. Somewhere between a full-fledged bookstore and a staff of graduate research assistants, my parents' fledgling business found a profitable niche.

While they were busy at the office and I wasn't busy at school, I turned my imagination to cars, soldiers, and planes. I had Hot Wheels and G.I. Joes and models from the hobby shop in Dobbs Ferry. Hasbro came out with the G.I. Joe Skystriker XP-14F, a just-to-scale fighter jet that looked an awful lot like the navy's F-14 Tomcat fighter jet. I knew this because I read about the real ones in the *World Book Encyclopedia*. I got two Skystrikers. I would turn our living room couch into a make-do aircraft carrier with constant takeoffs and landings. I had a picture book called *Sails, Rails and Wings,* by a cartoonist from *MAD* magazine. I knew every little scribble of the ships, trains, and planes in there. I'd copy the illustrations on tracing paper, then fill in the pictures using my sixty-four-box of Crayolas.

I was ten when the space shuttle *Challenger* blew up seventy-three seconds after takeoff and the book *Flight of the Intruder* came out. I was fascinated by both of them. I could imagine Christa McAuliffe being my social-studies teacher. I knew she wouldn't yell at me if I skipped an occasional assignment. And I couldn't get enough of Stephen Coonts's novel about a team of navy aviators and their two-man all-weather A-6 Intruder fighter jets. Those fliers hooked me on the Vietnam War. I could definitely see myself with Morg, Tiger, and Jake "Cool Hand" Grafton, gunning for "Gomers" in the north and grumbling about the navy's stupid rules of engagement. The Tom Cruise movie *Top Gun* had recently hit theaters. Goose and Maverick, Cougar and Charlie—they had the same easy camaraderie and perfect flier nicknames. And look at the toys they got to play with! F-14A Tomcats flying off the carrier U.S.S. *Enterprise* and engaging in dogfights with the bad-guy Soviets. I went to Regal Cinema in Yon-kers the weekend the movie opened. Then I saw it three more times.

What can I say? Some kids love fire trucks. Others love baseball cards. I liked war stories and military gear. I built soldier dioramas. I had a gray pseudo–flight jacket. On a trip with my parents to an army/navy store in the city, I bought pilot patches, flight wings, and a Jolly Roger skull-and-crossbones VF-84. With a joystick and a key-board, I played intricate combat flight-simulator video games. This was dorky stuff, my guilty pleasure while other kids were out playing soccer and basketball.

It was all a little unusual in Hastings, where most of the parents were extremely liberal and war was right at the top of the Do Not Glorify list. A lot of my friends weren't even allowed to have toy guns. That might have been one of the reasons kids liked coming over to my house. The few kids in our school who were interested in the military were the ones from the wrong side of the tracks. Their dads drove trucks for the Public Works Department or worked as prison guards. For the new families moving into Hastings, the military was something other people did. The Vietnam War draft was long over. No one's older brother was enlisting. This was the 1980s. Parents were already decrying the negative social influence of violent video games.

I don't know exactly where my interest came from. Maybe it was the books I'd been reading since I was little. Maybe it was hearing sto-ries about my French grandfather in the war. It certainly didn't come from my parents, who were born in war-torn countries and saw noth-ing romantic about war. Maybe I wanted to have something—some interest, some passion, some expertise—that made me stand apart from the other children and feel special somehow.

I didn't stress out over elementary schoolwork. I rarely did any. The last thing I was concerned with was grades. But just as I was stinking up my eighth-grade report card with another mess of Bs and Cs, my parents decided they'd had about enough of me screwing off in class. "It's time for you to clean up your act," my father told me in an unexpected burst of hard-assery.

The dreaded solution? Private school. More precisely, the Hackley School of Tarrytown, New York, a chichi prep school founded in 1899 by the philanthropist Mrs. Caleb Brewster Hackley. I got a keen sense of the soul of Hackley on my first day of classes, when I glanced across the student parking lot. It was filled with shiny new Porsches, BMWs, and Nissan 300Zs, a sporty number that had come out the year before. Suddenly, the Hastings-on-Hudson public schools seemed a little like *Boyz N the Hood*.

As I always had, I did my best to find a crowd to connect with, and it wasn't the A-students. I joined the football team, playing halfback and safety. Hackley wasn't exactly a gridiron powerhouse, and I made the varsity squad sophomore year. But somehow, my jokes didn't seem quite as funny at Hackley, and nothing about the private-school experience improved my grades. At the end of sophomore year, the Hackley headmaster politely but firmly suggested: "We really think you'd be happier back in public school." And my parents seemed to agree. They didn't see much reason to pay private-school tuition if I still wasn't ready to apply myself.

I felt like I'd been sprung from Leavenworth.

CHAPTER 2

FAMILY BUSINESS

The Russians just appeared.

One morning in the spring of 1988, when I was twelve years old, a man walked into my parents' office suite at 250 West Fifty-seventh Street, near Columbus Circle. He was tall and blond. He had blue eyes and a trim, athletic build. He appeared to be in his middle forties. He was wearing tortoiseshell glasses and a nice beige trench coat.

"Good morning," my father said. "Can I help you with something?"

"I would like to place an order for books," the man said.

He spoke in confident English with the slightest East European accent. He sounded well educated, as if he might be a professor or a resident wonk from a foreign-policy think tank. His tone was pleasant but stiff.

"Unfortunately," my father told the man, "we don't sell books to individuals. We are not a bookstore, despite our name. I'm very sorry." The confusion was understandable at a company called Books & Research, after all.

"Of course," the man said, as if he knew that already. "Please let me explain. My name is Tomakhin. I am with the United Nations. I am part of the Soviet Mission in New York."

My father gave his own name. The Russian held out a business card—not handing it to my father, just holding the card so my father could read what was printed there. PERMANENT MISSION OF THE USSR TO THE UNITED NATIONS, the card said in raised gold letters. It listed a 212 telephone number and a Manhattan address, 136 East Sixty-seventh Street. The card also said Tomakhin's rank was colonel.

"I work on weapons proliferation and disarmament," Colonel Tomakhin said.

My parents didn't get a lot of walk-in traffic, let alone colonels from the Soviet Mission to the UN. It wasn't that my dad was especially suspicious. He was just trying to get a clearer picture of who this Tomakhin was. "Can I ask how you heard about us?"

"You were recommended by a colleague at the United Nations," the visitor said. "My colleague said that you might be able to help us with some materials for a project we are working on."

My father thought for a second. "Do you know what you want?"

"Of course, of course," the Soviet colonel said. He was nothing if not agreeable and organized. He reached into the pocket of his trench coat and produced a sheet of unlined white paper, folded in half. The paper contained a neatly handwritten list of academic journals and books.

There were ten items in all, arcane scholarly titles that might be of interest to a graduate student in international relations or, yes, a UN military attaché. They were all what people in the research world call "open source," not restricted or classified. Any of these items could have been found in a decent college library but probably not across Fifty-seventh Street, at Coliseum Books. This was brainy stuff: the 1987 *SIPRI World Armaments and Disarmament Yearbook*. A special nonproliferation issue of the *Bulletin of the Atomic Scientists*. *The Tables of World Military Expenditures*. A *Foreign Affairs* report called

"Reluctant Warriors: The United States, the Soviet Union, and Arms Control." There were other, similar titles, from Oxford University Press, the Brookings Institution, and the Stockholm International Peace Research Institute, but nothing outside the normal interests of a military-focused diplomat.

After glancing at the list, my father said, "This should not be a problem. What address should we ship them to?"

"No," the Russian said firmly, "that won't be necessary. I will pick them up from you. Is two weeks enough time? Three weeks? I will pay you when I return."

"Two is fine," my father said before walking the Soviet colonel to the door, shaking his hand, and telling him goodbye.

My father wasn't sure what to make of any of this. But he felt no particular reason for alarm. He was open to developing new business at the United Nations. All those diplomats on the East Side of Manhattan could be a great profit center for Books & Research, he thought in passing. But he had more pressing matters to attend to. The minute the man was out the door, my father cleared the conversation from his mind, walked back to his office, shut the door, and got busy at his desk.

But not for long.

Barely thirty minutes after the Russian man left, there was a knock at my father's door. "Two gentlemen are here to see you," said Usman, one of the account managers. He looked slightly uncomfortable. "They said they need to talk with you in private."

One man was in his fifties, the other his middle thirties. They both had close-cropped dark hair and glasses. Like the Russian who'd just departed, the two visitors stood in the doorway wearing trench coats. Theirs were dark.

Why all the trench coats? my father thought as he motioned for the men to come in. "Please, have a seat," he said, closing the door behind them. "What can I do for you?"

The men introduced themselves as special agents with the Federal Bureau of Investigation. First the UN, now the FBI. It wasn't even noon yet.

The men said they worked in counterintelligence. My father had no trouble believing that. They seemed extremely somber, as if they were carrying some great burden they couldn't speak about. They wasted no time on small talk, as if they might be trying out for the Efrem Zimbalist Jr. role in a remake of the 1960s TV show *The FBI*. The younger agent pulled an eight-by-ten glossy photo from a manila folder and placed it on my father's desk. It was a head shot of the colonel from the Soviet Mission.

"Mr. Jamali," the older agent began.

They know my name, my father thought. *They know my name!*

"A short while ago," the agent continued, "this man came to your office. What did you speak with him about?"

The question came just like that, plain and direct, without any buildup or icebreaking pleasantries. The agents didn't detail the extent of what they knew or how they knew it. But their approach strongly suggested that my father might as well answer, since they already know everything.

My father knew so little, he didn't even know what everything might entail. "He was here earlier. He is from the Soviet Mission at the United Nations. He showed me his card, but he didn't leave it. He ordered some books from us. Is there a problem?"

The agents didn't answer the question directly. "We'd be interested in knowing what he ordered," the older agent said.

My father didn't see much percentage in arguing. "I have the list right here," he said.

He handed it to the younger agent, who read it carefully and passed it to his partner. They both nodded knowingly.

"Can we get a copy?" the older agent asked. Like most of his questions, this one didn't end with a question mark.

"Certainly," my father said. "Can you tell me a little more about what this is all about? I'm not used to this sort of thing. Who is this man?"

"Mr. Tomakhin is part of Soviet intelligence," the agent said.

"Soviet intelligence?" my father asked.

"Soviet intelligence," the agent repeated. "We would like your help with him. Would you be willing to help us?"

For my father, that question wasn't as simple it might be for some people. He loved America in the special way that many immigrants do. He had come from around the world and chosen to make America his home. He had no particular affinity for the Soviet Union. But he also came from a country where helping the authorities keep an eye on someone was fraught with implications. My father had never thought of himself as the informant type.

"Is it dangerous?" my father asked.

"No, not at all," the older agent assured him. "There shouldn't be any danger whatsoever."

"Well, what do you want me to do? Should I fill his order?"

"By all means," the agent said. "Complete his order. Treat him like you would any customer. When he returns—*if* he returns—we will be in touch."

My father wasn't sure how he felt about the agents and their request. But for now, he decided he would go along. Before shaking hands and saying goodbye, each of the agents handed my father a business card.

"Mr. Jamali," the older agent said, "we very much appreciate your cooperation in this matter."

What a morning!

My mother, who had been out of the office for an appointment, returned soon after the FBI agents had left. By then, my father had taken a few minutes to collect himself. He told my mother about the visitors. He'd just come face-to-face with both sides of the Cold War, he explained to my mom. "It's all so spy-versus-spy," he said. And both sides seemed to have agendas right here on West Fifty-seventh Street.

"How do you feel?" my mother asked.

"Well, it's kind of exciting, I have to admit that," my father told her. "But it was unnerving, too." He didn't have to tell my mother he wasn't the kind of man who was eager to report on someone to the government, any government. And he certainly didn't want to dive into the middle of some Soviet-American tug-of-war. "Honestly," my father said, "I don't know exactly what to make of it."

My mother had a thousand questions. "How did the Soviet man find us?" she asked my father.

"He said a colleague gave him our name."

"Who?" my mother asked.

"He didn't say, exactly."

"And you didn't ask him?"

My father didn't answer that. He didn't have to.

"Is any of this illegal?" my mother asked.

"I don't think so," my father said. "The FBI is involved."

"What does it mean?"

"I don't know. I just don't know."

"Nice to see you again, Naseem," Colonel Tomakhin said when he returned in two weeks. Give the man this much, he had a quick familiarity. "I came to see if my books have come in."

My father told him that they had. He walked back to the storeroom and returned with an unsealed cardboard box. The books and journals were packed neatly inside, along with an invoice for $163.75.

Tomakhin handed my father two crisp hundred-dollar bills.

"Let me see if I can find some change for you," my father said.

"My friend," the Russian colonel said, "don't worry about it. That's fine. Consider it a thank-you for getting these to me so promptly."

The two men traded some small talk before the Russian said goodbye. My father could banter with anyone.

"So how goes the disarmament business?" my father asked.

"A work in progress," the Russian said with a half-sigh, half-laugh. "It's always a work in progress. But we keep trying."

"We wouldn't want to put you out of business," my father said.

Before leaving the office, the Russian handed my father another list of journal articles and books. This one wasn't so different from the first one, except for one small wrinkle: The last two items were not books or articles but official U.S. government publications.

Again, nothing top secret. Nothing highly sensitive. Nothing that couldn't have been found in the library at Columbia or NYU. But for Books & Research customers, these items had to be ordered through NTIS, the National Technical Information Service, a massive clearinghouse for technical reports produced by the federal government. It's reasonable to assume that the UN mission of a hostile government would have had a difficult time opening a purchasing account at NTIS.

"I will be back in a month or so," Tomakhin said.

"I should have your order by then," my father assured him.

The FBI agents hadn't asked my father to call when the Russian colonel returned. They'd said *they* would be in touch. Three days later, the younger agent was on the phone. Somehow, my father thought, the FBI must be keeping tabs on the colonel. *Or is it close tabs on us?*

"He was here," my father said.

"We know," the agent said. "Do you have the titles?"

"I have them," my father said.

"Mr. Jamali," the agent said, "as always, we appreciate your cooperation."

For these agents, that was just another way of saying goodbye.

★   ★   ★

So began a strange two-decade relationship between my family and the government of America's sworn enemy number one, the Soviet Union—a nation that children from coast to coast had grown up loathing and their parents often feared. The Cuban missile crisis. Bomb drills in schools. Underground bunkers in suburban backyards. The Soviets inspired nuclear panic and Cold War nightmares.

And so, too, began our family's parallel relationship with the FBI, as America's top counterintelligence agents were never far behind. As those two relationships would unfold, the earliest cracks would begin to show in the great Soviet empire. Russian troops would retreat in defeat from Afghanistan. A strike would break out at the Vladimir Lenin Steelworks in Nowa Huta, touching off months of labor unrest across Poland. Demands for freedom would be heard in Estonia, Lithuania, and Latvia. Perestroika, the promise of greater openness from Soviet president Mikhail Gorbachev, would turn out to be not nearly enough to quell the call for change. Democratic uprisings would sweep across Eastern Europe. The Berlin Wall would fall. The Soviet empire would shatter like a Fabergé egg. Capitalism, a uniquely Russian capitalism, would become the order of the day.

The Russians would insist loudly that they were now our friends. And through the fits and starts of world-changing upheaval—the ups and the downs, the encouraging signals, and the dashed hopes—men with the accents of Moscow, Odessa, and St. Petersburg would keep showing up at the New York offices of my parents' Books & Research company.

Regime change in Moscow, the Soviet empire's utter collapse, damaging compromises by U.S. agents like Aldrich Ames and Robert Hanssen—my parents' relationship with the Russians would survive it all. All those years, my parents had been in a strictly reactive mode—waiting for the Russians to return, tipping off the FBI, then quickly getting back to work. They weren't looking to grow or build or expand. It was status quo, always. That might have been one of the reasons the relationship lasted so long.

If such a scenario arose today, it's hard to imagine it would have gone down so casually. But those were different times. My parents didn't seek advice from a lawyer. They didn't demand anything in writing from the FBI. They had no board members or shareholders or outside consultants to weigh the issues with. Their biggest worry was how their participation might affect their livelihood. They had some fleeting concern about their safety. But beyond that, there was no debate at all. My father, a classically trained ethicist, saw no moral ambiguity or dilemma. Nor did my parents feel threatened or pressured in any way by the FBI. They simply viewed themselves as grateful new citizens of their new country, a country they loved and one where they had started a home and were raising a family. Both had been born at the conclusion of war and violence. They never took for granted the safety and security the United States. gave them. What was there to discuss? What was there to worry about? As far as they were concerned, this was just the right thing to do.

CHAPTER 3

FINDING ME

While my parents were busy at the office, I reconnected with many of my old public-school friends at Hastings High School. I was even more committed to the principle that schoolwork should never interfere with hanging out or having fun. One day we had a substitute teacher for health class. I decided I should jump out the window. I raised my hand near the end of class.

"Yes, Naveed?"

Politely, I asked: "May I be excused early today?"

Maybe she felt that having the class clown leave would make her lesson go more smoothly. She answered, "Yes."

"Thank you," I said, stifling a smirk. I stood, glanced at the door out to the hallway, then turned and quickly scrambled through the window onto the empty lawn. As I pulled myself to my feet from the four-foot drop, I could hear my classmates laughing uproariously.

The teacher was not amused. She wrote me a pass to the principal's office. I proudly showed the infraction sheet to all of my friends:

"Student left via the window. Did not return." I was developing my own awkward sense of cool.

That summer, my parents gave me their old silver-and-gray 1984 Honda Civic. A car like that would have labeled me nearly homeless at Hackley. At Hastings, it wasn't the coolest car on campus, but my friends were happy enough to ride with me. I used it until spring, when my parents sold it and I convinced them to buy me a black-and-gold five-speed 1984 Pontiac Trans Am. The car had seen better days. It was slower than a minivan. But what a great-looking cruiser! With the T-tops off, my Orlando Magic cap on backward, and a small gold hoop in my left ear, I would lower the windows, turn up the radio, and cruise Central Avenue just to be seen, or head down to the city. How different could you get from my parents in their black Peugeot? That was the point. They were cluelessly nerdy. I wanted to look like I came from the Bronx.

We had life down to a careful science. I'd meet my friends outside the school on Friday and Saturday nights, then we'd head off to the houses of whichever parents wouldn't be around. We weren't bad kids, just a bunch of overprivileged brats who, like many teenagers, considered themselves untouchable (exactly how I don't want my own children to be). We had too much money, too much booze, and way too much time. Even we understood that. The Hastings Bubble, we called our lives back then. The cops might hate us and everything we stood for, but what were they going to do? If they tried to arrest us, someone's parents would only call the chief of police to express firm displeasure. Everyone knew how that would turn out.

My own parents watched with their usual distant dismay, convinced I wasn't using my gifts to their full potential but hoping that, when I was finally ready, I'd come around. Sadly, there wasn't the slightest sign of that in sight.

Senior year, this son of doctoral- and master's-degree holders applied to exactly zero colleges. I ducked my appointments in the guidance office. I deflected all questions from concerned adults. I didn't see any reason to rush into whatever it was that might be coming next. How could it ever be sweeter than this? At graduation, the principal called my name. I walked onstage in my cap and gown. My parents sat with the other parents in the audience. But I was the student who got the empty leather case with no diploma. When all my credits had been tallied, I had inexplicably come up one course short. I told myself I couldn't let that get me down. There was always a way to make something work. To become an official high school graduate, I enrolled in a life-drawing class at Westchester Community College. I chose that class because I'd heard they had naked models.

As things turned out, my drawing skills didn't show any special promise. But I was pleased to discover the naked-model rumors were true—right up to the second class, when the nubile female grad student was replaced by a pudgy fifty-five-year-old with man boobs and a beard. I told myself that was what the teacher must have meant by "suffering for your art."

That August, with an actual diploma in hand, I rode with my parents into the city and signed up for courses at Hunter College, part of the City University of New York. I wasn't enrolled in a degree program, though the courses I took could later count toward one. But at least I was out of the house in Hastings. I could say I was going to college. I could stay in an apartment my parents owned on Riverside Drive. And I could pick my own roommates. I wondered if I could major in Just Hanging Out.

I took a couple of political science classes and joined the Army ROTC. The Reserve Officers' Training Corps wasn't too popular on the Hunter campus—or at any of the other New York colleges, as far as I could tell. Our unit from Hunter was so tiny that we met on the Fordham University campus along with students from Columbia, NYU, and a couple of other schools.

I didn't depend on those few ROTC cadets for my college experience. I had lots of friends and friends of friends living in the city, and I made time for many of them. Early freshman year, I ran into a guy named Peter, who'd gone to school with my old kindergarten pal Jason. Peter was a freshman at Columbia, living on the fifth floor of Shapiro Hall at 115th Street and Riverside Drive, a five-minute walk from my apartment.

"We should get together," I said.

"Let's do it," he agreed.

I went up to his dorm a few times and met some of his Columbia friends. Columbia was an Ivy League college, but it wasn't all tests and homework for Peter. We spent hours playing *Doom* and *Duke Nukem*, first-person shooter video games.

Living across the hall from Peter was a cute girl named Ava Brent. She was thin with dark, wavy hair and an easy, quiet charm—friendly and open without being pushy or loud. I heard she was a biology major.

"Nice socks," I said one day as she was sitting in the fifth-floor TV lounge with her legs up on the coffee table. She laughed and said nothing.

Nice socks? I thought. *I'd better think of something smarter for this girl.* I vowed to find even more reasons to hang out at Peter's dorm. A week after the sock flirt, I saw Ava sitting in her dorm room with the door open. I stuck my head in and said hi. As we exchanged bland pleasantries, I noticed a book in her bookcase, Thomas Pynchon's novel *The Crying of Lot 49*. The story involves a California housewife, Oedipa Maas, whose rich ex-lover dies, leaving her as coexecutor of his estate. She gradually discovers and begins to unravel what may or may not have been a worldwide conspiracy.

"You read this?" I asked her, reaching over and pulling the book off the shelf.

"Yes."

"That book was totally formative for me," I told her.

"It's great," she agreed.

No one I knew had ever read that book, let alone called it great. "So is her boyfriend a secret agent, or is the woman going crazy?" I asked Ava.

"It could go either way," she said. "It's the shades of gray that make the story interesting."

I had no idea what a powerful life lesson that would turn out to be. But I do remember exactly what I was thinking as I stood in her doorway and we discussed Pynchon's postmodernism: *Wow! She's smart, she's pretty—and she reads Pynchon?* This could be good.

Maybe that's the way guys eventually grow up. I had an active mind, but nothing had grabbed my interest other than my odd obsession with military hardware. Then came Ava. This was a girl I could talk to. She wasn't just hanging out on campus, having "the college experience." She was actually *going* to college—you know, studying and learning stuff. And I even had the feeling she might like me.

I asked her when her birthday was.

"February fourteenth," she said.

"Mine's the twentieth," I said.

That had to mean something, right?

We made an agreement that night. We would get together for our birthdays, over two months away. "Neither one of us should spend our birthday alone," I said.

My material was getting better, I thought.

Our first real date was February 12, 1995, at a Chinese restaurant she liked, Empire Szechuan on West Ninety-sixth Street. On our second date, I took her to an Italian place I liked near the Off-Broadway theaters on West Forty-second Street.

She told me about her research and asked what I'd been reading. I said I'd been on a tear through recent Vietnam books. I was taking a course at the time on the My Lai massacre. Even though I was half-Pakistani, I told her, I wasn't into the wars and political turmoil of the Middle East. "Larger global things, mostly," I said. "The Cold War, the Soviets. The Middle East doesn't pique my curiosity."

It turned out we had all kinds of things in common. Ava was born in the city and moved with her family to Westchester. But her parents moved back to the city a year before the Jamalis fled to the suburbs. We both spent kindergarten in the city—she at Bank Street, me at Calhoun—living four blocks apart. The summer after seventh grade, we had another near miss at Buck's Rock sleepaway camp in Milford, Connecticut. The only reason we didn't end up as campmates was I was sent home with chicken pox during the first session and she came just for the second one.

"I remember that summer, eating a hamburger, trying not to scratch my chicken pox, and listening to the sound track from *Good Morning Vietnam*," I told her. "Louis Armstrong was singing 'What a Wonderful World.' I played that song over and over again—as a twelve-year-old!"

She didn't laugh at my childhood eccentricities. And now the two of us were hanging out together a few short blocks from where my mother and father had met three decades before.

"This is a little creepy," Ava said when I told her that.

"I know," I told her. "I don't care."

Despite all the biography we shared, Ava was in many ways my exact opposite. She was grounded and focused. She was an incredibly dedicated student. She worked in a lab. She took seven classes one semester, including developmental biology and James Joyce.

The dating grew more serious. At the start of sophomore year, Ava moved out of her dorm at Columbia. She split her time between my place on 112th Street and her old bedroom at home. We got two fish together, Franny and Zooey. I made some small changes of my own. I shifted into a degree program at Hunter. I couldn't deny it: Ava's seriousness about her schoolwork was rubbing off on me. I wasn't ready to take seven courses in one semester. But as I watched her with awe, I knew I could be working so much more intensely. She was studying hard and making progress and impressing her teachers, not to mention me, and getting maddeningly perfect grades. She didn't try to make me feel bad about this. But yes, I noticed the difference.

Gradually, I began to think: *Maybe I can aim a little higher here. Maybe I can live up to my long-rumored promise. Maybe I can do more.* In the fall of my sophomore year, on the typewriter in Ava's parents' apartment, with her sitting in a chair next to me, I typed out an application to New York University. That spring I learned I'd been accepted and quickly agreed to attend in time for junior year.

What finally motivated me?

I wanted to please Ava, to show her I wasn't just a charming fuckoff. But there was also something inside of me, a voice I'd been doing my best not to listen to, a voice that all through high school—even earlier—I had pretended wasn't there. Now, with my attention being focused by the most driven young woman I had ever met, I was finally willing to listen to that voice. "Time to quit hiding," it said. "Time to step on the gas and get on a road to somewhere. Time to cut out the shit." I answered the voice with a stern message of my own: "Don't. Fuck. This. Up."

CHAPTER 4

AMERICA ATTACKED

I knew Ava was going places. So I wasn't remotely surprised when she was offered a place in a highly selective PhD program at Harvard University in the field of biological and biomedical sciences with a special interest in genetics. Neither one of us especially wanted to leave New York. But Harvard was in Cambridge, Massachusetts, and seemed intent on staying there. So Ava and I loaded up our car, a 1999 Pontiac Trans Am Firehawk, metallic navy blue, and headed up Interstate 95, excited to be going off on this new adventure together.

We found a comfortable second-floor apartment on Queensberry Street in Boston's Fenway section. Ava dove into her graduate program, and I was lucky to land a programming position at Harvard.

Computer programmers aren't known for being early risers. Noon to two a.m.—those are programmer hours. Most of the programmers I've worked with put in long hours, often crazy-long hours. But even at big companies and major universities, the programmers hardly ever start before nine or ten a.m.

As in so many other facets of my life, I didn't fit the mold at all.

I liked to wake up early. I'd have a predawn breakfast with Ava before she rushed off to her lab. Then I'd head to the University Information Systems office at 1730 Cambridge Street, arriving by seven-thirty or seven-forty-five. I'd badge into the building. I'd grab a coffee in the food court. I'd climb the stairs to the UIS nerve center on the second floor. Then I'd weave my way past all the empty beige cubicles and darkened monitor screens, past the beanbag chairs and the dartboard, past the remote-controlled cars and bowls of Twizzlers, to the far side of our large open-plan workspace. I'd settle into my own beige cubicle and my ergonomic Aeron chair. Then I'd get in a quiet couple of hours of code writing before the rest of the animals came in.

The office was basically a frat house for nerds, as casual in its tone as the work was intense. This was Harvard, but preppy it was not. If I wore chinos and a button-down shirt to the office, people would immediately ask, "You going to a wedding, or do you have a job interview?" The same people who provided the tech support for this billion-dollar university would also "Hasselhoff" each other's computers, replacing all the icons with grinning photos of *Baywatch* hunk David Hasselhoff. Between eight-thirty and nine a.m., just before most people began trickling in, I'd head downstairs to check in with any other early arrivers.

September 11, 2001, started out like any other day at the office. But when I wandered downstairs a minute or two before nine, I noticed people clustered around several monitors at the far end of the room. Though I was too far away to make out faces, it was hard not to notice how still everyone was.

As I approached, no one looked up. They were laser-focused on what I could now see was the CNN.com logo and large-type headline: PLANE STRIKES WORLD TRADE CENTER.

It was a short alert at that point. No explanations. No on-the-record confirmations. Few actual details. No one was saying yet whether this was an accident or something scarier. All they were reporting was that at 8:46 a.m., on a bright and clear morning, an American Airlines Boeing 767 had flown into an upper floor of the North Tower of the World Trade Center in lower Manhattan. First responders were on the scene. There were mass casualties.

Looking back, I wish I'd said something insightful, eloquent, or profound. All I said was "Holy shit!" Then I said it again: "Holy shit!"

And that was just the start of it. Soon after the horrifying news broke, there was much we didn't know. That the plane had taken off from Boston's Logan International Airport, just a few miles from where we were watching, bound for Los Angeles International Airport. That fifteen minutes into the flight, five al-Qaeda members with box cutters had overpowered the captain and first officer. That one of the hijackers, Mohamed Atta, had taken the controls and veered the plane south toward New York. That 102 minutes after impact, the North Tower would crumble to earth with devastating results. That this flight was only the first of four planes, two from Boston, that were hijacked that morning, each with its own deadly results.

When the second plane crashed into the South Tower seventeen horrifying minutes later, we knew: This was no accident. It was a coordinated attack on America. But the full scope of the day revealed itself only gradually, to me and everyone. We had TV screens mounted around the office. But all they displayed were network and server loads, not actual TV. As more and more people around the world logged on to the Internet for World Trade Center updates, the CNN site refreshed more and more slowly. After a few more minutes, the site wouldn't come up at all. Even then, I recognized how ridiculous this was, to be at the technology hub of the greatest university on Planet Earth and, at the worst possible moment, totally unable to follow an unfolding, world-changing event.

We made our way to a conference room on the building's third floor, where someone found a big-butt 1980s television set with rab-bit ears. Thank God for Zenith.

By then, the second plane had hit the South Tower, and the TV had live pictures of frantic people waving from the upper floors while first responders raced into the buildings just as frantically from the chaotic street.

All the while, people were starting to show up for the day. Some had heard. Some hadn't. A woman named Susan, who used to work at the World Trade Center, burst into tears, thinking about all the people she knew who still worked there. Someone else mentioned that half a dozen people on the Information Services staff had been scheduled to fly from Logan that morning to a conference.

"Could they have been on one of the planes?" someone asked. No one answered. No one knew. It was too terrible to contemplate.

I called Ava at the lab but couldn't reach her. I left Cambridge in the Firehawk and put the car in the garage two blocks away from our apartment on Queensberry Street. As I walked home, I saw a young couple on the sidewalk, loading their car with two mountain bikes. Were they totally oblivious to what was happening? Were they head-ing to the country in a panicked retreat? I wasn't sure, but I thought I knew. In those earliest hours, the reality had not yet reached every-one's lives. Not yet.

The city was totally strange. There were people walking around, but no one seemed to be talking. The sky was quiet, too. Planes from Logan flew over the Fenway constantly, but not on this day. The airport had clearly been shut down. I looked up and saw two F-15 fighter jets flying low enough for me to see they had missiles loaded on their racks.

That was when I burst into tears, which I hadn't done in probably ten years. There I was, a self-conscious adult male, crying as I walked along Queensberry Street. I didn't care who saw me. I cried the rest of the way home.

I went inside the empty apartment and dead-bolted the door.

I don't know what I thought that would protect me against. It was instinct. I finally turned on a proper TV. The cable was working perfectly. I started flipping around the various news channels, CNN, FOX, MSNBC, and the local Boston stations. Every one of them had wall-to-wall coverage. I began calling people in New York. My parents in Westchester. A couple of friends I knew had jobs in downtown Manhattan. I felt like I had to speak to all of them.

America was under attack, and no one knew for certain who was responsible. Our military installations around the world were placed on DEFCON 3, the highest state of alert since 1973's Yom Kippur War between Israel and Egypt. When the towers collapsed, U.S. troops happened to be conducting exercises along the Russian border.

We'd had plenty of conflict and numerous enemies over the years. But on 9/11, it was our fiercest and long-running enemy who made the first call. President Vladimir Putin phoned President George W. Bush. The American president was aboard *Air Force One* when the call came in. Putin offered condolences and solidarity against brutal acts of terror. He told Bush that, given what had just occurred, Russian troops would immediately stand down.

Later, Bush spoke appreciatively about Putin's call, saying that under almost any other set of circumstances, our heightened military presence would have caused "inevitable tension." But Putin's call was "a moment where it clearly said to me he understands the Cold War is over."

My mind was racing all over the place but nowhere good.

Finally, Ava arrived home. "Is it bad?" she asked.

"It's bad," I answered.

We stared at the TV and made phone calls the rest of the afternoon. I finally caught my breath.

Within a few short hours, I'd gone from not thinking at all about my safety or the safety of the people I loved or the stability of American society to thinking of little else.

If someone had told me in that period that the Canadians had armed themselves to the teeth and were taking over America, I would have said, "Why not?" Anything and everything seemed possible. Who knew what normal was anymore?

Ava had lived through the 1993 attack on the World Trade Center. She'd been a student a few blocks away at Stuyvesant High School. If anything, she felt this new attack, far deadlier than the first one, even more personally than I did. She said she felt an overpowering urge to go back home. "Why are we still in Boston?" I asked.

On Friday, September 14, three days after the attacks, we drove south in the Firehawk. Driving was the only option. Commercial planes were still grounded. We had the radio on the whole way. As we pulled onto Interstate 95, Rev. Billy Graham was leading a national day of prayer and remembrance at the National Cathedral in Washington. It seemed like half the American political hierarchy was there, including President George W. Bush.

"We are here in the middle hour of our grief," the president told the overflow congregation. No one could deny that America's recovery was very much a work in progress—in the earliest of early stages. That afternoon, Bush flew up to New York. The president reached Ground Zero just as we were heading down the West Side Highway toward the Upper West Side. I turned the radio up as he spoke again.

"I want you all to know that America today, America today is on bended knee, in prayer for the people whose lives were lost here, for the workers who work here, for the families who mourn," he said through a bullhorn to a group of construction workers and rescue personnel down in the smoldering pit. "The nation stands with the good people of New York City and New Jersey and Connecticut as we mourn the loss of thousands of our citizens."

The president was interrupted right there. "I can't hear you!" one rescue worker called out from the back.

"I can hear you!" Bush called back through the bullhorn. "I can hear you! The rest of the world hears you! And the people, and the people who knocked these buildings down, will hear all of us soon!"

The workers erupted in a loud, throaty chant. "U.S.A.! U.S.A.! U.S.A.! U.S.A.!" They went on for a good long while.

As we pulled off the highway and onto the streets of the Upper West Side, Boston felt like a thousand miles and a lifetime away from where the real action was. Ava and I knew then and there that we had to move back to New York.

The next morning, we left her parents' apartment and started the long, winding walk downtown. The streets weren't quiet or empty. But everyone seemed to be in the same different, uncomfortable mood. The farther south we got, the stranger everything seemed. At Twenty-third Street, we turned west and walked the edge of Chelsea and Greenwich Village along the Hudson River waterfront.

That was about where the smell got strong. The pit, we knew, was still smoldering. It would for several more weeks. Ash and bits of paper floated in the air, which had an acrid smell, the sky a hazy glow. As we walked down those blocks, our eyes burned. So did our lungs.

Most of the way, we walked quietly. Not saying much to each other. Totally lost in our thoughts.

We'd heard about the tight security. We assumed that at around Houston Street or Canal, police or National Guardsmen would turn us back. But as we walked the edge of the West Side Highway, no one told us to stop.

We kept walking south until we got to Ava's old high school. Outside Stuyvesant was a line of battered New York police cars parked on the street. Some of them had their windows blown out. All of them were caked in dust. First responders frozen in time.

Ava knew the neighborhood well. We walked east, then north, then east, then south again. From where we stood, we had a straight-on view of the twisted steel and massive rubble pile of the collapsed towers. Four National Guardsmen were standing there. They had rifles and gas masks. They looked really young and really scared. So were we.

We turned north, then headed back up to Canal Street.

At Canal, there were huge lines of people trying to get south, unaware that they could loop around and avoid the barricades.

We kept walking north until we reached Washington Square. We finally stopped walking and began to talk.

"It's like a city without people," Ava said. "Like there's no more civilization here."

"The signs are what really get to me," I said. All over lower Manhattan, frantic people had taped up posters, desperately searching for information about missing friends and relatives. Most of them, we knew already, would never be found. We headed west and then north for the long walk home.

As we passed St. Vincent's Hospital, we saw people lined up to give blood. That was the hospital where the survivors would have gone. But the emergency room had been eerily quiet that day.

Around Fourteenth Street, we turned west with four firefighters in uniforms that didn't look familiar. Clearly, they weren't from the NYFD. We asked the men where they were from.

"Australia," two of them said.

"San Bernardino, California," said the other two.

"Thank you, thank you," I said, shaking all of their hands.

You couldn't help but be impressed—all these people coming from so far, so quickly, for no reason other than to help, bringing their talent, their experience, their energy, and their drive.

What could anyone say but thank you?

★   ★   ★

My experience of 9/11 was similar to that of many Americans. My loved ones all came home safely that day. But every little thing seemed magnified. Fear and worry were palpable. Cell phones were working only intermittently. Many people in New York, with no way to get home, were crashing with friends or coworkers. It took us several days to find my cousin JD, who worked in the Financial District. He was fine, but that was rattling.

I realized that morning there was no such thing as a safe world. This cocoon I'd been living in—skipping ROTC, working at Harvard with the Twizzler bowls and the Aeron chairs, our cozy apartment in the Fenway, the cushy job and the safe career, the decent money and nice cars—none of it could guarantee our safety. The world could change dramatically in a heartbeat. In fact, it just had.

That's what I was feeling. Then I started thinking: *What the hell can I do?* I had a sense that there was real work to be done out there somewhere, and I was home watching it on TV.

"I want to be part of this," I said to myself. "I want to feel like I'm contributing something here. I want to feel like I am making the world safer. I don't want to sit on the sidelines anymore."

Over the subsequent months, I made the full transition from dude who enjoyed a good time to dude who realizes there is something he wants to be part of that's bigger than he is. The only question was how.

CHAPTER 5

NAVY DREAMS

It would take longer than I wanted to make those changes in my life.

We stayed in Boston as Ava made swift progress through her doctoral program. My parents were working hard back in New York, building Books & Research, enjoying their lives in Hastings, feeling satisfaction at all they'd achieved as first-generation Americans. My Pakistani father had even become a U.S. citizen. For him, it wasn't so much an expression of American patriotism or a question of national identity, although he did love America. He had gotten interested in local politics in Hastings and all riled up about a school-tax increase. He hated the fact that he couldn't vote in village elections. So he took the U.S. citizenship test—aced it, of course—and was sworn in during August 2001, just before lower Manhattan was transformed into a massive crime scene.

My friends from high school and college were mostly making money on Wall Street or hiding out in graduate school. None of them seemed to be feeling a whole lot of angst about the state of the world. So why did I have this empty feeling?

It wasn't like my life was in shambles. It was actually going pretty well. I'd been working at Harvard barely a year when I was promoted from a programmer position in the human resources department to managing my own team at University Information Systems. This was a great opportunity for me and something new for the university. It was as if we were running our own business under the umbrella of Harvard. We were allowed to be creative and entrepreneurial—actually encouraged to be. I could run my team the way I wanted to. And if I did well in this position, I had every reason to think more good things lay ahead.

I had a fine education. I'd been coddled all my life. I had all the benefits of growing up in New York's affluent suburbs. Ava and I were young and in love. We had a great apartment and the Firehawk. We'd bought a commuter car, too, an easy-to-park black 1993 Honda Civic for quick trips around town. I'd been blessed with all these opportunities and advantages, but what had I done with them, really?

Not nearly enough. Nothing I was doing seemed important at all.

This was a life? Building websites for Harvard president Larry Summers? Sitting through endless meetings with pretentious people discussing initiatives I couldn't care less about? Was this how I wanted to spend the next forty years? Liberally hiding behind high Ivy walls? It was a nice job with a nice future, cozy as could be. But I felt oddly disconnected. I was Peter Gibbons, the disgruntled programmer in Mike Judge's *Office Space*. "We don't have a lot of time on this earth," Peter comes to understand. "We weren't meant to spend it this way. Human beings were not meant to sit in little cubicles staring at computer screens all day." He was right. I felt totally adrift and out of the action, not that I knew where the real action might be. My great-great-great-grandfather, he knew action. I had the feeling I was wasting my life away. Nine-eleven definitely shone an uncomfortable light on that. My life was all about safety and comfort, and that didn't feel right anymore. I was twenty-five but acting more like a complacent, settled-down forty-year-old. I had to do something. I had to make a change.

But what? How? Where?

Nine-eleven had not only inspired patriotism. It had reminded a lot of people that there were opportunities to do something worthwhile. The more I thought about it, the more I knew: There had to be something larger and more meaningful I could do. That was when I came up with the idea of joining Naval Intelligence.

I'd always read a lot about the military. Ever since I was a boy, I had played with toy soldiers and model planes. I'd seen more than my share of war and espionage films. Lately, I noticed, I'd been diving even deeper into that stuff. On the Saturday trips Ava and I made to the Barnes & Noble in Newton, I'd pick up a lot of geopolitical books, titles like Con Coughlin's *Saddam: King of Terror*. None of this related to my IT job. I just loved reading about far-off adventures and knotty international crises. I imagined being immersed in some great world event and thought about how I would handle the issues. I read about great leaders faced with great decisions. I devoured books that told the inside stories, the real details that didn't make the regular history books. I wanted to know how these leaders responded when they were confronted with unimaginable odds and impossible judgments. Did they do the right thing? Did their choices influence history? Did President Kennedy blink during the Cuban missile crisis? No. Would the Berlin Wall have fallen without Ronald Reagan? No. Was General Westmoreland a brilliant strategist, or did he totally botch the Vietnam War? Both. I teased out all these riddles. I rated the successes and failures of supposedly great men. And when my thoughts weren't on real military, I was as obsessed with the fictional kind. In my mind, I went down all kinds of crazy paths. Which role did I see myself in? *Saving Private Ryan* or *13 Days*? Was I tactical or strategic? Was I the guy kicking down doors and shooting people or the guy sitting back and putting the puzzle pieces together? Both roles are critical. But I was pretty sure my gifts were on the cerebral side.

I'd been watching those movies and reading those books and playacting the scenes in my head ever since I was a kid with my G.I. Joe Skystrikers and the Jolly Roger patches on my gray pseudo–flight jacket. As a child, I played those games between homework and bedtime. Now that I was older and had friends who were wearing real air force or navy flight jackets, one thing hadn't changed: I'd chosen to leave the real adventures to other people.

Not anymore.

I had a plan. It would start with me doing what I was already an expert at—using technology to find out stuff. If there was one skill I had in abundance, it was data mining. I was hoping my technical abilities would loop me back to where I was always meant to be.

We were still on rudimentary search engines like WebCrawler, Dogpile, and Ask Jeeves, and we posted on message boards. The Internet was growing slowly, allowing connections with people we wouldn't ever be likely to meet. Someone I met in an IRC chat room pointed me toward military.com, where he said I could get all kinds of advice about getting into Naval Intelligence, and fast.

Fast was critical. Patience was not my strongest suit. I wasn't looking for a twenty-year process. I didn't want to sit on a ship out at sea. *Come on,* I thought. *My life is almost one third over. I'm not getting any younger here. How much longer can I wait?*

The people who posted at military.com—current and former officers and enlisted personnel—knew an amazing amount, and once they decided I was serious, they couldn't have been friendlier or more willing to share. I wasn't shy about asking. I said I wanted to be an officer in Naval Intelligence. I said I had a tech background, and I wanted to find a way to do it fast. Several posters mentioned something called the direct commission officer program, which I had never heard of.

But it sounded perfect to me. It was part of the U.S. Navy Reserves. This wasn't the career path for gung-ho eighteen-year-olds fresh out of high school. The DCO program was for people who had already started their civilian careers and had special skills the navy might need. Physicians. Engineers. Lawyers. Chaplains. Meteorologists. I could imagine the local TV weatherman from the eleven o'clock news stripping off his makeup with a baby wipe and racing over to the local base, radioing destroyer captains about squalls up ahead. Hey, why not?

I might not have the background to predict low-pressure systems. But the requirements for Naval Intelligence officers weren't all that precise. You just needed "significant civilian occupational experience in disciplines related to intelligence or cyber-related professions." That could mean anything, right? I knew I was on the right track. I had the basic skills to spy.

I'd spent a zillion hours in the computer lab at NYU. Everywhere I'd worked, I was known as a kung fu master at research and turning vague ideas into code. I had brand-name colleges and employers on my résumé—NYU, Columbia, and Harvard—that were bound to impress. I didn't have to mention my unfortunate time at Hackley or my empty diploma case at Hastings. I was one of those techies who could actually talk to people on both sides of the digital divide, the super-bright code writers who were on my team and the foggy academics who were our clients. And I figured being half Pakistani couldn't hurt. I didn't speak Arabic, but I could probably pass on a street corner as someone who did.

The whole idea of naval intelligence called to me. It was a key part of our military strategy. But it wasn't about overrunning the enemy. It was about outsmarting him. That was a realm I thought I could thrive in.

As much as the idea appealed to the adventure-loving adolescent inside me, I knew that being a real-life Naval Intelligence officer wouldn't be all car chases, secret drop-offs, and John le Carré. There'd be some grunt research and report writing and all the other boring stuff. But it had to be more fun and more exciting and far more meaningful than working in a university computer lab.

I made a point of learning as much as I could about navy intelligence. Assuming I was accepted into the program—and given my background, how hard could that really be?—they'd whisk me through a two-week indoctrination at the Direct Commission Officer Indoctrination Course in Pensacola, Florida. The day I signed my contract, I'd be a full commissioned officer in the U.S. Navy Reserves. No service academy, no ROTC, no Officer Candidate School, no endless waiting around to begin the next phase of my life. As one of the posters at military.com told me: "You'll be busy on your first assignment. People will be saluting you."

It was a commitment I was eager to make. I'd have to agree to serve for eight years. That could involve one weekend a month of training and two weeks of summer camp. Or, more likely, given the way things were headed in this post-9/11 world, an extended deployment on a naval base in the United States or in a war zone in Afghanistan, Iraq, or who knows where. Probably a little of both, the people on military.com explained. A path that was perfect for me. An adventure I was right for and ripe for.

Waking up with a goal was incredibly invigorating. And it didn't take me long to head off in search of it.

I filled out the "for more information" form on the navy's direct commission website. I clicked the box for "intelligence officer." A couple of days later, I got a reply email from Lieutenant Commander Lino Covarrubias, the officer recruiter in New England for the direct commission program. With titles like that one, it sounded like the navy was as bureaucratic as I remembered the army being when I was in ROTC. The lieutenant commander said he'd be happy to meet with me. But first, he said, I should attend a direct commission information briefing for my intended specialty, naval intelligence, at Fort Devens, a reservist military installation near Worchester, Massachusetts, about an hour east of Boston. And I should go for a basic navy physical exam at MEPS, the Military Entrance Processing Station, in South Boston.

"The information briefing will be conducted by a navy intelligence officer," the lieutenant commander wrote. "That's the best way for you to get an idea whether this might make sense for you. Send me an email after you attend the briefing if you are still interested. We can meet, and I will answer any questions you might have. Maybe I'll take you to lunch."

"Rgr that," I wrote.

I knew it was a high-end crowd when I saw the cars in the Fort Devens parking lot. A Mercedes. A Jaguar. A couple of BMWs. Strictly in terms of sticker price, my Firehawk was in the back of the pack. I found my way to a fluorescent-lit classroom with time to spare before the seven p.m. information session began. I wasn't the first one there. A group of what looked like professionals had already gathered, about two dozen people in all, mostly men but three or four women, too. I introduced myself and joined a conversation with two lawyers, a stockbroker, a sales executive, an accountant, and a couple of mid-level corporate drones. No one was old, but I was one of the younger people in the room. And maybe one of the less successful. In the short time since 9/11, the navy had obviously seen some changes in the recruitment pool.

A woman in khaki pants and khaki shirt came in and introduced herself. She was squat, with a no-nonsense helmet haircut. She said she was a lieutenant commander in the Naval Intelligence Reserves. Then she repeated much of what I'd read on the website, only she said it like she was trying to convince us we shouldn't bother to apply.

"You may have some misconceptions about the life of an intelligence officer," she said. "It's not all cloak-and-dagger. It's not all James Bond. In fact, it's mostly *not* James Bond. There is a lot of information gathering. A lot of analysis. A lot of finding out things maybe our nation's enemies don't want us to discover.

"My job is not to glorify this," she went on. "My job is to tell you the truth. The navy appreciates your interest. But we want you to do this—if you decide you want to do it—with your eyes open wide. We are at a unique time in history now." One of the realities that we shouldn't take lightly, she said, was the distinct possibility of being deployed overseas. "I know we call it the reserves," she said, "and I know that's different from active duty. But let me warn you, there is nothing passive anymore about the Navy Reserves. Do not join if you are not open to having your life turned upside down."

I knew she meant it as a warning. This lieutenant commander was an expert at discouraging anyone who wasn't 110 percent certain. But I heard a different message. *Turn my life upside down?* I thought. *Yes! Go ahead!*

"If you are accepted into this program, there is a high likelihood that you will be deployed." She paused and waited for that to sink in. "There are significant costs that you should consider carefully." She began ticking them off. "There's risk to your job, risk to your family, risk to your income—people who have high-paying jobs may very well have to take a pay cut." I noticed several people stiffen. "I saw a lot of fancy cars driving into the parking lot," she said. "If you like those cars, this probably is not the right program for you. We have people who were stockbrokers, making four or five hundred thousand dollars a year. Now they're making seventy thousand as an ensign. Prepare for this. Ask yourself, 'Can you do it?' No hard feelings if you decide it's not for you."

I noticed a couple of people in the room shaking their heads and shifting uncomfortably in their seats. I was nodding. Leaning forward. Excited.

*   *   *

I did have some concerns about my physical condition. One concern, actually. On the navy's official health-screening form, I was able to check the "no" boxes for cancer, heart disease, and a long list of other dire and not so dire ailments. No, I am not addicted to heroin, cocaine, or other narcotics! No, I do not suffer from a brain tumor! No, I don't have flat feet! But the truth was, I wasn't in such great shape. Working at Harvard wasn't so different from being at a lot of tech jobs: We put in absurdly long hours. We sat at ergonomic workstations in ergonomic chairs, constantly on guard against repetitive-stress injuries. We chain-guzzled high-sugar, high-caffeine beverages. Hardly anyone went out for lunch. The whole workplace was designed to keep us at or near our keyboards, updating system architecture, building next-generation websites, writing never-ending lines of programming code. The heaping bowls of Twizzlers, the humming cappuccino machines, the twenty-four-hour buffet table—they were all designed to keep us there and sedentary but not starving. There *was* such a thing as a free lunch at Harvard—a free breakfast and dinner, too. It was our waistlines and cholesterol that paid.

I knew that could be a problem for me. So right after getting the email from the recruiter, even before I went to see the great dissuader at Fort Devens, I'd put myself on the Atkins Diet and started working out again. I weighed about 177 pounds when I got started. I am five-seven. The height-weight chart said I had to get myself down to 168. I got busy doing that the Atkins way. I ate bacon, hamburgers without the bun, and endless plates of broccoli. I ate no bread or pasta or anything with carbs and, truthfully, not too many other vegetables. What I sacrificed in variety, I made up for in determination.. The night before I had my MEPS appointment, my bathroom scale said 168.

I was due in South Boston at four a.m. This was so crazy early that Ava agreed to drive in with me. She had just gotten the proofs back for an article she'd submitted to a science journal. She said she would wait in the car, doing her proofreading, while I went inside to be poked, probed, tested, and barked at. Ava was encouraging, but I thought I saw her smirk at what I was putting myself through.

I gathered up all the paperwork I needed—my health survey, my immunization card, a copy of my high school diploma, a state-issued ID. We left Fenway at three-fifteen and drove the easy-to-maneuver Honda into South Boston. MEPS was at 495 Summer Street, near the mouth of the Ted Williams Tunnel.

"Good luck," Ava said as I kissed her goodbye.

I couldn't help but notice how different the cars in this parking lot were. These were aging Chevys, Toyotas, and Fords. I saw a couple of minivans and a dented pickup. And instead of stockbrokers, lawyers, and accountants, it was mostly eighteen- and nineteen-year-olds in the waiting room. Several of them were talking about the night they'd just spent at a Holiday Inn Express, possibly their first time alone away from home. More than a few seemed somewhere between excited and terrified. These guys were there to join the real navy. Assuming they got through MEPS, they'd be shipping out the following morning to basic training.

The staff here seemed different, too. Instead of a lieutenant commander patiently answering condescending questions from after-work stockbrokers, the brusque MEPS personnel didn't seem like they'd put up with anything. If Fort Devens was *An Officer and a Gentleman*, MEPS was *Platoon*.

I was shuttled through MEPS as if through an automatic car wash, station by station by station, each with a special function, until every square inch of me had been attended to. Muscle tests. Joint tests. I was given an eye exam. They checked my hearing, too. I went upstairs to have my blood drawn. Urine and blood tests. Drug and alcohol tests.

"Walk like a duck," one of the proctors said to us. And a whole line of recruits did just that, duck-walked across the room.

I carried my stack of papers in a large manila envelope. The weigh-in was at the end. That was the station I was most nervous about. A corpsman with a clipboard stood by a beat-up Toledo doctor's-office scale.

"This is where it all ends for me," I said, trying to manage a charming smile. "Any advice?"

He was not about to be charmed. "Up" was all he said, and I climbed on the scale, recalling all those bunless burgers and bacon sides.

He slid the smaller weight to the right until the metal arm balanced at what looked like exactly 168 pounds. "Where are you headed?" he asked me.

"Navy," I told him.

"Then you're fine," he said. "We'll put it down as 167."

He stamped my card and sent me on my way. It was past six-thirty by the time I got out of there. Most of Boston was still in bed, but my girlfriend had waited in the car for me almost three hours. I couldn't wait to tell Ava I had passed the weigh-in. And I had one request: Could we please make a quick stop at Au Bon Pain? Finally, I was free to eat a mouthwatering toasted bagel with way more than a schmear of scallion cream cheese.

When she asked how it went, I said, "Fine. And please don't ever ask me to walk like a duck."

CHAPTER 6

COMMANDER LINO

I wanted to *be* Lino Covarrubias. I knew that five minutes after we sat down together at the Imperial Terrace Chinese buffet in Quincy, Massachusetts, and I asked him what he'd done in the navy before he became a recruiter.

"Surface warfare officer," he said. "A jack of all trades, a master of none. In the Med and the Adriatic. On frigates, cruisers, and an aircraft carrier."

That was how he spoke—simply, directly, like he had no need to embellish or to brag about anything. I nodded across the spring rolls at him.

"When the Balkans blew up in the early nineties," he said, "we joined a NATO task force trying to keep weapons out of Serbia and Montenegro. The idea was to draw the violence down by starving out the weapons and ammo. We were out there inspecting ships, stopping black-market arms from coming across from Italy. A few got through at night on cigarette boats going sixty miles an hour. We couldn't shoot at them. But that was maybe a few dozen firearms at a time. We were focused on the larger ships that could deliver thousands of weapons. It was a miserable winter, the sea so choppy, cold winds blowing down from the Alps. But we kept a lot of arms out of Serbia, I'll tell you that."

I was spellbound. I had read all those books about the military. I'd seen hundreds of war movies and TV shows. I'd heard stories as a boy from my French grandfather about his harrowing experiences in World War II. I'd had my short career in ROTC, for whatever that was worth. But none of that made me feel like this did, sitting across a restaurant table from this lieutenant commander in the navy, having adult-to-adult conversation about life on the inside.

"That must have been exciting," I told him.

"It was," he said.

I had taken the steps Lino had asked of me in his email. I'd filled out a whole stack of forms and applications, checking "no" in all the right spots. I had driven the Firehawk to the U.S. Naval Reserve Center at 85 Sea Street. Now it was time to meet the man who'd laid out the steps for me.

Quincy is an old industrial city on Boston's South Shore. To an outsider, it looks less like its own city and more like another Boston neighborhood on its way to being gentrified. It has winding streets, triple-decker houses, and idle factory buildings turned into offices and condos. But Quincy still has a strong identity of its own. "QUIN-zy," the old-timers like to say, as if the "c" were a "z." I had read about Quincy's place in American history. Settled in 1625, the city got its name from Colonel John Quincy, maternal grandfather of Abigail Adams. Her husband, John Adams, the second president of the United States, was born in Quincy, as was their son, John Quincy Adams, the sixth president. So was John Hancock, the Massachusetts governor known by children across America for his bold and stylish signature on the Declaration of Independence.

This part of Quincy didn't look all that historic to me. The architectural style was more like "surplus cinder block." I passed a couple of strip malls and a Blockbuster, a McDonald's, a Burger King, and a Friendly's. The brownish one-story navy building looked more like a decommissioned junior high school. I parked the car in the lot and walked inside.

The recruiters shared the building with the MBTA Transit Police Academy. The police recruits were down one hallway, the navy prospects down the other.

"I'm here to see Lieutenant Commander Covarrubias," I told the navy clerk, doing my best with the five-syllable last name. The clerk nodded, and I took a seat.

I waited about ten minutes as people in blue uniforms came and went. I couldn't tell what they were doing, but they all seemed busy doing it. I stared at the recruiting posters featuring fit young men and women gazing off ship decks, leaping out of helicopters, and running purposefully through the surf. I could hear the police recruits down the hall.

Suddenly, a stocky man in his early forties breezed into the waiting room. He was wearing a khaki officer's uniform. He said a quick "good morning" to the people in the blue shirts before looking over at me. He was about my height and had a shock of thick black hair parted on the left side. I counted five rows of ribbons on his shirt. I couldn't say what all of them were, but I saw silver jump wings, a recruiter pin, and a gold surface-warfare badge.

"Hey," he said brightly to me, reaching out his right hand. "How's it goin'? I'm Lino. You wanna grab some lunch?"

His easygoing friendliness caught me off guard. "Yes, sir," I said, standing up quickly.

"It's Lino," he said, brushing off the formality.

"Yes, sir," I answered. "Lino." I'd have been just as comfortable calling him "Lieutenant Commander."

We walked a block to a Chinese buffet, probably chosen for convenience. It couldn't have been the ambience. The room was dark and mostly empty. The food was all-you-can-eat, that's the best I can say about it. Lino piled his plate with dumplings and spring rolls, and I did the same.

"So how did you get into this?" I asked him.

I started eating, and Lino began to talk. Even with this dim lighting, I could see the grease shining off his plate.

"It's what I always knew I'd do," he said. "You meet some of the greatest people in the navy. It's something you really feel part of. I had some amazing times out there." He started ticking off the ports that he and his shipmates had visited. "Toulon, France. Málaga, Spain. Corfu in the Greek Islands. Haifa, Israel."

"Was that totally amazing?" I asked.

"Oh, yeah. It is. There is nothing in the world like the Atlantic fleet coming into a port after a couple months at sea. We're a dry navy, you know. No alcohol on board the ship. In a lot of your other navies, as long you're off duty, you can have a beer or a rum, watch a movie, and go to sleep. In the U.S. Navy, no. You're weeks or more at sea with nothing to distract you. So you've just hit port. You haven't had a beer in a month and a half. That first beer hits you in the head like a rock. That picture of U.S. sailors out drinking, it's quite true. Two or three days in port, you get in as much as you can."

The way Lino told it, he made even the bad things sound good. No beer on the ship—for no matter how long—sounded like no big deal when he described the raucous camaraderie of another port call. The sailors, he told me, did more on land than drink, womanize, and unwind. They also tried to help people wherever they could.

"We would build a playground," he said. "Or we would rehab an orphanage. We bring money into the restaurants and bars, but we also do these projects. People appreciate it. Most of the places we're sent to, people are very happy to see the U.S. fleet come in. Most people like Americans."

He seemed happy enough to talk, like it was a relief to have a recruit who was asking questions about *him*. I knew we would get around to discussing the direct commission program and my chances of getting in. But I kept pumping him about his own background.

"Covarrubias—is that a Greek name?" I asked him.

"Spanish," he answered. "My family is Mexican-American. I grew up in Southern California, outside El Centro. It's a pretty poor area near the Mexican border. There's a Naval Air Facility in El Centro. It's the winter home of the U.S. Navy Blue Angels. You've heard of them?"

Of course I'd heard of the Blue Angels, the legendary acrobatic flying team. "As a little kid through high school, I watched the Angels every winter," Lino explained. "They had air shows at the base. I was sold on the navy from the very start. It was the only thing I wanted to do. That was the way to get out of the poverty of the barrio."

He enlisted right out of high school in 1984. After basic training, he was tapped for the BOOST program (Broadened Opportunity for Officer Selection and Training). "The navy needed more officers," he said. "BOOST was for enlisted personnel from the fleet, a one-year prep school in San Diego that would prepare you for a Navy ROTC program at a college somewhere."

Lino must have done well in BOOST. He was one of only ten students in his class offered a place in the U.S. Naval Academy in Annapolis, Maryland. But he wasn't sure it was what he should do. He'd also been accepted to the ROTC program at UCLA. He'd seen the full-color brochures of the Los Angeles campus. It looked pretty sweet.

"My chief pulled me aside," Lino remembered. "He said to me, 'Covarrubias, you come from a poor background, right? Your parents, they don't have any money. ROTC pays for tuition and books, not room and board. Who's gonna pay for room and board? Your parents will pay for that? Most people have to work. I tell you what you're gonna do. You'll be flipping burgers. You ever been to Maryland?' I hadn't traveled anywhere. 'Best seafood ever. You don't have to work. Everything is paid for. It's twenty-four/seven navy. No flipping patties.'

"The reason I went to Annapolis wasn't because it was a fine institution or a prestigious school or anything like that. I went because my family couldn't afford room and board, and I didn't want to flip burgers."

He graduated from the Naval Academy in 1989 and headed out to sea, this time as an officer with a big career ahead of him.

Our conversation shifted. He started asking questions about me. I told him about my own background. The French mother, the Pakistani father, the techie son now dating a brilliant Jewish woman from New York.

He seemed to like all that. "America is a nation of immigrants," he said. "I particularly like candidates who come from immigrant families in the first generation or two."

I told him that when 9/11 happened, Ava and I both felt bad about not being in New York. When she finished her doctoral program at Harvard, we would probably move back there.

That was fine, he said. If I got accepted into the program, the navy would tell me where to report, but they wouldn't care where I lived in my off time.

As we talked on, he repeated some of the things I already knew about the extreme selectivity of the program, and he emphasized that the most selective specialty was Naval Intelligence.

"We need skilled people for that," he said. "A lot of the surveillance we're doing now is with computers. We need techies. Maybe next year we'll have too many techies and we'll need people who can think. Then they'll be telling me, 'Send us all those professors and PhDs.'

"After nine-eleven," he said, "my phone started ringing with all these people who never would have thought about joining the military. Professional people. People with Ivy League degrees. People who'd already had good careers. They're saying the same things: 'I've had a great life. I have a great family. I have a great education. I'm making a great living. But I haven't done anything for my country, and that doesn't seem right.' Any of this sound familiar to you?"

I told Lino he was reading my mind.

"You might be a good fit for this," he said.

He told me he'd gone over my application. Nothing was guaranteed, but he thought I had a solid chance of getting in. "You have good paper," he told me. "You have strong technical skills. Working at Harvard is nice. You have the diversity piece. You seem to be doing this for all the right reasons. You know what you're getting into."

He said he did have some concern about the depth of my work experience. "You are really just getting started in your career," he said. "But I think you'll be a competitive candidate. As far as I'm concerned, you make the initial cut."

Lino kept talking. And I kept asking him questions. About the great people he'd met in the navy. How serving had brought meaning to his life. About all the fun he'd been able to have. He lit up as he described one memorable cruise across the Mediterranean and an exchange program with the Turkish Navy. "There's just a lot of opportunity to contribute," he said.

Up until that point, I'd had no idea what an intel officer did day to day. There wasn't much explanation in the official paperwork beyond the fact that applicants needed a college degree. The rest I'd tried to learn in military chat rooms, though I'd noticed the intel officers weren't big on sharing details until they really trusted you. I asked Lino if he had dealt personally with any intel officers. He nodded without saying too much. "They've always been professional."

I asked what specifically I might be doing if I got in. "You'll know better once you are attached to a command," he said. "They'll tell you what you'll be doing." It was all a little vague, all very Maverick in *Top Gun*: "It's classified. I could tell you, but then I'd have to kill you." But I liked the fact that he spoke as if I was likely to be accepted. "When you get in," he said, "you might want to choose a unit to drill with that's close to home so it won't impact too much on your home or work life. The reserves are very compatible with having a normal, civilian career."

He didn't get much more specific, and I couldn't tell how much he really knew. I asked if he thought I could get pilot training while I was an intelligence officer. He was very good at not saying much while still sounding encouraging. "It's not impossible," he said. "No doors are closed. A lot of different things can happen."

I didn't want the lunch to end. I looked up and noticed a couple of other people in uniform in the restaurant. "I've heard good and bad about navy food," I said. "You've been around. Where is the best?"

"The submarine service has the best food," he said without missing a beat. "Those guys have long hours underwater and not a lot of distractions."

"That makes sense," I said.

I could have listened to Lino talk all afternoon. But the main thing he left me with was the sense that as a navy intelligence officer, I would immediately be doing something important to help the country and that I had a good shot at getting in. That was all I wanted to hear.

I knew I was in the company of one bad-ass military dude. I wanted to do what he had done: spent his young-adult years running around the world to exotic hot spots as part of the world's greatest navy. That sounded pretty enticing.

By the time I walked out of that Chinese buffet in Quincy, I was hooked.

The letter reached Queensberry Street on Saturday morning, June 7, 2003. Ava was with me when I got the mail from the lobby box. The return address said Navy Recruiting Command, 5722 Integrity Drive, Millington, TN 38054-5057. The envelope was thin.

Walking upstairs to the second floor, I remembered what my high school friends had said when they were waiting to hear from colleges: You always want a thick envelope, packed with course selections and housing forms and moving-day tips and return-mail envelopes. When it comes to news-bearing envelopes, thin is never good.

"Dear Mr. Jamali," the letter began.

"Your application for appointment to the U.S. Navy Reserve Direct Commissioning Program has been carefully reviewed, but regrettably, due to program restrictions, you were not selected."

I read the first paragraph again. It didn't get any better the second time.

The usual happy horseshit followed. "Your application will remain on file for two years with this command. You should maintain contact with an officer recruiter should the program reopen in the future. He or she may request reactivation of your application should that occur."

And then the don't-feel-too-bad-about-this part: "Please be assured that your nonselection is not an adverse reflection on you, but an indication of the intense competitiveness of the Naval Reserve Program." And finally: "I regret a favorable decision could not be made in your case. Your interest in obtaining a commission in the Naval Reserve Intelligence Officer Program is greatly appreciated."

The letter was signed, "Sincerely, S. M. Heller, Lieutenant Commander, U.S. Naval Reserve." His title continued: "Head, Inactive Reserve Section, Officer Programs Division, Operations Department."

At the bottom was one last line: "By direction of the Commander." That made the rejection sound even more official.

I've heard people say that when they got bad news, it felt like they'd been kicked in the gut. Well, I felt like I'd been kicked in the gut by a Clydesdale.

"You really wanted this, didn't you?" Ava asked, sounding very concerned. "At first I thought you were just playing around with the idea, like you thought it might be cool or it just sounded interesting. I figured you would lose interest along the way."

"I don't think I've ever wanted anything more in my life," I said. "How do I go back to work Monday? Everything seems so pointless." I was oozing self-pity and acting like a victim.

Ava's reaction was not to throw me a pity party. Instead, she grabbed my hand and made me look her in the eye as she spoke firmly. "Hey! What happened to the kid who didn't get into college and then applied and got himself into NYU? Did that kid give up? Stop feeling sorry for yourself. You're going to do just what you did at Hunter. You're going to put one foot in front of the other and try again. If this is what you want, it doesn't matter how many times it takes or how long. You. Don't. Give. Up."

For a brief minute I thought she might punch me. But then her face broke into a giant smile. "It's beautiful outside, and I don't need to be in the lab. Why don't we take the T-tops off the 'hawk and go for a ride by the shore?"

I called Lino on Monday morning. He'd already heard. "Don't take it personally," he told me.

I knew he would say that. I also knew I would take it personally. How could I not?

"What do you think happened?" I asked him.

"It's probably the work experience," he said. "You haven't been out of school that long. You're just getting started in your career."

I've been out for five years already, I thought. *How long am I supposed to wait?*

"Geography might have something to do with it," he said. "For a program like this one, New England is probably the most competitive. It's not just Harvard. It's MIT, Yale, Brown—I mean, there's a lot of them. Maybe if you'd come from Texas, it would have been easier. There's a lot of good paper here."

He repeated what he and others had told me, that not getting in the first time was not that unusual. He said I had several other options. I could enlist in the navy, gain some experience, and move into intelligence work that way. Or I could get more experience on the outside and then apply again.

"If you want something bad enough," he said, "you keep trying. You may not be selected the first time. I know people who haven't been selected the second and third time, and they kept trying and finally got in. They wanted it. They did what they had to. They got it done."

He asked if Ava and I were still planning to move back to New York. I told him we were.

"Here's what I would do," he said. "The most important thing is you need to get experience that is relevant to this program. Being an IT person at Harvard is great. But just because you are Harvard, that isn't enough. What you really need is experience in the intelligence field, something that would make you more competitive against these applicants. You might consider working for the State Department or the FBI or a law-enforcement agency that does intelligence. You should apply for that kind of stuff. We have people who are dual-agency, who work in other state or federal law-enforcement agencies, and they're also in the Navy Reserves. That works out great for everyone. It doesn't have to be that, exactly, just something so you can show 'I have some actual experience in the field.' Does that make sense?"

"Okay," I said, trying not to sound too discouraged.

"And Naveed?" Lino said before wishing me luck and saying goodbye. "Let me hear from you, okay? Let me know how you do."

I knew Ava and Lino were right. I couldn't give up. Immediately, I started trying to figure out what I should do next. The obvious thing was to get a master's degree. When in doubt, hide in graduate school. Since Harvard offered free tuition at the Extension School, I thought, *Why not?* So I applied and, much to my delight, was accepted into the master of liberal arts program. After reading Samantha Power's *A Problem from Hell: America and the Age of Genocide,* I decided to focus my studies on state sovereignty and the concept that some crimes are so heinous, they justify its breach. I debated passionately with my fellow classmates about when evil is so profound, it permits or even compels military intervention. This was during the early months of the war in Iraq and growing condemnation of U.S. imperialism. I can say that my prointervention arguments were not too popular on the Harvard campus. Additionally, I decided to take on the role of Harvard freshmen academic adviser and found myself helping a gaggle of eighteen- and nineteen-year-olds navigate an unfamiliar campus. I traded in my old 1999 Firehawk for a silver 405-horsepower fiftieth-anniversary Corvette Z06. I dove deeply into the car scene in Boston, doing track days at New Hampshire International Speedway and Lime Rock Park and weekend car cruises across New England.

To anyone halfway paying attention, it would have seemed I'd settled back into my pre-9/11 contentedness. But I still felt that these were all poor substitutes for what I really wanted: a commission as an officer in the United States Navy. I was still going nowhere. In January 2005, after Ava was awarded her doctorate in genetics, the newly minted Dr. Brent and I loaded our two cats into a box truck and headed with all our worldly possessions back to the city of our birth.

CHAPTER 7

SPECIAL AGENTS

Boston was quickly feeling like yesterday.

Ava and I were New Yorkers on an atomic level. With my hopes of joining the navy on hold, leaving Boston—and with it, my unfinished master's degree at Harvard—hadn't been hard at all. At first I debated whether to take a semester off from my studies and then commute or transfer to a graduate program in New York. But even that felt like another excuse for delay.

New York was a new start for both of us. I went back to work—temporarily, I told myself—at Books & Research. We'd barely unpacked when I suggested to Ava that we do something major now that we were back home. "Let's get married," I said.

It wasn't a big wedding. Neither of us wanted that. On February 9, 2005, a week before our birthdays, we went to city hall and said "I do."

One Saturday morning a few weeks after that, Ava Brent Jamali was reading journal articles as I paced in the living room. "Hey, Ave," I asked for perhaps the thirty-seventh time, "now that I'm not in school, what do you think if I tried to get some work experience for the navy? You think that would help?"

"Uh-huh," she replied without looking up.

"Well, I was thinking, you know, maybe I should try and do an internship, like with the FBI, maybe. What do you think?"

I noticed my voice sounded intense and high-pitched. Ava had put down her articles and was looking at me. "Seriously, Naveed," she said. "Are you scheming again?" The last time I'd decided to join the navy.

"No, just listen."

"Okay, Naveed," she said, "why don't you just call the FBI and offer your services? But in the meantime, if you want to save the world, would you pick up some kitty litter? We're out."

Challenge accepted—on both counts.

That Monday, I asked my mother for the phone number of the latest FBI agent she and my father had been dealing with, explaining that I wanted to see if one of the agents might have some advice for me about the navy. Perhaps pitying me—her little boy was still trying to decide what to do when he grew up—she gave me a number. In her heavy French accent, she said: "Be careful, these are not people to trust."

A product of the seventies, I thought. *Suspicious of "the man."*

Excitedly, I dialed the number my mother had given me. The agent answered on the second ring.

"Is it okay if I call you Bambi?" I asked after introducing myself. I was trying to sound friendly and casual.

"If you want to, sure," she said, sounding slightly confused. "But if you'd like me to answer, it's probably better to call me by my actual name. I'm Randi."

I should have known better than to ask my mother for the agent's name. With the French accent, "Randi" had come out like "Bambi," and I'd just made a fool of myself with the agent I was eager to impress. So much for instant rapport!

I explained that I was calling on behalf of my parents. That was true enough and a better opening line, I thought, than "Hi, are you hiring part-time help?" I said that the man from the Russian Mission had stopped by, and I had been the one to take the order. "As you know," I said, "my parents are getting older. They'll be retiring soon. From now on, I'll be the one dealing with the Russians."

Maybe she was having a slow day. Maybe she just wanted to lay eyes on the idiot kid who'd called her Bambi. But she suggested that I come downtown and meet in person with her and her partner. We settled on a meeting place—outside the FBI's New York office at 26 Federal Plaza, near city hall and the courts in lower Manhattan. "We can walk somewhere from there," Randi said.

It was a beautiful spring morning when I went to see the agents. They seemed happy enough to meet me.

Randi seemed to be a smart and savvy young woman. Her family came from Colombia in South America. She said she had recently returned to New York from Seattle, where she'd been shocked to find that traffic stopped for her the minute she stepped off the curb, whether she had the light or not. "Very different out there," she said.

Her partner was named Terry. He seemed to be the junior agent. He couldn't have been much older than I was. He was thin and wore glasses and spoke in a slightly nasal voice. He came from an Italian-American family in Pennsylvania.

We darted across the heavy Broadway traffic to a Dunkin' Donuts. When Randi warned, "Be careful, Terry," he teased her about her concern for his street-crossing habits. "You've been in Seattle too long," he said, laughing.

Terry asked if I wanted anything to eat. "No," I said, "that's okay. Just some water."

With a slight smirk, Randi asked Terry if he wanted some fruit. He looked annoyed and didn't answer. "How 'bout an apple turnover?" she asked. "I hear they have good apple turnovers here."

Terry just scowled. I liked the fact that, even though they were FBI agents, they seemed to have some personality. They seemed looser than the stereotype. "Terry won't eat anything natural or with certain colors," Randi said to me. "Literally, he has not eaten any fruits or vegetables or anything green in years."

It seemed weird. But Terry shrugged, so I let it go.

He got three bottles of water. We grabbed a table in the corner and had a little talk. I repeated what I'd said on the phone to Randi, that my parents were transitioning out of the business and I would be dealing with the Russians. "I know there has been a long relationship between the Bureau and my family," I said. "I have been hearing about this for most of my life. The time has come for me to be more directly involved."

I didn't tell the agents what I was thinking. Frankly, I was a little hazy on the details myself. But Russian diplomats, FBI, surreptitious visits, secrets reports—that had to add up to something interesting. I was pretty sure I wanted to be part of it, even if I didn't know how.

The agents were obviously thinking on a smaller scale. "We appreciate your cooperation," Randi finally said. "We'd like for it to continue. But it's entirely up to you. If you want to keep doing this, that's fine. If not, we understand. Your cooperation is totally voluntary."

I understood, I said, and I was happy to continue. More like eager to continue. "So how should we proceed?"

"What do you mean?" Randi asked.

"Help me understand what you're looking for," I said. "What would you like me to do? I'll get the lists, but are there other things I can be helpful with?"

The agents didn't seem to pick up on my ambition to do more than provide copies of the Russians' shopping lists.

"We have a good relationship with your family, Mr. Jamali. Everything seems to be going well. Keep us informed. Let us know what happens. Just do whatever you're comfortable with. And please let us know when you hear from them again."

I promised I would.

The agents were perfectly pleasant and professional. They gave me plenty of time that day. But any ideas I had about getting more involved than my parents had been or buffing up my résumé with intel experience—clearly, that would have to wait. I didn't cook up any fresh business at the get-to-know-you meeting, and I wouldn't say they were excited to get to know me. They definitely didn't suggest an internship. But I did gain a glimmer of intel from that meeting. I noticed, as our conversation wound down, neither agent got up to leave.

"Should I leave first?" I finally asked. The agents nodded together. And I did. Without knowing it, I was getting a glimpse at inside methods of counterintelligence operators, something that would be important to me in the months and years to come. There were many must-know rules, it turned out. When possible, talk in person, not on the telephone. Agents work in pairs. They take a careful measure of the people they agree to work with. Protect the secrecy of the relationship. Trust and comfort are built over time.

Just telling the agents that I'd be taking over for my parents meant I was involved in something covert. I'd collect the list from the Russian man, then secretly turn it over to the Bureau. I was, at the lowest possible level, an FBI asset. I felt like a less bombastic Ed Norton in *Fight Club*, learning the rules at the same time I was supposed to play by them.

I stayed in touch with the agents like I'd promised to.

The next time a Russian from the mission dropped off a new

order, I called Randi and reported what was on the latest list. I was pleasant. She was pleasant. But that was about as far as it went. When I asked how else I might be helpful, she brushed aside my offers. "We appreciate what you're doing," she said. "It's very helpful." I don't think she knew what more I was asking to do. Truthfully, neither did I. Not yet. I didn't know where any of this was heading, if anywhere.

Randi and I spoke again three months later. I'd been out of the office this time when the Russian showed up. He'd collected his order and left a new list with my father. When I got back, I reminded my dad that I'd like to be the one calling the agents. He didn't care.

"I have the info for you," I told Randi when I got her on the phone. "Can we set up a time to meet?"

Since that first day when I met Randi and Terry, I'd never stopped thinking about how to expand our mundane relationship. At the very least, I knew I wanted to do something with the FBI that would impress the direct commission people in the navy. There had to be something I could do. I kept thinking back to the family dinner-table conversations from childhood, when my parents and I used to joke that the Russian men in trench coats *had* to be spies. Twenty years later, even after the Soviet Union fell and so much else had changed in the world, the Russians were still coming to Books & Research and the FBI was still keeping tabs on them. There had to be some reason for that, right? On both sides, I was sure. Whatever those reasons were, I kept telling myself, I was in a great spot to do some digging and maybe have something to write to Lino and his colleagues about.

I didn't want to report over the phone. And I wasn't thrilled about having FBI agents coming to the office. There were too many people around for us to talk privately. "Would you mind if we met before work near my apartment?" I asked Randi. She didn't ask why, but we agreed to connect at eight-thirty the following morning before I left for work.

I think I mentioned to Ava that I was meeting with the agents in the morning. Or maybe I didn't. I'm not sure. Either way, it wasn't a big topic between us. And she'd already left for her lab at NYU when Terry rang my phone from the street. "We're in the middle of the block across from your building," he said.

I rode the elevator down and met the two agents on the sidewalk next to their car, a black fourth-generation Ford Taurus. From a distance, I could see they were laughing, sharing what I imagined was some kind of special-agent inside joke. Terry was wearing a gray suit with a red tie. Randi had on a dark blue pantsuit. They didn't stand out in our Yuppie neighborhood. They could have been on their way to a job at a bank or a law office. Nobody would've glanced twice or thought FBI, much less counterintelligence.

As I approached, the agents' demeanor changed. They appeared much more serious.

"Why don't we go somewhere and talk," Randi suggested.

"You want to come upstairs?" I asked.

Randi and Terry hesitated. But then they glanced at each other and shrugged. "Okay," Randi said.

We crossed the street and went into the building. I nodded but said nothing to the doorman as we passed. We rode the elevator in silence till the doors slid open. I unlocked the apartment and led the agents inside.

Common sense and good old-fashioned paranoia should suggest to federal agents that it isn't wise to meet with an asset at his home. And even if all my parents and I ever did was provide the FBI with Russian reading lists, we qualified as FBI assets. There's no better way to take the covert out of a covert operation than for the government agent to be seen entering or leaving the asset's home. But discussing sensitive matters isn't always easy in public places, and I wasn't the kind of asset they needed to meet in the shadows. It wasn't likely the Russians would detect Randi and Terry slipping into my building. And they must have figured if coming upstairs made me more comfortable and helped us bond, it was worth the negligible risk.

So here we were at the ten-seat dining room table while I made my presentation.

"Here is what he ordered. . . . Here is a copy of the list. . . . Here is the new stuff. . . . Here is what it's gonna cost." Terry and Randi expressed bland interest: "Okay. . . . Uh-huh. . . . Right."

I watched Randi for a reaction. She was sitting military-straight with a blank expression on her face. Terry was watching her, and he looked worried. I believed I knew what both of them were thinking: *We have a good thing going here. It works. Why fuck with it?* The Bureau's relationship with my parents had always been a low-yield return, but it hadn't taken a whole lot of effort, and it was a return nonetheless. Neither one of the agents said that, of course. But I don't think my impression was wrong. And who could blame them? I didn't have that much to report. But since this was my first official briefing, I was trying to be as efficient and thorough as I could. I wanted the agents to think of me as skilled and professional. I was hoping I could quickly convince them I was creative enough to expand the nature of our relationship.

I explained to the agents how my parents' business was growing steadily, how we would be moving to a new office and hiring more people, how our customer base was expanding and we were breaking into more technical fields and performing more high-visibility projects. I also explained that I needed to be certain that my involvement with the Bureau, no matter what level it reached, didn't put the business at risk.

Randi waved her hand dismissively at that last part. "Your cooperation is not something that should impact your business," she said.

I thought about that, then squinted at her with mild annoyance. "I get that it *shouldn't* impact my business, but what if it does?"

"Look, you're obviously a very intelligent and well-spoken person," she said.

I smiled at the flattery but cut her off. I knew what she was doing, and I had to laugh. "One of the things I've learned in dealing with military customers from the South," I said, "is that you can absolutely eviscerate somebody as long as you end with 'Bless his heart.' 'Tom is a total fuckin' idiot, bless his heart.' " I wanted her to know they couldn't play with me. "Is that your bless-my-heart speech?"

Terry looked concerned, if not a little confused, and spoke up. "Naveed," he said sharply, "what are you thinking?"

"I'll tell you," I said. I dove in, suggesting a whole new level of involvement with the Russians. I took it as a given that they were engaged in something more than traditional diplomacy. The FBI had told my parents two decades earlier that Tomakhin was Russian intelligence. It seemed reasonable to assume that the present-day Russians were involved in more of the same. "Is there any way to steer the Russian who comes to the office away from the real business? What could I suggest to him that he might find alluring? Something that wouldn't put me or the business in any real jeopardy? I'd like to think of a new focus here."

There was another pause while Terry and Randi reflected. Looking back, I should have been more surprised by their response. They didn't shut me down immediately. They almost sounded interested.

"Take his lead," Randi said as the tension seemed to abate a bit. "We can't direct him to one particular path," she warned. "It has to be from him."

We talked a while longer, but that was about the extent of it. They didn't give me any useful guidance. Or a plan. But at least they hadn't ordered me to back off. As things seemed to be winding down, Randi asked, "Do you mind if I use your bathroom?"

"Of course not," I said. "Go ahead." I pointed her in the direction of our bathroom, which had original subway tile and a window that looked west to the Hudson. "It's all the way at the end of the hall."

As Randi left, I looked at Terry, who looked at me. We both sat there as if somebody had just pushed *pause*. He said nothing, and neither did I. I wondered what he thought of me. He seemed like a careful, deliberate, and observant person. Was this the FBI spin on good cop/bad cop—verbal agent/mute agent?

As I heard the water running, I couldn't help but wonder: Was Randi rifling through the medicine cabinet and writing down the names of the pills she found? Wasn't that what FBI agents did? Was she investigating whether I was on Lorazepam? Or was it Cialis? Either way, I was pretty sure that whatever she found was going straight into my personal FBI file. Briefly, I wished I had stuffed some exotic meds in there to fuck with the agents or filled the cabinet with candy: "Asset has a penchant for green M&Ms."

She came back from the bathroom. We said goodbye, and they left the apartment.

I had the impression that our Venn diagram wasn't quite intersecting. Where was the common ground here? We hadn't found it. Not yet. Randi and Terry seemed happy enough with the way things had been going. I was tense and impatient and fidgety, itching for things to change and develop and grow.

My cell phone rang. It was the office. I didn't have time to wrestle with my questions. I had to get off to work. I grabbed my laptop and headed to the garage to get the car.

I spent the day tied up in the boring duties of work and pretty much forgot about my meeting with the FBI agents. When I got home, it was already dark outside, and the lights were on in the front room of our apartment, so I knew Ava was there. I kicked my shoes off in the living room and called out, "Hello." She didn't answer. I walked back to the bedroom, which was where we spent most of our time. Ava was just standing there. Arms crossed. Looking really, really pissed.

Uh-oh, I thought. *This can't be good.*

"What's going on?" I asked her, hoping I sounded casual, hoping I was wrong.

"I don't know," she said. "You tell me."

Now, I knew that was a trick question. I wanted to be careful answering it. *What have I done? What do I admit to? Did I leave the apartment a mess in the morning? Should I not have told the fart joke at her lab dinner?* At a time like this, there is no right way to answer, no way to dig yourself out of whatever hole you don't even know you are in.

"Something you want to say?" Ava asked again.

Did I miss a birthday? What the hell did I do?

I was desperately trying to step around all the land mines in my head. A couple of possibilities came to mind. The one thing that did not register at all was the visit I'd had that morning with the federal agents.

We had a set of bookshelves in the bedroom. As she turned, I noted on one shelf a conspicuously out-of-place bright yellow plastic wrapper. Ava walked over and picked it up. I couldn't tell exactly what it was. "What is this?" she asked.

"I don't know." I really didn't. I just knew it played a part in whatever wrong thing I'd been caught doing.

"It's a maxi-pad wrapper, you dolt."

Now I was even more confused. *How did it get there? It's a female thing. Why does this involve me?*

"Did you have anyone over today?"

"I've been working all day," I said, which didn't exactly answer the question but had the benefit of being technically true. When in doubt, start with the truth. *Did I leave the keys with anyone? Did we have workers in?*

"You're telling me this just magically showed up?"

"I don't know about these things, Av—"

"Well, it isn't mine!"

We kept going back and forth. I was stalling for time, hoping I could think of something.

Then it hit me.

Terry and Randi had been in the apartment. And Randi had used the bathroom.

How do I explain this? Will Ava believe me? What bold assertion of mine would ease the wrath quotient? Should I say I'm having an affair? I have a weird maxi-pad fetish? I don't like to get up to pee and I find women's hygiene products more convenient than using a Coke bottle?

I wondered how crazy it would sound if I just said, "Ava, baby. I swear. I was just meeting with two FBI agents who were debriefing me about someone who may be a Russian spy." The truth sounded more preposterous than any stupid lie.

But I did tell her the truth. "I was meeting the FBI agents Randi and Terry this morning. I thought I mentioned it. I told them to come up here. We talked in the dining room."

"You brought them up here?" Ava demanded. "They saw our house? You let them use the bathroom? Did you clean the bathroom first?"

"No, I didn't clean the bathroom."

Ava was mortified. No longer at the maxi-pad wrapper or the imagined orgies I was conducting in our apartment in the middle of the afternoon. Suddenly, the issue was housekeeping. I hadn't exactly jumped from the frying pan into the fire, but I'd sure landed in a second frying pan—and this one was just as sizzlingly hot.

In my head, I cursed the FBI. This was their famously deft investigative technique? Their idea of being discreet? Strewing feminine hygiene products everywhere they went? What would be next? Getting made by the Russians because I had toilet paper stuck to my shoe?

"Did you make them take their shoes off?"

Oh, yeah. Right. As if I was going to insist that a couple of armed federal agents remove their shoes before they'd be allowed inside! But I was floating helplessly, so I grabbed for the life preserver of a little white lie. Trying to sound as stung as she had, I said, "Of course I made them take their shoes off. I did."

That day was just the first of many when the various parts of my increasingly complex life collided. My job, my wife, my career, my parents, the Russians and the feds, my obsession with cars—I had quite a few balls in the air. They sometimes placed competing demands on me. And I wasn't always perfect at juggling everything.

But I learned two very important lessons that day. First, never again lie to Ava Jamali. Period. It's not worth it. It's really not. And second, when building cover for a counterintelligence operation, you have to build layer after layer after layer. It takes time. It takes effort. It takes skill. And it can all be undone in a heartbeat by something as trivial as a feminine hygiene pad.

CHAPTER 8

MEETING OLEG

The first time I met Oleg Kulikov, my father was also there.

This was early December 2005. The days had gotten shorter. The Christmas lights were already up. The temperatures hadn't hit freezing yet, but the wind was snapping off the Hudson, and winter was closing in. Just a month earlier, we'd moved the office from Hastings to a larger suite at 145 Palisades Street in Dobbs Ferry, a four-story white stucco riverfront fortress down a steep driveway half a mile from the Dobbs Ferry Metro-North train station. The building had been a naval research facility in World War II and then a Bible factory. Our suite of offices was on the second floor, with picture-window views of anyone who came or went.

Shortly before eleven on a crisp Tuesday morning, I was talking with one of our account managers. The large metal door swung open, and I saw a short middle-aged man step inside.

He didn't say hello to anyone. He didn't walk over to us. He didn't sit on the couch in the reception area. He just stood in front of a large white bookcase filled with sample books that publishers had sent us. We invited visitors to help themselves to one or two if something caught their eye. The man was scanning the titles and mumbling to himself.

I knew immediately he had to be Oleg.

Over the years, half a dozen Russians had come through the business, maybe more. Typically, they served three-year terms at the mission in New York. There had been a lull in the early 1990s when the Soviet Union fell, and my parents wondered if they were done with the Russians for good. But after a year or so, fresh Russians returned with the same old requests—books, articles, and research materials they couldn't find otherwise.

There was Sergei. There was Alexi. There was Ivan. There were a couple of others who made hardly any impression.

Most of what they requested was open-source and seemingly benign. Occasionally, they'd slip in a request for something restricted or otherwise classified as U.S. government secrets. My parents always said no to those, and the Russians never pressed the point.

There had been a couple of creepy incidents over the years.

One Saturday morning, my father and I were at a hobby shop in Dobbs Ferry. I was looking at model airplanes. He looked up and saw two men staring at us from the other side of the store. One of them was Sergei from the Mission.

My father was about to walk over and say hello, then thought better of it. He said nothing. Sergei said nothing. But the Russians' appearance, so far from their residential compound in the Riverdale section of the Bronx, made one thing obvious: They knew where my parents lived, and they'd noticed my parents' son.

Another time, my mother noticed a gray sedan driving slowly back and forth in front of their house. No one said anything. No one did anything. But my mother was sure she recognized the driver as a Russian from the Mission.

I had heard my mother and father describe the latest Russian, who had been to the office in Hastings two or three times that summer and fall.

"He's different from the others," my mother said.

"Not as sophisticated," my father agreed. "He has a stronger accent."

"Not as friendly, not as outgoing," my mother said. "I liked Alexi. And Tomakhin."

"Or as educated," my father added, picking up her thought. "This one doesn't have anything to say."

He had none of the charm of the other men from the Russian Mission who'd come by to order books. They seemed intelligent, well traveled, and generally personable, whatever dastardly activities the FBI claimed they were engaged in. They might be spies. For all my parents knew, they might be stone-cold killers. But that didn't mean they couldn't be nice. The Russian diplomats carried themselves pretty much like my parents' other friends did. Not Oleg.

"He's a peasant," my mother said.

"That's it," my father said. "He's rough around the edges. He's thick."

And now he was over near the bookcase, standing by himself.

I took a moment to check him out. He was maybe five-six. Maybe. He had light-colored hair that was streaking toward gray and a neatly trimmed mustache. He was very pale, almost to the point of looking unhealthy. Even from where I was standing, I could see he had piercing blue eyes. He was wearing a white button-down shirt, a thick red tie, a boxy light gray suit, and a too-large tan trench coat.

Men's Wearhouse, I thought. Or maybe Jos. A. Bank. I knew that Paul Stuart and Barneys were a short walk from the Russian Mission. This man was not shopping at either of those.

As I was finishing my conversation with our account manager, I heard my father greet Oleg. "Oh, good. You found the new place. Sorry. Was it a problem?" I guessed my father hadn't mentioned we were moving.

"Uh-kay," Oleg said, his soft voice turning almost singsongy. I swear he sounded like a slightly watered-down version of Borat, Sacha Baron Cohen's Kazakh character from *Da Ali G Show* on HBO. "I found my way."

He spoke in concise phrases with a slight Russian accent and a tiny lilt dropped in. His English was solid. Was he trying to avoid being recorded? Was he in the theater club in high school? I could only speculate. But his tone was soft, calm, and nonconfrontational.

This was my chance, I knew. I didn't care so much whether my parents found him charming. After my conversations with Randi and Terry about helping the FBI with the Russians, I was eager to meet the new one.

"This is my son, Naveed," my father said as I walked over. "He is helping with the company now."

Oleg shook my hand and nodded.

"Let me get your books," my father said.

As my father walked away, I tried to strike up a conversation with the Russian. "So how do you like New York?" I asked.

I got five words back: "It's the center of everything."

"My wife and I moved back from Boston," I told him. "I much prefer New York."

"You are working here now?" he asked.

"Yes," I told him. "I've come into the business. My parents aren't getting younger, you know."

None of this struck a spark. The Russian seemed impatient, like he just wanted to get what it was he had come for and be on his way. As far as I could tell, he didn't have the slightest interest in me or my assessments of the relative merit of various American cities.

So I tried to loosen things up. Humor had always been my secret weapon. I wasn't sure it would work on the sour Russian. But I took a chance on a vintage glasnost joke. So much was different now, I figured even the dour Oleg could laugh at the bad old days.

The joke went something like this: Viktor and Boris were stand-ing on line in Red Square for their daily ration of cabbage and borscht when Viktor turned to Boris. "I don't understand," he said. "With glasnost, I thought things were supposed to be better."

"I agree, comrade," Boris said. "I'm so mad I could shoot Gor-bachev right now. In fact, would you hold my place in line?"

Four hours later, Boris returned. "So? Is it done?" Viktor asked him.

"Sadly, no," Boris said. "There is a line for that, too."

Oleg shot me a withering look. "I don't know anything about that" was all he said.

Yeah, I can be a dumbass sometimes. My father had the good sense or the lucky timing to rescue us before I could make more of a fool of myself. He set a cardboard box down on the table and handed an invoice to Oleg.

"Has my son told you he is interested in the military?" my father asked. "Naveed has been studying for his master's degree at Harvard. Tell him about your thesis, son."

That was just like my father, to exaggerate my achievements and mention Harvard, then make me sort everything out. I'd been gone from grad school for almost a year, and it didn't look like I'd be going back. But I resisted the temptation to nitpick my father's own awk-ward attempt at conversation and took one last stab at chatting up the Russian diplomat.

"I've been writing about universal jurisdiction and its impact on national sovereignty," I said. "Issues like the International Criminal Court and the point at which a nation's activities are so egregious that other nations have the right to step in. One of the things we studied was the Cuban missile crisis. It's interesting how, over the last few years, so much information from the Cold War has been declas-sified. You can study it much more openly now. It seems like things have really changed."

"Okay," Oleg said.

"There was a Russian colonel," I continued. "I can't remember his name. But he was in charge of the nuclear missiles in Cuba. Do you know his name?"

"No," Oleg said.

"Well, a lot has changed since then," I said.

Oleg stood there. He seemed to have no trouble following the conversation. But he definitely wasn't doing anything to prolong it.

"Okay," my father said finally, "we were able to get you everything except"—he ran his index finger across an item two thirds of the way down the list—"this book was backordered."

Oleg seemed satisfied. He just said, "Fine." He paid his bill with three hundred-dollar bills, rounding up the tally by forty-some dollars and declining the change. He didn't strike up any further conversation. He just handed my father another list of books and articles, promising, "I will be back for these."

As I said, "Good to meet you," and my father said, "See you next time," Oleg didn't leave the office. Not immediately. He reached inside his trench coat and retrieved a neatly folded black plastic garbage bag. He walked back to the large white bookcase and removed a book from one of the sample shelves. I couldn't see the title from where I was standing. But he dropped the book into the large bag. He grabbed another and another and another. Pretty soon he was sweeping them off the shelves like a six-year-old wrecking a house of cards. He was moving so swiftly, he couldn't possibly have read the titles as the giveaway books tumbled into the garbage bag.

What was he going to do with them? Send them back to Moscow? Sell them on eBay? Fill up his bookcase at the Riverdale compound so his colleagues would think he was well read? I didn't know, and he didn't say.

It seemed strange to me that our latest Russian customer, who'd earned what I assumed was a prize posting and a sought-after job, was also a free-book hog. I wasn't sure what to make of that. I also noticed how eager he was to leave. Fifteen minutes tops, from door open to door close, he was in and out of there.

I returned to my desk, plopped in my chair, and gazed out the big picture window. Just as I did, there was Oleg walking briskly up the steep driveway with his box and his bag of books. The load he was carrying had to be awfully heavy. But I have to give him credit. The short, pale Russian UN diplomat really flew up that hill.

"What's with him grabbing all the free books?" I asked my father as soon as Oleg had left with his heaping cardboard box and heavy Hefty bag. "What a piece of work! When he goes to the diner, does he fill up doggie bags with the free mints?"

"I don't know what he's doing with all those books," my father said. "Maybe he is selling them to the Strand," the legendary resale bookstore in Greenwich Village. "Or he just likes to read."

I knew my father didn't believe that. "Oleg doesn't seem like a big reader to me," I said.

I had very much wanted to start off well with the latest Russian. If I was going to make any real inroads with the FBI, if I was going to get the kind of experience I needed for the navy, I had to convince the Russians to trust me. And I had barely gotten two grunts out of Oleg. In that short visit, I saw firsthand what my parents had been talking about. He was different from the other Russians who'd been coming. Less sophisticated, less cultured—let me just say it, less couth.

"Maybe I shouldn't have told the glasnost joke," I said to my father. "The whole thing was pretty awkward. And I expected him to be taller."

"Height is not his biggest issue," my father said.

By this point, my mother and father had met Oleg two or three times. They didn't know him well, but well enough. "He makes no effort at all to be charming," my father said. "What I really notice about Oleg is that he so obviously doesn't want to be here. He seems to find dealing with us almost contemptible, like it's beneath him somehow."

That reminded me. "Why would you have to bring up graduate school?" I asked. "That's what you want the Russians to know about me? I'm not even there anymore."

"You said you might go back."

"It's been a year," I said. "I'm probably not going back. I didn't finish. I left."

"Well, there's no harm in letting people know what you've accomplished. It's all very impressive."

I just rolled my eyes.

The not-so-hidden message, I knew, was I should go back to graduate school. I should get a brand-name education. I should stack as many letters as possible at the end of my name. My father really knew how to deliver the Pakistani guilt. It was like he was asking me: "When are you gonna give us grandkids?" Was he going to push that, too? Maybe next time he could tell the Russian, "Naveed is working on making us grandparents. Tell him about your progress, son."

Ava and I were enjoying being back in New York. Now that she was finishing with her postdoc at NYU, she would soon be going from crazy hours to bankers' hours. We had far more predictable lives. We were taking on the normal trappings of a couple in their late twenties: building careers, thinking about starting a family, and genuinely settling down.

An hour after Oleg left the office with his books, the ones he paid for and the ones he didn't, I dialed Terry's number at 26 Federal Plaza. I knew this was my chance to pique his interest. I decided cryptic was the way to go.

"Hey, Terry, it's Naveed," I said. "I have some information for you."

He paused. "Oh-kay," he said slowly. "What do you have?"

"I had an interesting experience today."

He paused again. "Hold on," he told me. This time I swear I could hear a clicking sound over the phone line, as if he'd just pushed a little red button marked *record*.

"So tell me," Terry said.

"I met with the latest Russian," I said. "It was, ah, it was very revealing. I have a new list for you. Would you like me to bring a copy of it?"

"Sure," Terry said. "Let's meet. You wanna shoot for Thursday?"

FBI agents, I was discovering, aren't so good at appointments. Their schedules are unpredictable. Stuff comes up. Even a day or two later is far in advance for them.

"Thursday is good," I said. "Can we do it before work?"

"Sure."

"I'll meet you in the city," I said.

"We can come up to your neighborhood," he said. "We'll call when we're close."

After Oleg left and I'd reached out to Terry, I took a moment to reflect on the three things I needed to accomplish, and they all had to do with my own independence. One, I had to get Oleg to deal with me solely, instead of my parents. Two, I had to continue to build my own relationship with the FBI. And three, I had to get both sides to meet me outside of the office. Our office was the worst place to talk privately. The space was wide open. I never knew when my parents would be around. As far as I was concerned, an upper Broadway park bench in the middle of December, or a terrible chain restaurant in the suburbs, was a far more hospitable environment.

That Thursday morning, a little before nine, while I was getting ready for work, Terry's number came up on my cell phone. "We're downstairs," he said.

I came down from the apartment. Ava was off at work. Tucked

into my winter jacket pocket was a copy of Oleg's latest list. As soon as I hit the sidewalk, I saw Terry standing outside his car, which was parked at a fire hydrant, directly across from our building.

Randi wasn't with him this time. Standing beside Terry was a very large man.

"Where's Randi?" I asked when I walked up.

"She transferred," Terry said.

Oh, shit, I thought. Did someone hear about the maxi-pad debacle? But how could they? I hadn't told anyone besides Ava. "Is she okay?" I asked.

"Yeah," Terry said. "It's something good."

I was glad to hear that, even if Terry's lack of detail left a lot to the imagination.

"This is Ted," Terry said. No last name. Just Ted. He was blond and thick and muscular. He had very large hands, like someone who could open a stuck jar from your refrigerator in record time. He and I shook hands firmly. He gave me a big smile. He seemed more outgoing than the subdued Terry. Neither one said so, but I got the clear impression that Ted was the senior agent, just as Randi had been senior to Terry. But Ted, like Randi, seemed friendly enough.

"I have your list," I told them.

As we spoke, I noticed a couple of my neighbors coming out of the building. Luckily, they didn't cross the street on their way to the subway. But I knew it was only a matter of time until someone walked past us and said "Good morning." It occurred to me that this was not exactly discreet, the unshaved me in gym clothes talking intensely with two well-groomed gentlemen in suits.

"Hey, guys, this is a little awkward," I said. This time I didn't invite them up to the apartment. "Do you mind if we don't do this right in front of my building? There's a park over there."

Straus Park is a one-block landscaped triangle where Broadway and West End Avenue come together. The little park is famous for a bronze statue, erected in 1913, of a nymph gazing over calm water. The statue honors Isidor Straus, a U.S. congressman and co-owner of Macy's, and his wife, Ida, who died together on April 15, 1912, when the S.S. *Titanic* went down in the North Atlantic.

The Strauses lived in a house on Broadway a block south of the park. As the doomed ship took on water, Ida refused to climb into a lifeboat with other women and children, insisting on staying with her beloved Isidor. A passage from 2 Samuel 1:23 is carved into the memorial: "Lovely and pleasant were they in their lives and in their death they were not parted."

Ted, Terry, and I sat on a bench to the left of the nymph. On this chilly December morning, the three of us were the only people sitting out there.

"How did Oleg react when you approached him?" Terry asked, getting the conversation rolling. "He was expecting just your father, right?"

"Well, I wouldn't exactly call him friendly," I said. "Unfortunately, I made a joke. It didn't go over too well. He didn't think it was too funny."

"You made a joke?" Ted asked. "What kind of joke?"

"A glasnost joke."

The agents looked at me and then each other. "You know any glasnost jokes?" Terry asked Ted.

"I don't think so. You?"

"Me, neither," Terry said, and then to me: "What was the joke?"

"You want to hear it?" I asked.

"Yeah!" the agents said almost in unison.

I told them about the guy who was so sick of all the lines in the old Soviet Union, he went to shoot Gorbachev, but the line was too long.

"And Oleg didn't find that funny?" Ted asked.

I figured Ted was messing with me.

"I think it's hilarious," Terry said.

"You would," Ted told him.

I told the agents how Oleg wasn't much of a talker and seemed more comfortable interacting with my father than with me, not that he seemed too comfortable interacting with anyone. I said I'd been able to chat him up a little, discussing what I'd studied in graduate school and how I was in the company now.

"I think I made a little progress with him," I said, exaggerating the stiff interaction a bit.

I gave Terry the new list. I said I was sure Oleg would return in a few weeks to pick up these books and place another order. Then, as vividly as I could, I described the kind of person Oleg seemed to be. I gave special emphasis to the freebie books.

"What a cheap ass he was!" I said. "Are these guys that broke? They have to come to small businesses and take free shit? A box of wire hangers from the dry cleaners? A bucket of ketchup packets from McDonald's?"

Ted started laughing. "I believe it," he said. "They're awful."

The senior agent said that some of the diplomats got subsidies from the UN to pay for their tolls on New York bridges and tunnels. "Then they go out of their way to use the free bridges. They complain that the tolls are supporting the American government—and really, they just want to pocket the money themselves."

I told them that my father had a theory about the booze the Russians often brought after they went home to Moscow. "My father says they don't actually buy it there," I said. "They get it dirt-cheap from the Mission, or they pick up a few bottles at the duty-free store."

"Sounds about right," Terry said.

I count that conversation in Straus Park, which lasted no more than fifteen minutes, as my first operational meeting with the FBI, the first time I was reporting to the agents about something I had picked up in the field. It might not have been much. It was just my initial impressions and a few stray details. But I'd had my first face-to-face conversation with a Russian diplomat, and I'd passed my own intelligence to the FBI. I'm not saying any of it was valuable. But that is how trust is built, and I hoped I was building some on both sides of the post–Cold War divide.

Nine weeks later, Oleg returned to Dobbs Ferry, for all the usual reasons: To pick up the books he had asked for. To order some new ones. And yes, to fill his Hefty bag with sweeping armloads from the restocked shelves. It was the dead of February, and as usual, Oleg simply showed up. No call beforehand. No prescheduled appointment. No heads-up of any kind. Expecting this, I'd been making sure to be around the office as much as possible, arriving early, staying late. I didn't want to miss Oleg. My other hope was he'd arrive when my parents were out.

Success on both counts: I didn't miss him, and they weren't there.

He stepped inside the front door but came no farther. After he stood there for a moment, I walked over to him.

"Hello," I said.

"Good morning," he said in that soft, flat voice. "Is Naseem here?"

"He isn't," I said. "My mother isn't, either. Is there something I can help you with?"

He paused. "I see. Will they be back later?"

"Not today."

"I see. Perhaps I should come back another time."

The whole point was having Oleg establish a rapport with *me*. My parents were out. This was the perfect opportunity. I didn't want to let it slip away. Who knew when Oleg might return? If he thought something was wrong here, would he come back at all?

I pedaled hard. "You're more than welcome to come back later," I told Oleg. "But my parents are spending less time in the office. They told you they're retiring, right? Their schedules are very erratic, you know. I'd hate to have you return and miss them again."

I could tell he was studying me, trying to process what I was telling him. For the first time it occurred to me that there was a very real possibility the Russians had done some research of their own and decided my parents were safe to do business with. I was an unknown.

"I'm sure I can help you," I told him.

He took a breath and finally agreed. "I am here to pick up my order," he said.

"It's not a problem," I said. "I can go and grab it for you."

"Uh-kay," he said.

I didn't get the feeling that he disbelieved me. It was more like this was a new development for him and he was taking it in. He didn't seem like someone who reacted well to surprises.

I headed back to the storeroom and found his cardboard box. As usual, the box wasn't sealed yet, and the invoice was sitting on top. I carried the box out to the reception area and placed it on the coffee table. "I believe we have everything here," I said. He didn't check.

I handed Oleg the invoice. He looked at it carefully. He paid his money with the usual sweetener added on. He left another list. Then he reached into his trench and pulled out his trusty Hefty bag and got busy at the bookcase.

As he left, I had the feeling that this time I'd made some actual headway. He hadn't expected me to be in the office. He assumed he'd see my mother or father, like he and all the Russians before him usually did. I could tell he didn't like that. But at least he and I were talking. And even that little conversation gave me hope that we might be heading somewhere.

CHAPTER 9

NETWORKCENTRIC

To get their hands on secret information, the Russians liked a technique perfected at American convenience stores by generations of thirsty sixteen-year-olds. In my town, we called it "slipping it past 'em."

"Okay, I want a Lean Cuisine, a jar of applesauce, two D batteries, a child's toothbrush, a six-pack of Bud—oh yeah, and an *Us Weekly*." We'd say that as casually as we could, hoping the clerk wouldn't respond, "Hey, wait a second! You're a teenager! You can't buy beer!"

They must have had something similar in Russia.

Over the years, I had laughed with my parents when one Russian or another tried to bury a classified document or a restricted report inside a routine order for research books. But the first time I witnessed a Russian slip it past 'em was in 2006, when Oleg showed up at the office in Dobbs Ferry—unannounced, as usual—one steamy August day.

He issued a few awkward pleasantries, then cast his gaze, as he always did, on the book-giveaway shelf. As I went to fetch his order, he began loading the freebies into his plastic garbage bag. Nothing out of the ordinary so far. That was Oleg. After paying me in cash for the order, rounding up generously, he handed me his latest wish list. It contained a dozen or so books and articles, plus a printout about a conference that had been held in Washington earlier that year.

"What's this?" I asked him with all the charm of a harried 7-Eleven night clerk.

"Oh, yeah," he said as if he'd almost forgotten. "Are you a member of this organization? Would you be able to get the proceedings from this conference for me?"

I glanced at the printout he'd handed me. "IDGA," it said. "Institute for Defense and Government Advancement. 5th Annual Conference on Networkcentric Warfare."

Hmm.

I'd heard of networkcentric warfare. It was a theory of war articulated in the mid-1990s by Admiral William Owens and others in the U.S. Defense Department. The basic idea was that we had far better computer technology than most of our enemies did, so we should try to translate America's information superiority into practical military advantages for our troops on the battlefield. Network sensoring systems, shared situational awareness, full-spectrum dominance, rapid target assessment, reduced operational pause—those were the buzzwords of networkcentric warfare. It was a hot topic in defense circles when Oleg expressed his interest to me. I knew nothing about this particular conference. As far as I knew, it could be a walk-in presentation open to anyone with a single-ride MetroCard. But I promised Oleg I'd find out what I could.

As much as I wanted to keep a dialogue going, maybe finally crack this guy's stiff facade, it was a little creepy having him in the office. I noticed a couple of people casting uncomfortable glances in his direction, as if to say, "Oh, him again."

"I'll look into it for you," I promised before he left the office that day. "I will let you know either way."

He was gone as quickly as he came.

The IDGA, I vaguely recalled, catered to government officials, mostly from the Pentagon, and people from the technical side of the defense industry. Part networking group, part training platform, part idea lab, the organization and industry events were "dedicated to the promotion of innovative ideas and latest developments in public service and defense."

Defense wonks trading information for fun and for profit, if you prefer the English translation.

From a quick Google search, I learned that the IDGA's network-centric warfare conference was held in January at the Ronald Reagan Building and International Trade Center, one block from the White House. And yes, the conference seemed to be a whole lot more than a gathering of IT hobbyists. It was, to quote the brief hype material I found online, "a unique opportunity to learn from and network with over 800 senior-level military and industry colleagues." The speakers' first-string players from this muscular-defense world: General Richard Myers, former chairman of the Joint Chiefs of Staff, gave the keynote. John Ashcroft, former U.S. attorney general, also spoke.

I passed Oleg's request to one of the researchers in the office, as I would any order. I was trying to pretend that Oleg was just another customer. "Get what you can," I said.

The researcher came back a couple of days later, saying he had tried everything he could think of but had pretty much struck out. "It's not generally available" was the way he put it to me. "I don't think we can help with this one. You have to be a member of the organization to get this kind of access, or you have to have attended the conference." There seemed to be a complicated credentialing process for any of that.

I asked the researcher if he had any other ideas. He said he didn't. This wasn't going to be easy, I concluded. We weren't likely to get these conference proceedings by simply strolling in the front door at IDGA. And I couldn't see myself arriving on cables suspended from the ceiling like Tom Cruise did in *Mission: Impossible*.

But I wasn't ready to give up yet. I saw Oleg's request as a golden opportunity. He was asking for material that was clearly off-limits to him. If he'd asked my parents, they would have simply told him no, as they'd told him and his predecessors many times before. Had Oleg picked up on my signals of openness? Or had he decided to roll the dice on me? Either way, I hated the idea of returning to him empty-handed. If I wanted to deepen our relationship, I'd be missing an opportunity.

I was eager to talk to the agents. Maybe they would have an idea. Ted and Terry agreed to meet me in the rose garden at the Cathedral of St. John the Divine. As long as we had business to do, I thought we might as well do it somewhere nice. That stinky August, the cathedral garden was one of the few pleasant and secluded spots in all of New York.

"I've been trying to get these conference proceedings for Oleg," I explained to the agents. "They're different from the usual things he's been asking for. I don't think that's by accident. But I've basically hit a dead end."

I told them I wasn't ready to give up yet. "I have this feeling that he might be probing me," I said, "trying to figure out what I have access to, what I am able to get for him, how I feel about the rules of secrecy, how far I am willing to go for him. I'm not even sure how much he cares about the conference. I guess what I'm saying is I think he's testing me."

"For what?" Ted asked, the obvious follow-up.

"Hell if I know," I admitted.

Ted and Terry didn't agree to jump in immediately. But they

seemed to like the fact that I was thinking strategically and trying to tease out the Russian's motives. At least they didn't dismiss me out-right, as I'd feared they might.

"That's all very interesting," Ted said.

"I can tell Oleg, 'Look, I can't get this for you. I'm sorry.' But what would I do if this was real, if I really was ready to spy for him? I'd try to get it for him, right?"

Ted and Terry seemed to get my logic. But we ended our rose-garden conversation on a noncommittal note. "Okay," Ted said, "let's think about this."

There wasn't any rush. We knew we had three months or so before Oleg would return.

Ah, not quite.

Oleg turned up again at the Dobbs Ferry office in mid-September, less than a month after he'd last popped in. As usual, he came without any warning. I just looked up, and he was there. This habit of his was becoming annoying. He made planning impossible. I didn't want to miss him. I felt like I had to hang around the office. That was no fun. And he continued to make the other employees uncomfortable. Our customers were spread across the country and around the world. This wasn't an office where the customers dropped in at random. Besides all that, I wasn't ready for him.

I hustled Oleg outside as quickly as I could. After some perfunctory small talk, he turned quickly to what I assumed was the reason for his speedy return. "You have those conference proceedings for me?"

All I could do was put him off. I didn't want to tell him I'd tried and hadn't gotten the material. "I've been swamped around here," I said, which was true but not the reason. "I'll get on it soon. I'll try and get them for you."

As soon as Oleg left, I was on the phone with Ted and Terry. "He's still asking about that conference," I told the agents. "I can try one more time on my own and see if I can get this. But I have to be careful. I don't want to stir up a whole bunch of suspicion. And I really can't spend too much time on it. People in the office are already wondering about him. I can't let this fuck up my business. We should decide if we want to get this for him—and how."

"So how do you read it?" Ted asked me. I liked that he was seeking my opinion. "What do you want to do?"

"I wish we could find a way to get him that conference material," I said. "I think it might build some trust between us."

"Well, give it one last try," Terry told me. "Let us know how it goes." I said I would. I thought they could have been a little more helpful, but at least they weren't telling me my analysis of the situation was wrong.

I found some additional conferences. There was a networkcentric warfare conference in Europe. I could attend that one and report back to Oleg. Traveling abroad sounded like fun. But that didn't answer his request for the Washington event. I got about as far as I expected on that one, which was nowhere, not that I had very long to try.

Oleg was back again in October, another one-month turnaround. Our rhythm was definitely changing here. I looked up from my desk one rainy Thursday morning, and there he was. This time I walked him out to the parking lot. We stood out there like a couple of drug dealers haggling over gram prices. He got around to the conference soon enough. Clearly, the former Russian military man was not someone who liked to let things linger. The man had to have an iron to-do list!

"I'm working on it," I told him a little impatiently. "But this isn't like ordering a book for you. It's taking time. I think I can get it, but I have to jump through some hoops." I lowered my voice. "You know, this is different. A completely new category. I'm not even sure I can get it. I may have a friend who might be able to help. But it's going to cost you something. It won't be cheap. You understand?"

He said he did.

As soon as he left, I went back to my office and called the agents again.

"Look," I told Terry. "I have discussed with Oleg the difficulties. I need to be clear on what I should tell him. Are you guys gonna leave me hanging forever? Or can you help me get it?"

"Maybe," Terry said, making me think he meant probably. "I'll see what we can do." I felt relief. Even without any solid assurances that he'd help, we began to discuss how I would explain to Oleg where I'd gotten the documents.

"The logical thing," I said, "would be to say I relied on someone else to procure them. Either that or I signed up with IDGA, paid the fees." I was thinking fast, coming up with ideas and tweaking them on the spot when I saw a problem. "Perhaps," I continued, "just joining would yield results, but that would produce a paper trail, and I couldn't be sure Oleg's people hadn't already tried and knew it wouldn't work. This could all be a test. It would be better, I'm thinking, to let him believe I had someone on the inside helping me." I liked the idea of planting the thought that I knew lots of people in lots of places. "To me," I said, satisfied with my analysis, "that seems like the way to go."

"We can't provide you with a script," Ted said. "You have to be natural. You have to be in the moment, believe what you're saying. If you don't believe, why should he?" If Oleg was going to trust me, our interaction had to be real and fluid, like a genuine relationship. There are no teleprompters in espionage. "So the important question is 'How do *you* think you would have gotten these materials?' And don't forget, it's okay sometimes to leave it vague."

"Vague might work," I agreed. "In the past, the Russians have never asked how I got the books. They just took the stuff we gave them and went away."

Increasingly, the agents had been making me feel like I was part of the conversation, that we were three smart people trying to dream up a sensible strategy and get our heads around a challenge. It definitely brought out the mentor in Ted. I kept asking him questions. I wouldn't call him fatherly. We had too much of a smart-ass banter for that. But he seemed to like giving me advice.

Were they working me? Were they flattering me? Or did they actually appreciate what I had to say? Let me put it this way: They made me believe we were on to something.

A few days later, Terry was on the phone again. This time he was calling me.

"We got you what you wanted," he said. "We put it all on one CD for you. You gotta see the PowerPoint transitions our guys used!"

"Ugh, PowerPoint!" I said.

I hated PowerPoint. I knew Terry was trying to appeal to my geeky side, but he'd chosen the wrong software to praise. In the hands of a boring speaker, PowerPoint squeezed the life from the very ideas it was supposed to enhance. Whatever the topic—replacing a toilet seat or invading Iraq—PowerPoint imposed its mind-numbing uniformity, turning even an interesting subject into an undifferentiated blob. The famous speech by Martin Luther King Jr. wasn't "I Have a [pause/dissolve/new slide] Dream." If I had to sit through another list of PowerPoint bullets, I might have to put one of them in my head.

"Come on, Naveed," Terry said. "You should look at it. There is some nice work in there."

"I guess that's why they pay you the big bucks, dude," I told him. The fancy graphics didn't excite me. The fact that I had a CD did.

It was pretty impressive what the agents had pulled together about that conference. A detailed agenda. An attendees list. Summaries of the panel discussions on "Actionable Intelligence on the Network and

Airborne Networking Flight Test Results." All the PowerPoints. Copies of slide decks. Even the notes from the speakers. So much was packed on that single CD, it was the next best thing to being there. Give the feds this much credit: When they got in gear, things moved.

Ted never told me who the agents had spoken with or what explanation they gave. I'd tried every way I knew to get this information—or even a small part of it—with no results. I consoled myself with the thought that they had operated with a distinct advantage. Quasi-government research is significantly easier when the first words out of your mouth are "Hello, we're calling from the FBI."

They got what I couldn't, and I was very glad they did.

Oleg kept up his rapid-return rhythm. He was back in November. When I saw him trudging down the driveway to our building, I ran downstairs and cut him off before he ever reached the door.

"Let's take a ride," I told him. "I have something for you."

We climbed into my gold 2005 Acura RL, the latest in a rapid succession of vehicles. We drove toward Cedar Avenue, the main drag in downtown Dobbs Ferry.

"Here," I said, handing him the FBI's CD. "It's got everything from the conference. "I mean everything, right down to slide decks and the speakers' margin notes. Am I fuckin' amazing or what?"

Oleg didn't answer that. Actually, I'm glad he didn't. But he said thank you, and he seemed to mean it. And he handed me a white legal-sized envelope stuffed with American cash. "Will a thousand dollars be okay?" he asked me.

"Ten would be better," I told him, "but a thousand will get us started." I immediately thought I'd accepted too little. "This is not indicative of the cost going forward," I emphasized, "but it's a fine place to begin."

Oleg didn't press me on how I got the conference proceedings.

I never got a chance to trot out my helpful-friend cover story, which was extremely lucky. It couldn't have withstood thirty seconds of follow-up. *Who was this friend? What was his motivation? How much did you pay him? Will he help us again? Can I meet him?* "It was a little bit of work" was all I said to Oleg. Mainly, he seemed pleased that I'd been able to get what he'd asked for. He turned his attention to my parking skills.

"That is a very small spot," he said as I pulled the Acura in front of a bagel shop on Cedar Avenue. "I don't believe you could park there."

"Oh, yeah? Just watch," I said.

Why did I feel so competitive with Oleg? And why would that competitiveness assert itself over a suburban parking spot? All I know is that as I put the car in reverse and eased my foot against the accelerator, a little voice in my head was whispering about American honor. And as I cut the wheel hard to the right, I could have been Sylvester Stallone pounding Dolph Lundgren in the fifteenth round of *Rocky IV*.

The Acura had very delicate handling and back-up sensors, which I'm not sure Oleg had ever heard before. I don't want to say I needed the beeps to get into that parking place on Cedar Avenue. I was always a pretty good parallel parker on my own. But I did cut the wheel at the extra perfect moment, and the sensors didn't hurt. I glided the Acura snugly into the tiny spot. Cue James Brown's "Living in America."

"Very good," Oleg said.

We didn't stay long at the bagel shop, just long enough to grab coffee and have a short chat. We hadn't begun to bond. But I wanted to get him used to the idea of leaving the office with me. And I wanted to float the idea that things could be changing between us soon.

"My parents are ready to retire," I said. "I'm trying to find new revenue streams. Selling paper has a limited shelf life, I think." Oleg looked intrigued. I couldn't tell if he understood what I was saying or was afraid to admit that he couldn't. He didn't seem to like showing weakness of any sort. "Perhaps this creates an opportunity for you and me?" I asked.

He perked up at that. "Yes," he said. "I am interested in opportunities."

What the fuck? I thought. *Who isn't interested in opportunities?* It was time to test the waters. "Perhaps there are some things I could do for you?" I suggested.

He smiled. "Naveed," he said, "I am so glad we were able to leave and get coffee. It is a good way to discuss business, drinking coffee." He raised his paper cup as if toasting with a crystal glass of chilled Russian vodka. "Now, tell me, how would you like to do business?"

Uh-oh. It hit me that I hadn't thought this through. I'd violated the rule that every baby lawyer learns, hopefully before walking into a courtroom for the first time: Never ask a question you don't already know the answer to. Now that I'd opened the door, I had no choice but to walk through it.

"My goal," I told him, expanding on what I'd said earlier, "is to switch from ink on paper to more technology projects. I'd really like to change the direction of the business a little bit. We are working on some different projects for the navy and other parts of the government, mostly with military data. There is a lot of opportunity there for you and me. I am convinced of that."

"Very interesting," Oleg said. "That could be very interesting."

"We also have some library-related projects," I said. "Do you think you can help me find a librarian in Russia I can speak to?"

He didn't come up with a name for me, but he didn't seem perturbed by the question, and he didn't shut me off. "I will think about that," he said. "So do you like working in this business? Is this your—how do you say it?—your profession?"

"Well," I said, taking a breath before I tried to explain how I'd gotten drawn into technology. Out of the corner of my eye, I thought I saw somebody watching me. I vaguely recognized the older gentleman as someone I knew through my father. I tried not to make eye contact with him, knowing he would invite himself over. But it was too late. With a smile and a wave, he was making his way toward us.

"Naveed, right?" he said. "Naseem's son? How is your father? How's business? I thought you were in Boston!"

"Things are really great," I said. "You should give him a call."

I didn't introduce the man to Oleg, and Oleg didn't say anything at all, but I could tell he was paying attention. He was leaning forward without actually leaning forward. He seemed to enjoy my flustered expression.

"I'm sorry," I told the man. "I'm just in the middle of some business right now. Let's catch up later." I gave him my card and all but told him to leave. He looked at the card, realized he had interrupted something, and backed away.

"I'm so sorry," I said to Oleg after the man had left. "This is the difficulty with small towns—they're small."

Oleg waved away my concern like he would a tiny mosquito. But he seemed to have lost interest in continuing our conversation. He was out of his seat before I could finish my sentence, pulling his jacket on.

I already knew that this was a crucial day in my growing relationship with Oleg. The lead-up hadn't been easy, but the rewards were going to be great. I'm not sure what would have happened if the FBI hadn't gotten the conference proceedings. I'm just glad they did. Message delivered. Thank you very much.

I knew from the beginning that if Oleg and I were ever going to commit espionage together, our interaction would have to change. He'd need to become more than a customer to me, and I'd have to become more than a vendor to him. We'd have to get out of the office. The subtleties would have to end. I'd have to betray my own country, and he would have to ask me to.

The agents and I had dangled the bait that Oleg found enticing, and he had bitten.

★   ★   ★

A few days later, I met with Ted and Terry. They told me to bring the white envelope Oleg had given me. I was glad to hand it over, along with the thousand dollars. For as long as the Russians had been ordering books and paying us—always a little more than the invoice—any extra money we got from them just went back into the company.

But the dollars were growing, and I knew I couldn't just pocket the money. This was more than simply ordering books. I didn't know the right way to handle it. So I asked Ted and Terry.

"You can't take money from the Russians," Ted told me. "Give it to us. We'll voucher it. You'll sign a receipt. We'll give you the same amount of money back."

So that was what we did. It was all very official. Terry handed me the receipt to sign. "What if I don't want to sign this?" I asked him.

"Then we can't give you the money."

That seemed fair enough to me. I hadn't gotten into this for the money. Given all the time it was taking, I'd have been better off putting an ad on Craigslist for babysitting work. But I was incurring expenses. Our growing operation was taking time away from my regular work. I couldn't have Books & Research financing the counterintelligence efforts of the United States. And Ted and Terry seemed to like the idea that, in a roundabout way, the Russians were paying me to double-cross them. I liked that, too.

"I'll sign," I told Terry.

CHAPTER 10

OUT AND ABOUT

"Oleg!" I snapped when he showed up again the week after Thanksgiving. "You can't keep coming here randomly every time you feel like it. This doesn't work for me."

I hustled him out to the parking lot even before he'd had a chance to snag a single free book. We stood next to the Acura and spoke for a few minutes. "From now on," I said to him as firmly as I could, "we have to start meeting someplace different. Do you hear me?"

With the CD, I knew we had crossed some kind of threshold, Oleg and I, even if I wasn't certain what was on the other side. He had asked for something difficult, and I had delivered it to him with the help of the FBI. He had paid with a crisp stack of U.S. dollars. This double-agent business wasn't easy, I could see that already. But I was starting to think I might have some talent for it.

Though that delivery was going to seal my credibility with the Russians, some loose ends needed to be tied down. The most pressing item on my agenda was getting Oleg out of the office for good. There was no way he and I could talk there. Every time he showed up was another potential disaster. He never came and went discreetly. Even if he stayed for only fifteen minutes, it felt like he was lurking around. His visits were an obvious focus of curiosity and suspicion for the other employees. They couldn't help wondering about the weird Russian guy and his coat-pocket garbage bags. And each time Oleg left, I had to go through a routine to avoid their questions: I would busy myself with phone calls that couldn't be interrupted or meetings that couldn't be disturbed, hoping that by the time I came up for air, attention would have shifted elsewhere.

There was no need for Oleg to keep popping in like this, especially with his appearances being so frequent. I wasn't just his vendor anymore. The relationship had already moved beyond what it had been in my parents' day, a box the New York Russians could check off regularly and report to their minders back in Moscow. I needed to find a way to separate the book business from the spy business.

The Books & Research part of my relationship with the Russian Mission was still part of the equation. Acquiring information, even open-source information in an open society, had genuine value to them. The kinds of reports, articles, and books the Russians wanted might be available, but that didn't mean America's longtime enemy had easy access. Almost everywhere the Russian diplomats went, their trench coats, accents, and documents were sure to raise eyebrows and suspicions. *Why do you want this?* people would ask. *Is it legal? Will I get in trouble if I give it to you? Isn't your country the enemy of my country? Why should I help you?* Even when there were no legal prohibitions, our nations had a history that made getting these items maddeningly difficult. Where else were the Russians going to go? This stuff wasn't stocked at Barnes & Noble. Mail orders left paper trails that could lead to questions of intent. These topics were too technical, too narrow, too arcane for general distribution. And even if no one ever asked directly about their true objectives, my assumption was that the Russians had a near-obsessive desire to operate as discreetly as they could. It was clear they didn't want the FBI or any other U.S. government entities knowing what they sought. With our experience and contacts, my family's company was able to get this stuff easily without raising concerns. There were no forms to fill out. No purchase orders in triplicate. And we were based in New York. That allowed Oleg and his predecessors to make in-person visits to a private office. They never stayed very long. They didn't even like to sit down. Our company offered the diplomats of the Russian Mission an agreeable alternative to the things they most wanted to avoid.

Now things were shifting and growing more complicated. While dealing with my parents had been safe and convenient, I wasn't just a sporadic asset. I had become someone they were working regularly with—and valued, I hoped.

The decades of business-as-usual civility shifted noticeably when I got grumpy with Oleg that morning in early December. But he was surprisingly agreeable to my change-of-venue demand. Maybe he didn't like visiting the office any more than I liked hosting him.

Almost immediately, the benefits of being out of the office were made clear. We were able to talk without fear of being overheard. He asked for my cell phone number. I gave it to him. He offered me an email address, a generic Yahoo! account. I wrote it down but told him I probably wouldn't be using it. "When things go over email, there is always a record," I said.

"At least you will have it," he said. I think he liked my caution, though.

It was chilly in the parking lot that morning. A sharp breeze was blowing in from the river. But our conversation felt comfortable and natural. And then Oleg came back to the reason we were freezing outside.

"I have thought about what you were saying," he told me. "After today, we will meet in different places. If I order books, you will bring them when we meet. I will not come here anymore. Our relationship is changing."

Damn, that was easy!

"I must be away for the holiday," Oleg continued. "But we will have many things to discuss when I return. The next time we meet, will it be okay if we meet in a restaurant?" He went into his pocket and pulled out a business card. "Do you know where this is?"

"Uno Pizzeria & Grill," the card said. "Original Chicago Deep Dish Pizza." The address was on Central Avenue in Yonkers, on the main suburban-sprawl drag through this part of Westchester County.

We were going to Pizzeria Uno? Was this really where treason was committed these days?

"That will be just fine," I told him.

"I will call you on your phone when I return," he said.

"And if something happens and I'm busy and can't meet you, how will I contact you?"

I worried for a minute that I was asking too many questions, but Oleg didn't seem to mind. "It will be fine," he said. "I will wait and if you do not come, I will leave. I will call you. We will meet another time."

I have to say I was a little disappointed by Oleg's choice of restaurant. I imagined us whispering at a back table in Manhattan's glamorously ostentatious Russian Tea Room or conspiring over late-night Iordanov shots at a sleek vodka bar on the far West Side. Pizzeria Uno? Not even close. Instead of a perfect-30 Zagat rating, I was getting a pizza chain with an "ample parking, ample portions" Yelp review. Instead of blinis with sour cream and caviar, I was headed for prima pepperoni and cheese stix. I wasn't really sure why he chose the pizza chain. Maybe that was all his Russian Mission stingy expense account could cover. And if Pizzeria Uno was Oleg's idea of fine American dining, that was where we'd go. I was just happy he wouldn't be coming to the office anymore.

When I told Ted and Terry, they sounded as psyched as I was. "He gave you his email?" Ted asked me. "And you gave him your cell? That's all good. He's setting up the structure for clandestine meetings. He's gaining confidence in you."

"Yeah, but Pizzeria Uno," I said, shaking my head in disbelief. "Where are we going next? KFC?"

Two weeks before Christmas, I met a flatbed truck off Interstate 87 in Yonkers. Strapped to the bed was a new-to-me black-on-black 2006 Corvette Z06. I'd been researching the purchase heavily. In my estimation, the Z06 was everything that was right about America. Confidence. Power. Craftsmanship. Performance. It was powered by an LS7, an old-school pushrod seven-liter, 505-horsepower V8 engine, and a manually shifted six-speed transmission. That's a lot of get-up-and-go for a vehicle that size. The Z had so much torque. Jeremy Clarkson, of the BBC's *Top Gear,* exclaimed that it's "an actual fact" that the Z06 "will go from a standstill to 175 miles an hour in one gear!" That Corvette clocked better times at Nürburgring than cars ten times the price—and still had modern creature comforts like XM satellite radio, navigation, and dual climate control. It could get you there in a hurry, and you'd still enjoy the ride. This was the rare American car that the boys from Maranello, Stuttgart, and Bologna couldn't afford to shrug off, much as they'd like to. Just looking at that car made me feel patriotic. I was in love.

In my view, cars were meant to be driven. Any vehicle I ever owned, I used as part of my daily life. Lots of people are enthralled by the chase scene in *Bullitt* when Steve McQueen overtakes a black

Barracuda in a green fastback Mustang. But what enthralled me was that his character drove the car daily and parked it on the streets of San Francisco.

That's what the Z06 meant to me. It was beautiful and exotic and fast as lightning. And I took great pride in parking it on the streets of Manhattan while all those fussy Ferrari owners parked their beloveds in high-priced garages, too nervous to drive their cars to one of the outer boroughs. If I was going to have a car, I was going to drive it— anywhere, anytime—including hauling my butt around on a counter-intelligence operation that required constant navigation between a Russian diplomat and agents from the FBI. I never felt like the money I poured into cars was remotely wasteful. I stood firmly with the great Northern Irish footballer George Best, who famously said: "I spent a lot of money on booze, birds, and fast cars. The rest I just squandered."

On the long road ahead, the Z would play a consistent support-ing role. In addition to serving as my getaway vehicle after many of my meet-ups with Oleg, it would also become a much-needed release for me, helping me blow off some of the pressure that was constantly building inside. Dealing with Oleg could be awfully frus-trating. I would learn that over and over again. Dealing with the Bureau could be even more so, as we painstakingly gamed out what I should say and how I was going to say it. I worried about the operation getting canceled, being found out, or worse. In any of these scenarios, I knew the blame would fall on me. I have the kind of mind that dances all over the place, so I thought about every cir-cumstance and how it would play out—sometimes good and some-times bad. Being able to wipe all that out of my consciousness for even a few minutes at a time, to step on the gas and send the Cor-vette flying, produced a special Zen for me. I never liked to miss a chance to experience that rush. Tearing up the switchbacks at Bear Mountain. Hitting the apex just right. Gliding confidently into the next left turn.

Just as I had in Boston with my first Corvette, I began spending time with a group of like-minded car aficionados who were not looking for notoriety. When they wanted to sound formal, they called themselves the New York Motor Club. They just sought the bliss that pure driving brought. We would meet extra early on Sunday mornings outside the city, then blast up the back roads and rural highways, hitting speeds that would never be possible a few hours later with traffic on the road. It was on one of those weekends, when slower family cars began to clog those back roads, that we descended into the misty Hudson Valley and met in a tiny town to grab a round of coffee and top off our gas tanks.

As we sat together on the curb in front of my wide Z06, my friends Matt and Larry and I started talking about some of the coolest people we'd ever met.

"My uncle worked for the CIA," Matt said. "He was very quiet. Nobody knew what he did at the time. But he was a total badass, in a highly discreet way."

"It's crazy to think that there are people who do that," Larry said. "But you'd never know. You think he killed anyone?"

As much as I wanted to jump in, I kept my mouth shut except to say: "I doubt it. But he probably hurt a few people's feelings."

I stole that line from Robert De Niro in *Ronin*. I'd been waiting for years to use it.

When we weren't going to the Lime Rock racetrack or doing early-morning runs, we would hang out and plan what we called ego runs. We'd descend together on Times Square or some other high-traffic, high-visibility spot. We'd park the cars and say nothing. As we stepped aside and watched, the wide-eyed out-of-towners would go crazy, asking questions, posing for pictures. It was embarrassing and exhilarating all at once as strangers shook our hands and begged for rides in our highly polished automobiles.

The car runs and associated lifestyle would become one of the little secrets I hid from the FBI. The agents were becoming so entangled with me, it felt good to have some things I didn't share. Some people drink. Some people do drugs. Some people jump out of airplanes or hit a dimpled ball over a stretch of well-kept grass. I wasn't interested in any of that. Instead, I drove like a maniac.

I knew the FBI wouldn't approve of the recklessness of the driving or some of the car people. It was likely they would see racing as a weakness, evidence that I lacked the reliability or maturity necessary to carry out the plans we were developing. They certainly didn't want a risk-taker on their hands, especially when they hadn't had the chance to carefully measure the level of risk.

But what they didn't know couldn't hurt me. So on that mid-December morning when that car came off the truck, I took my first drive in the Z and felt the thrill of all that power in my hands. I felt full of confidence. There wasn't anything I couldn't learn to drive with a little practice—automobile or espionage.

Oleg and I met four times in the first half of 2007, all at casual restaurants on Central Avenue. Twice it was Pizzeria Uno, in January and February. In April, we met at Charlie Brown's, a family-friendly regional-chain steak house. In June, it was the retro—real retro, not ersatz retro—El Dorado Diner. Not a bowl of borscht or a hot Russian hostess at any of those places.

Each time we followed the same pattern. Oleg would call my cell phone and ask if I was available to meet for lunch, usually the following day. Never dinner. Never breakfast. Never cocktails. Always lunch. I always said yes, agreeing to meet him even if it meant rearranging an appointment or canceling other plans. He always set the place and the time, handing me a card or a take-out menu as we were saying goodbye. "This is where we'll go next time," he would say. Then I'd wait for his call to tell me when.

It was a long, slow dance between us, progressing a few agonizingly unhurried steps every time we met. There's a scene in Vin Diesel's spy thriller *XXX* in which his character Xander Cage meets with a Russian spy named Yelena, who's been monitoring suspected terrorists in central Europe. "I've been undercover here for two years," she tells him. He can't believe she's been at it so long. "Two years?" he asks. "What was your plan? To let them die of old age?"

He may as well have been talking about me.

As slowly as I felt things were moving, Ted and Terry's excitement was clear. They encouraged the dance, sometimes offering vague guidance for their nouveau operative. Their advice mainly consisted of telling me to be natural and to let it "be a conversation." They offered no opinion on how I should steer Oleg. They just acted like the important part was me reporting back to them.

There were rare occasions when they did offer me clear advice, often consisting of dire warnings. Ted once told me: "Under no circumstances are you to get into a drinking competition with Oleg."

That's a funny way to put it, I thought. "What? You mean like beer pong?"

The normally unflappable Ted seemed unexpectedly tense. He repeated his warning with even more emphasis. "For them," he said, "drinking is not a sport. It is a skill developed and nurtured at an early age. Whatever you think you can do, you cannot outdrink them."

I wondered if either of these guys had ever been to an American college frat party. But I listened. *Okay. Do not drink with Oleg. Ever. Check.*

Armed with that warning, I made my first trip to Pizzeria Uno at noon on a Tuesday in mid-January. Oleg ordered a beer. I ordered an iced tea.

It was a pleasant meeting, but not what I'd expected. I brought his book order in the Corvette and delivered it to him. He showed up in a bland gray business suit with a medium-width red tie. He had a lanyard around his neck with an ID card he'd tucked into the right front pocket of his shirt. He still looked like a business drone but a more comfortable one than the man who had been visiting our office. For the first time since I'd met him, he spoke at length about himself. He told me that he'd grown up in western Russia, not in Moscow. He'd attended the Maritime Academy in Vladivostok, a tough port city not far from Russia's border with China and North Korea. He said he'd wanted to join the navy since he was a boy. The academy was how he could go in as an officer, not unlike our own service academies or ROTC. "It was tough," he said. "We had to do running and pull-ups and all these physical activities. I worked very hard. But I was determined. I made it through."

The way Oleg told his story, he didn't leave much room for doubt. Despite his outward appearance, when he talked about himself there was some swagger and a lot of pride. And maybe, I thought, a little exaggeration.

He mentioned a wife and a teenage daughter, though he didn't say either of their names. I noticed he had on a wedding ring and a gold submarine pin, the way a U.S. Air Force pilot might wear miniwings or a Navy SEAL might wear a trident on the lapel of a suit jacket. "Were you an officer on a submarine?" I asked Oleg. "Yes, a submariner," he said. "Very important duty." He said that part of protecting the homeland had involved patrolling the coast of the United States with nuclear missiles pointed at us. He had been stationed in a lot of places, he said. He mentioned Turkey. He'd had a diplomatic posting in Canada, he said, before he came to New York.

And now he was here, very much enjoying the big city. "It is the center of the world, the center of everything."

I had no way of knowing how much of his story was true, but I had the sense that most of it was. Oleg was a professional diplomat and, as was becoming more and more apparent, a man inclined to spy. I suspected that he had absorbed, in whatever training he had received, the same important lesson about lying that I was learning now: Lies are far better hidden when they are wrapped in demonstrable truth. As far as I could tell, none of this stuff really mattered, so why not tell it mostly straight?

But I did wonder why Oleg was going on like this. He didn't seem like someone for whom confession came naturally.

He said he liked my parents. He told me how important education was and asked where I'd gone to college. I said NYU and mentioned that I had been part of the ROTC there, but I'd been drawn away into technology. I detected a pattern immediately. He would say something nice to butter me up, then slide in a seemingly innocent question. He said he enjoyed watching American football on TV— bond with the young male American!—and asked if I did, too.

"Cars are my sport," I told him, promptly skipping over a topic he'd probably studied for my benefit.

It seemed like white noise at first, our conversation in the pizzeria. It occurred to me only later what Oleg was doing. He'd been loosening me up, using his own apparent openness to make me more comfortable revealing myself. His plan, I saw now, was to lull me into a state of ease so that I would reflexively answer his questions. To some extent, I did. It was a testament to Oleg's skill as an interrogator, I suppose, that while I was there, I felt comfortable and momentarily let down my guard.

As I'd been chatting, he'd been operating. I had to step up my game. There was an obvious potential for danger. I'd heard stories that I hoped Ava wasn't aware of, like the chilling tale of Alexander Litvinenko, the investigative journalist and fugitive Russian FSB officer who was poisoned to death the previous November in London. Oleg was thoroughly unassuming and assertively nondescript. But he did work on the same side that was suspected of kill-ing Litvinenko, and I had no illusions of what his countrymen were capable of.

I couldn't linger on that. I'd never again be that unguarded. I had work to do. But I wouldn't let myself be paralyzed by my dark imagination.

I also decided that just as Oleg seemed intent on learning more about me, I needed to know more about him. The information he'd shared about his time in the navy had been enlightening but was intentionally orchestrated to encourage me to open up. There was more to this man who bragged about being a Soviet submarine captain turned Russian diplomat, and I wanted to know everything.

The first time I'd told Terry his name, I'd gotten a clear sense that Oleg was someone our government was keenly aware of and interested in—someone very much on the FBI radar. The agents weren't quick to share the biographical details. But when I poked around on the Internet, checked some public databases, and made a couple of educated guesses, I pieced together that Oleg wasn't just any Russian diplomat. He served on the United Nations' Military Staff Committee. In that role, he interacted at a high level with military diplomats from countries around the world. And my instincts about his special focus had been right all along. Oleg was an officer in the Main Intelligence Directorate of the General Staff of the Armed Forces of the Russian Federation—the GRU, which stands for Glavnoye Razvedyvatel'noye Upravleniye.

The quiet, slightly awkward man in bad suits and worse trench coats was a middle-to-high-ranking officer in Russian military intelligence. And there was more. He was a case officer, my case officer. He'd been trained in the management of human agents and the recruiting of prospective foreign assets. His mission was to spot people whose knowledge and access might be of value to the Russian Federation—and then to work diligently on bringing them into the fold.

People like me.

I was familiar with the title *case officer* from books and articles I had read. It was a special role in the Russian military-intelligence service, a real upwardly mobile position. At least one had gone on to the highest heights of all: During his time with the KGB, as he worked his way up to president, Vladimir Putin had been an intelligence-service case officer.

As January turned into February, I grew increasingly impatient for Oleg to call. What was he doing? What had I told him? Had I discouraged him? Had he just disappeared? During the day, I busied myself with work, trying not to dwell on my budding double-agent career. But I didn't try too hard. Each night I'd read books on spies like Ames, Hansen, and Pollard. I analyzed the tactics they employed and wondered if I could do better than they had. In many cases, it was their arrogance that had done them in. It had given them confidence at first, but then it made them sloppy. The more I thought about this espionage business, the more I came to see what a huge challenge fooling someone at this level was—truly the ultimate challenge. And the more I read about and dissected the methods used by these renowned spies, the more eager I grew to be back in play with Oleg.

While I waited, I had several long meetings with Ted and Terry. As eager as I was to press forward with Oleg, I also didn't want to get myself killed in the process. I didn't think Ava would like that. I was pretty sure I wouldn't, either. There was a thrill to living close to the edge, but I didn't want to fall over it. Slowly, clumsily, in fits and starts, I tried to find a balance I could live with.

In one of my FBI meetings, I brought up one nagging concern. "You think he's armed?" I asked Terry.

"I would say probably not," the agent answered.

"Probably not?" That *probably* stood out.

"I don't think they'd risk having a high-ranking diplomat carrying a gun with him. What sense does that make?"

"So why aren't you sure?" I said. "What's *probably* about it?"

"In this business," he said, "*probably* is all we get."

When Oleg did call, it was on a freakishly warm Thursday morning in February. He asked if I could meet him for lunch that day, and I said yes. Thirty minutes before our appointment, I stopped first at my parents' house and threw up. Radioactive poisoning. Guns. My brain was working overtime. I splashed some cold water on my face and pulled myself together. Then I drove the Z06 like a madman, trying not to be late. On my way there, I made one last call to Terry and let him know I was off to see the man—"just so you know."

"Just be cool," he told me. "You'll be fine."

Despite my aggressive noontime driving, I was fifteen minutes late for Oleg. I found him sitting near the hostess stand, feigning interest in an Uno's menu.

I saw a glimpse of anger as I walked in, but he quickly gained control. Whatever he was really feeling, he assumed a look of relief as I stepped toward him. "My friend," he said with a smile, vigorously shaking my hand. "It is good to see you!"

I smiled back faintly. That brief flash of anger had made me nervous. I couldn't help glancing for a bulge in his waistband. I didn't see anything. "I am so sorry," I said. "Something got tweaked at work, and it took a little longer to sort out."

He looked confused at that. "Tweaked?" he asked. I guess he hadn't heard the word before. I noticed he hadn't let go of my hand. Was that just a matter of social awkwardness? Was it a test of some sort? Was he feeling if my pulse was racing as I tried to explain why I was late? Nothing Oleg did seemed like an accident.

"We had an unhappy customer," I explained. "It took a little longer on the phone."

He looked at my face maybe a fraction of a second too long, smiled, and let my hand go. "Shall we sit down?" he asked.

Once we did, Oleg continued the friendly banter from our last lunch at Uno's, offering tidbits from his own life and seeking some from me. He said his daughter was studying French in school and recalled that my mother came from France. "Do you speak French?" he asked me. "Do you have a French passport? Do you travel there?"

"I speak it," I said, leaving my answer at that. I didn't have a French passport, though I'd traveled to France many times with my parents. I got the feeling Oleg was asking the travel questions for some reason beyond curiosity.

But he didn't press the point. "French is a beautiful language," he said. He didn't point out that my father was Pakistani or ask if I spoke Urdu.

I had prepared a tidbit of my own that I wanted to mention—the fact that my wife had a relative who was somehow related to Trotsky, the Marxist revolutionary theorist and first leader of the Red Army. I thought Oleg would like that, and he did.

"*Leon* Trotsky?" he asked, lighting up at the name.

"The one and only," I said.

I'd impressed him. But quickly, he was back in control. He asked me if I was an electrical engineer. "Was that your subject in college?"

"No," I explained. "Computers. My background is technology."

All these questions seemed harmless enough. He wasn't asking for anything I wouldn't divulge in small talk with a stranger sitting next to me on a plane. And that made it difficult to keep up any defensive wall. He asked innocent-sounding questions, and I couldn't think of any good reason to lie. Part of me really welcomed the openness. I wanted to bond with Oleg, as he wanted to bond with me. But with each new query, the knot in my stomach grew tighter. It wasn't that I was divulging secrets. It was more that I recognized how single-handedly he was driving the conversation. I was committing myself to a specific, detailed biography without knowing what the endgame was. At the very least, I would have to remember what I had told him so I wouldn't contradict it later on. The tone remained cool and friendly. But the longer we talked, the more nerve-wracking it became. I felt like he was leading me somewhere, and I knew that couldn't be good. My whole life, I'd never been comfortable in the passenger seat, especially when I didn't know where I was going, much less the route.

I called for the check. Oleg paid it in cash. It was always in cash. As we stood to leave, his wallet slipped out of his hand. I caught the falling wallet in midair and handed it back to him. "Thank you, thank you," he said.

I was thinking again: *Was that a simple accident? Was it a test? Was he checking to see if I'd casually try to look inside? Was there something he wanted me to see? Am I being paranoid?* His benign-sounding questions had my mind racing. If it was a test, I guess I'd passed. But every time we were together, I came away with the feeling that Oleg was trying to climb inside my head. And if placing a hint of paranoia in there was one of his goals, he was succeeding.

I had to find a way to take some more control. These meandering quiz sessions weren't only stomach-turning, they were too risky for me. With my vague but honest answers, the Russians wouldn't be able to figure out what to do with me, and then I'd have wasted all this time. Or just as bad, before I could make a move, they'd come up with some request or plan that I wouldn't like at all. I could only imagine: *Okay, we've figured it out. We want you to rent a van and drive around Washington taking pictures of sensitive buildings. No, forget that.*

We want you to marry this redheaded woman named Anna so we can get her a green card. No, thank you very much! I had to be in the driver's seat.

"They are opportunists," Ted warned me when I shared my concerns. "They probably don't know yet what they can do with you. When they figure that out, believe me, they will try."

That rang true. When they did make a decision about what they wanted me to do, I needed to be sure it was something I could deliver—or, more precisely, make them think I could.

CHAPTER 11

WHY SPY

I never had the opportunity to change my name or my basic identity. The Russians had known my family for two decades. Using my real name left me more vulnerable. If the Russians wanted to come and get me, they knew exactly where I was. I wasn't overly talkative with Oleg about personal details. I never talked about my neighborhood or about Ava, beyond the mere fact that I had a wife. But I had no illusions about protecting my privacy or the Russians' ability to dig into my life. I assumed they'd already done that. It couldn't have been very hard. I had a listed phone number. I drove cars registered in my name. A simple records check would tell them where I lived, who my neighbors were, who I was married to, where I went to college, where I used to work, and for all I knew, how many times I'd forgotten to pay my parking tickets until they double and tripled with interest and penalties.

(Just a couple of times. I swear!)

I said to Ted one day: "They must know a lot about me. How much danger am I in?"

He answered in his usual measured way. "Not a tremendous amount, as far as we know."

"Not a tremendous amount? As far as we know? What does that mean?"

"We have no reason to believe you are in danger. Why would they want to harm you? They're hoping you'll be useful to them."

I knew he was trying to be comforting. It wasn't working. "Can they check up on me?" I asked.

"They can do open-source searches," Ted said. "Sure."

He didn't specify what he thought that might entail, but I knew more about open-source research than he did. It included Lexis-Nexis and Google and checking out my Facebook, Twitter, and LinkedIn accounts. The Russian could dig up whatever Equifax or the other credit-reporting agencies had on me. Pretty much anyone could get his hands on that. They could talk to my neighbors, my former employers—could they also bug my apartment or tap my phone? Were they following me? What about Ava? "It's illegal for them to perform surveillance," Ted assured me, deftly avoiding the question.

Was that really the best he had, that the Russians wouldn't do anything illegal?

"But Oleg is GRU," I said. Again, Ted didn't respond directly, but his lack of denial was enough for me. I went on, "You're telling me that, against their number one enemy, Russian intelligence doesn't have resources to burn? Diplomats in this city don't even pay parking tickets. And they're going to follow more serious rules? They'd like to follow the guy who's helping them spy on the United States, but they won't because that would violate some GRU Boy Scout oath?"

Ted laughed at that.

I was new to all this, but give me some credit. I had to assume that Oleg had people checking me out, even if he wasn't doing the checking himself. And those people would no doubt attempt to verify anything and everything I said. I'd better not out-and-out lie to him about provable factual details except when I really had to.

I could narrow the frame of reference. I could stretch the truth. I could hide troublesome factoids and focus on stray details. But however I presented my own biography and motives, all of it would be painstakingly examined by the Russians abroad and at home. They would check enough to give themselves confidence in me. So everything I said had to be defensible, even if it wasn't 100 percent true. There could be no idle chatter. Nothing could be uttered thoughtlessly. Whatever lies I wove had to be supported on a bedrock of truth. The Russians had to believe. It was as simple—and as complicated—as that.

Though I was stuck with my name and basic biography, my personality and motivations were all up for grabs. Oleg already knew *who* I was, but it was up to me to show him what I was all about. The double-agent business, I discovered, is not a come-as-you-are affair. In fact, I had to dream up a whole new persona that would serve me better than the real me would. Getting that right turned out to be immensely important and tons of fun.

Basically, I got to be a much bigger asshole with Oleg than I ever was in real life. Constantly impatient. Quick to anger. Cocky. Obnoxious. Self-absorbed. Focused on money above all else. I convinced myself this was the most effective way to be. Oleg was a very tough character. He'd endured the Russian navy and earned a coveted post in the United States and a prime posting in New York. Most impressive, he'd made the transition from Soviet Union to Russian Federation on his feet. Those are not the achievements of a weak or wobbly man. If I was going to hold my own against a guy like that, I thought I had to be one tough motherfucker, too.

For the first time, I was freed from being the friendly, agreeable, decent guy I had always tried to be. With most people, I was self-deprecating to a fault. I liked to make people laugh with me. I wanted them to like me. My alter ego was an amoral, narcissistic psychopath. He got to do all kinds of things I never would have dreamed of. I probably shouldn't admit how quickly I took to the major-jerk role. When I was in character with Oleg, I didn't care if he hated me or wanted me to die. All I cared was that my behavior worked, that it kept me focused, sane, and effective under circumstances I was totally unfamiliar with. That can be quite liberating, I found out.

I didn't feel like I had much choice. The guy my friends, parents, and wife knew would be incapable of selling out his country for cash. I had a moral compass. I cared too much about the respect of the people I respected. I liked to sleep at night. If this grand deception was going to be believable, I had to create a character who would plausibly engage in espionage. That character needed to be strong-willed and fully formed. And ruthless. Personality, attitudes, manner-isms, all of it had to shout: "Sure, I'll sell out my country. But I won't do it for free."

The good news was that I had some built-in faults I could draw from. I swore too much. (I plead "native New Yorker" to that.) My sense of humor has often been compared to that of a fourteen-year-old boy, and it's not usually meant as a compliment. I still laugh when someone says "sperm whale." My idea of entertainment truly does intersect with that inner fourteen-year-old's: I'd seen far too many cynical movies and played far too many twisted video games. So in some ways, I had a solid base for building the Naveed that Oleg was getting to know. Imagine how hard this transition would have been if I were a total candy ass!

But my shortcomings weren't sufficient inspiration. For top pro-fessional guidance in becoming a thoroughly amoral prick, I turned to the undisputed experts of the character-creation world: Holly-wood. If anyone knew how to make up characters, the people writing for TV and the movies did.

So as I got deeper with Oleg, I began staging my own personal Spooks, Spies, and Double Agents Film Festival on the flat-screen TV in my living room. I went looking for characters I could copy and learn from. There was no shortage of them. *Miami Vice, Spy Game, Ronin, Heat, Collateral, Casino Royale, Manhunter, Bullitt*—I watched until I grew bleary-eyed and had to go to bed. Movies I'd seen before, movies I'd barely heard of, random episodes of old TV shows. I practically memorized all of it. Then I'd stand in front of the bathroom mirror and practice some of the juicer lines like a Stella Adler wannabe cramming myself into an especially challenging role.

"We didn't come down here to audition for business. Business auditions for us." Jamie Foxx, *Miami Vice*.

"The wrong decision is better than indecision." James Gandolfini, *The Sopranos*.

"I'm funny how? I mean, funny like I'm a clown? I amuse you? I make you laugh? I'm here to fuckin' amuse you?" Joe Pesci, *Goodfellas*.

This may sound goofy now, but I swear it taught me a lot about building a new, rougher legend for myself. It helped me slide into character like nothing else could. A few rounds in front of the mirror, and I was transforming into this other me. In the thirty seconds it took me to imitate Al Pacino in *Scarface*—"I always tell the truth, even when I lie"—I could pivot from Naveed Jamali, regular guy, toward Naveed Jamali, pissed-off double agent.

Those were some of the baddest-ass dudes I was emulating. In many of those films and TV shows, the main character played a double of some sort, an undercover cop or clandestine spy. I was fixated on how those characters reacted when they were accused—as they inevitably were—of not being who they claimed to be. As far as I could tell, the best defense was a powerful offense.

I loved the way Crockett and Tubbs (Colin Farrell in the old Don Johnson role and Foxx stepping in for Philip Michael Thomas) react in the *Miami Vice* movie when the cartel lieutenant Yero demands: "Other than Nicholas, who the fuck knows you?"

"My mommy and daddy know me," Crockett seethes, his voice dripping with condescension. Then he plops a hand grenade on the table, removes the pin, and begins questioning Yero's cred. "You want to 'know' shit? Who the fuck are you? You got a side deal with U.S. Customs to open up the coast in a few spots. In exchange, you flip them some gringo runners? Like us?"

"You wearing a wire?" Tubbs demands, ripping open the kingpin's shirt.

"Or DEA?" Crockett jumps in. "The Feeb?"

The agents are suddenly back in control.

I could see myself pulling something like that on Oleg—minus the hand grenade, of course.

There was so much to choose from here and so much work for me to do. Once I had my basic character down—little patience, explosive temper, money-obsessed—I had to learn to act like a criminal. I'd done my share of stupid things, but I had never committed a crime, much less something as serious as treason or espionage. All I had in my arsenal of experience was exceeding the speed limit or slipping into a bar below the drinking age. When I was growing up, that stuff would hardly get you a written warning from the jittery Hastings cops. Definitely not a mug shot and rap sheet.

So what would a real criminal say and do? More important, what would Oleg and the Russians expect a criminal to be like? As a professional military officer and a diplomat, Oleg probably hadn't had a tremendous amount of exposure to real criminals, either, let alone traitors who were willing to sell out their country for fat envelopes of cash. I assumed that he was building on his expectations from American TV and movies just like I was: I'd always heard that Hollywood is America's greatest export.

On film, even the soft-spoken criminals had explosive tempers. They were never afraid to storm away from a deal if it didn't skew sufficiently their way. They had their own language and their own unique set of rules.

In *Spy Game,* Brad Pitt's Tom Bishop complains to Nathan Muir, the Robert Redford character, that he let an asset get killed:

Muir: He was your asset, somebody you use for information.

Bishop: Ah, Jesus Christ, you just . . . You don't just trade these people like they're baseball cards! It's not a fucking game!

Muir: Oh, yes, it is. It's exactly what it is. And it's no kids' game, either. This is a whole other game. And it's serious and it's dangerous. And it's not one you want to lose.

Spying is a tough business, all the movies seemed to say. It isn't for the faint of heart. There is no room for complainers or wimps. It's like what the grizzled cop Vincent Hanna, played by Al Pacino, says to Neil McCauley, the De Niro bank-robber character in *Heat*: "My life's a disaster zone. I got a stepdaughter so fucked up because her real father's this large-type asshole. I got a wife, we're passing each other on the downslope of a marriage—my third—because I spend all my time chasing guys like you around the block. That's my life."

Says McCauley: "A guy told me one time, 'Don't let yourself get attached to anything you are not willing to walk out on in thirty seconds flat if you feel the heat around the corner.' Now, if you're on me and you gotta move when I move, how do you expect to keep a marriage?"

God bless the movies and TV.

Then there was the question of my motivation. Why would someone like me commit espionage? I got busy reading up on what makes people spy. History and fiction, both ancient and modern, had lots to offer on the subject. Spy books, spy movies, spy TV shows—they all have theories about the hidden and not-so-hidden motivations. Early in my research, I came across the theory of MICE.

According to MICE, people commit espionage for four basic reasons—money, ideology, coercion, or ego. Sometimes it's a mixture of two or three, but people who've thought about this far more deeply than I have say that those are the four solid categories. Each is powerful in its own special way. And it's easy to find examples of all four.

Money may be the most common reason. To supplement income or in a fit of desperate financial need, people have often spilled their country's secrets. That's why anyone applying for government clearance is put through a credit and finance check. Many traitors have been revealed by sloppy, lavish spending. John Anthony Walker is a perfect example, though sadly, nowhere near the only one. The former U.S. Navy chief warrant officer convicted of spying for the Soviet Union from the late 1960s to the mid-1980s seems to have been motivated largely by the lure of cold, hard cash. Secretary of Defense Caspar Weinberger acknowledged that Walker's treason gave the Soviets access to a wide array of U.S. arms secrets—"weapons and sensor data and naval tactics, terrorist threats, and surface, submarine, and airborne training, readiness and tactics."

Ideology is another common motivation. From early patriots like Nathan Hale to sainted abolitionists like Harriet Tubman, some of America's greatest heroes were ideological spies. Spying for ideology has been a factor in almost every nation and every war. Name a cause and someone has famously spied for it. Communism: Kim Philby and Klaus Fuchs. Anti-Nazi: Fritz Kolbe and Juan Pujol. Pro-Cuba: Ana Montes. The list goes on and makes for fascinating history.

Coercion, though less common, also plays a role. Torture is the most obvious and extreme example, though threats can work just as well. Once captured, some spies motivated by M, I, or E predictably claim they were coerced. But it does happen, sometimes quite ingeniously. During World War II, Mathilde Carré, working with the French Resistance, was captured by the Nazis and threatened with torture or worse unless she became a double agent. Svetlana Tumanova was told by the KGB that her family in the Soviet Union was in peril unless she played ball. To somewhat greater skepticism, Ronald Humphrey claimed he helped North Vietnam only to smooth the release of his Vietnamese wife. For centuries, military officers and diplomats were coerced to spy by the threat of being outed as gay. Worried about this possibility, intelligence agencies routinely investigated the sexual histories of applicants, fearing that "deviants" might be subject to blackmail. That kind of coercion is mostly a thing of the past, but anyone in a sensitive position is still a potential target of espionage blackmail.

Ego, excitement, thrill, arrogance—call it what you want to. Lots of people spy because it's so much fun, even when other motives play a partial role. Robert Hanssen is a prime example. An FBI agent who spied for the Soviet Union, he was involved in what was called "possibly the worst intelligence disaster in U.S. history." He was truly propelled by his own cockiness. Jonathan Pollard was another one. A civilian American intelligence analyst, he was convicted of selling secrets to the Israelis, but he couldn't imagine that someone as brilliant as he was could ever get caught. Christopher Cooke, a U.S. Air Force lieutenant who slipped Titan II missile data to the Soviet embassy in 1981, suffered from the same outsize ego. He was so fascinated with espionage that he could barely stop himself from diving in. At least that was what he told unsympathetic investigators.

So what was going to be my motivation? Was I an M, an I, a C, or an E? I had to have something. It had to be believable, and it had to be me. I was certain that Oleg had read as much about MICE as I had. He knew what to look for. Wasn't all that restaurant conversation designed to pin this down? He wasn't just enjoying the cheese stix!

Money was the answer for me. Of all the plausible motives for my treason, money was by a mile the most believable. If I was going to pretend to spy, nothing else felt true enough to act out. I wasn't an ideologue. I wasn't an Islamicist any more than my father was. I wasn't up for endless discussions with Oleg about religion or communism or the glory of the Russian Empire or anything like that. I didn't have passionate feelings against the United States—quite the opposite, in fact. I didn't belong to a single subversive organization, unless you counted my fast-driving club. I wasn't a card-carrying member of anything except maybe the public library and Blue Cross Blue Shield. I didn't even have a Blockbuster card anymore.

Money was simple. It was clean. I understood money. Like most people, I liked what money could buy. Leisure time. The comfort of my family. And really fast American cars. I thought if I exaggerated my desire for money, it would be something that Oleg could understand. He'd grown up in the Communist Soviet Union. For decades they'd derided Americans for greedy capitalistic ideals. But he seemed to have adjusted to the wide-open capitalistic jag his country now seemed to be on. I suspected he, too, liked money, and he could easily see how I lived—the cars, the clothes, the job—as much proof as he wanted.

As did a lot of real spies, I added some E to my primary motivation. There is something fundamentally arrogant about deciding to commit such a grave act, the kind I was pretending to. Pollard and Hanssen were arrogant. So were most of the others. The real me—and the double-agent me—shared some of that. I couldn't deny it. Adding a dose of superiority to what I wanted the Russians to believe was my motivation, that was easy. Around Oleg, I constantly wanted to convince him that I was smarter than he was. Lots of times I played the same head games with the FBI. And not for a second did I doubt my ability to outwit both. Like my real-deal role models from espionage history, I knew I was craftier than my trackers were.

That was a character I could play, money-hungry and abundantly sure of myself. It wasn't me exactly, but it was close enough.

These movies and books might not have been the perfect teachers. But along with Ted and Terry, they were the teachers I had. Luckily, I had those agents to bounce my self-taught methods off. Before I saw Oleg again, I shared with Ted and Terry what I thought I had learned.

"It's gotta be about money for me," I said to the agents, "with a little arrogance thrown in. Nothing else makes any sense. I'm not a Communist. I don't hate America. I just like stuff. I can't pretend to be a nuclear physicist. I just won't be able to pull that off. I can talk about most things. But I can't convince a genuine subject-matter expert that I know more if I don't. There's no way of knowing what secret vaults of knowledge Oleg has hidden away. Wanting money is a story I can always keep straight."

"I like it," Ted said.

With their seal of approval, I climbed into the car and got to work.

Once I was out of the apartment and away from the highly obser-vant Ava, I made the switch. Only then could I see firsthand how much about me I'd changed. My demeanor. My strut. My aura. The way I drove. (Okay, maybe not the way I drove. I never drove bash-fully.) Though I was unarmed, I had to ooze confidence and display no hint of fear. So even though I wore my regular clothes, left from my real apartment, drove my actual car, and gave the Russians the only name I had, I adopted the mannerisms and personality of some-body who was fully manufactured for Oleg.

To complete my transformation, each time I'd drive to meet Oleg, I had a carefully chosen playlist of music. It really did help to psych me into my new character. On my way there, I listened to a lot of things that amped me up—Jay-Z's "99 Problems," M.I.A.'s "Paper Planes," Audioslave's "Shadow on the Sun." On the way home, as I eased back into real Naveed, I would substitute the harder-edged stuff for mellower music to cool me down—Eddie Vedder's "Hard Sun," RJD2's "Ghostwriter," and a dash of Wilco. "Theologians" was perfect for that.

I'd have a packet of documents at my side, props I could use to enhance my credibility. Those papers gave me the confidence that I had something tangible to trade and the arrogance that my brain was worth more to the Russians alive then dead.

By the time I pulled into a parking spot, I was a different person. Any fear had evaporated. It was like I had flipped a switch. I turned on an almost clinical out-of-body view of what I had to do next.

Yes, playing a double agent was unfamiliar territory, but I didn't mind the newness of the experience. I was actually wired for it in more ways than one. My technology training served me well: I was used to using new technology. In my industry, that was the expectation. Whether it was a query, a loop, an object, or a select statement, if you understood the basic concepts, it just needed to be applied to the latest format.

It was the same with spying and counterspying. I didn't know much about espionage. But I knew human nature, and I knew I could learn. This was just another new experience with its own basic concepts and language. And I was learning to adapt.

When I put it all together, I knew I had what it would take to convince the Russians I was the real deal.

CHAPTER 12

GAINING CONTROL

It was selling time, and the product was me.

When Oleg and I connected in April at Charlie Brown's in Yonkers, I didn't wait for him to quiz me. Over a couple of buffalo chicken wraps, I described my plans for the company, how I was committed to turning a modest family business into an international data and research powerhouse. I had large ambitions, I explained. "Ink on paper is so yesterday," I said. "The world is going digital, and we should, too." I said I was committed to grabbing far more of the international market share. "We should be a much bigger business than we are," I told him. "And I am going to make that happen."

I expounded proudly for my lunch partner. My ego was bulging! There was money to be made! I was capable of anything!

All this had the advantage of being largely true, even if I wasn't quite on the edge of world financial domination—yet. As I suspected, sticking with the money story was way easier than railing against oppressive American imperialism or quoting lengthy passages from the Koran. To support my young-businessman-on-the-make persona,

I buried Oleg in a stack of Excel spreadsheets showing steady growth and increasing momentum for the company. He seemed impressed. The truth, even somewhat exaggerated, is easy that way. The ambitious business talk came tumbling off my tongue.

I told Oleg I'd been writing new software that would make it easier to keep track of what orders were filled. Everything had been on paper before. It wasn't easy to get an overview. "Now," I said, "we'll be able to track and inventory items using bar code technology, checking every single book in and out."

I mentioned that we might be hired to digitize some large volumes of technical military data. I talked about the National Defense University and some other projects that were winding up. "As we close out these projects," I told him, "we're starting some other new projects you might be interested in."

"Yes?" he asked. He leaned forward, waiting for more.

"Just as a hypothetical," I told him, "say you were interested in Tomahawk cruise missiles. Currently, you don't know what information is available out there, right? I might have access to certain databases. It seems like you are missing a lot of stuff here. Hypothetically," I repeated, "would you be interested in something along those lines?"

"We might be," he said. The more I spoke, the fewer chances he had to quiz me about my family, my background, and my personal life. "You are very ambitious," he told me.

Story, motivation, access—the pieces were coming together one bad lunch at a time.

Before I met with Oleg again, I had my usual strategy sessions with Ted and Terry. We discussed what I could dangle in front of him. I said I was eager to come up with something enticing—and soon. I teased the agents about who was slower and more bureaucratic, the

FBI or Oleg. One day while we were hashing over various possible scenarios, Ted slipped in a question for me, Russian-style: "Oh, by the way, would you mind wearing this watch the next time you meet with Oleg?"

He was holding a large black G-Shock wristwatch with a black Velcro band. It was the kind of watch that a special-ops commando might wear, or a SWAT-team member, or an especially flamboyant rapper. It had a digital readout and a built-in compass and—you couldn't see this last part unless you turned the watch over—a tiny digital tape recorder secreted inside.

Ted's request didn't bother me. The way he put it, I didn't feel like there was any trust issue with him or Terry or the FBI. All along, I'd assumed they were listening in on my conversations with Oleg. I figured they had the table wired or undercovers sitting next to us or—anything is possible, right?—maybe the waitress wasn't a waitress at all. Maybe she was a special agent with an order pad.

From here to the end, I knew that surveillance and countersurveillance would be part of my life, even if I never knew when or how. I tried not to become too obsessed with it. I tried to compartmentalize. But I couldn't help wondering as I went about my daily chores: *Is that van on my block following me? Is the couple in the next booth listening in? Maybe. Maybe not.* But I discovered eventually that if I wanted to keep paranoia from mingling with observation, I had to keep my frisky imagination on a very short leash. If I had a question or a concern, I couldn't obsess about it. I should note it, report it, and move on. I wasn't alone. I did have some professionals on my side.

We joked about the watch. "I have a small wrist," I told Ted and Terry. "This thing is huge. It looks like a Flavor Flav timepiece, to tell you the truth. You buy it off Flav? Was he selling it on eBay?"

"Hey, it was either this or a key fob," Ted told me.

"A key fob?"

"Yeah, a key fob. One of those little things that hangs off a key chain."

"I know what a key fob is," I said. But there were all kinds. I'd seen teenage girls with Hello Kitty key chains. Grandmas with fobs that opened their 1990 Oldsmobile 98s. "You were gonna put the recorder in a key fob?"

"We could have," Ted told me. "But we chose to go with the G-Shock instead. I think it's cooler. They made it just for you. No one else has this."

On balance, I agreed the watch was better. Jason Bourne never busted anyone with a key fob.

The watch came with a charging station. I had to leave it plugged in so it would be ready when I went to meet Oleg. As far as I know, he never paid attention to the watch at all.

That watch changed many things. In subtle ways, it changed the character I had created. When I started recording our meetings, I felt like I had become a genuine double agent.

"We'll have to meet with you afterward and download every-thing," Ted warned me.

"I understand."

"Every time you meet with him, you'll have to record every-thing," he said. "Everything you tell us will be verifiable."

From that day forward, my FBI handlers would know if I was full of shit. I was already confident they believed what I was telling them. They'd invested enough time and energy in me. But I was strangely happy to relieve any doubt that might be lingering. My debriefings had all been on the level, but only as well as I could remember what was said. Now the agents could independently verify any part of it.

There was one other reason I liked wearing the hidden recorder: It would show Ted and Terry how deftly I'd been handling Oleg, what a crafty negotiator I was. (Ego.) I was proud of my talents as a manipulator, and I didn't mind for one second that the agents would get to hear me in action from now on.

They got an immediate earful.

Oleg called in early June. We met at the El Dorado Diner on Central Avenue in Scarsdale. Before going inside, I made sure no one was watching and did what Ted and Terry had taught me: I removed the watch from my wrist and pressed the two buttons that activated the recorder. I checked to see that a tiny light hidden on the underside was flashing. That told me the recorder was running before I slipped the watch back on.

I carried a stack of papers in my computer bag. I thought it was important to validate for Oleg two specific points: that the business was experiencing an exciting new-revenue spurt and that I was truly in charge. As soon as I settled into the booth, I set the papers on the table between us and, one by one, showed them to him. Contracts. Government certifications. And most of all, copies of the stock certificates that showed my parents had transferred their shares in the company into my name. I was the owner of record.

Oleg shook my hand warmly. "Congratulations," he said, beaming. "It looks like we have something to celebrate today!" Though he'd grown up in the collectivism of the Communist Soviet Union, he knew that owner was better than worker any day.

He asked me about France again. "France is nice" was all I said.

Then he asked me about Ava. "What is your wife's name?" he asked.

I didn't like him asking about her. But I knew it was public record, and there was no point in attempting to evade his question or lie. When I told him Ava's name, he came back with a follow-up: "Do you have any children?"

Oleg was quizzing me again and not as gently as before. I didn't want any part of it, but I told him anyway.

"Well, God is great to bless you with this success," he said. It was so out of character, so forced. So obviously designed to test if I was Muslim. He was probing to see what might motivate me. I wanted to control that story line. I didn't want him to. I had to stop the phony-friendly interrogation. Thankfully, my story was thoroughly crafted. For the first time in a public place, I erupted at Oleg. "Look," I shouted over the clacking plates and shouted orders of the busy suburban diner, "don't fuckin' talk to me about my wife." The waitress glared over. I didn't miss a beat. "And don't fuckin' talk to me about God," I said. "We are here to do business. I don't want to talk about my family. We have covered enough of that. Let's discuss how we can do business."

Suddenly, I really was in the business. And I got down to it. Remaining deadly serious but lowering my voice, I asked directly, "What can I do for you, Oleg, that you can pay me for? I can't help you unless you tell me what you want. I'll tell you if I can do it. I'll tell you how much you have to pay. You decide. It's binary. It's simple and clear. That's all that matters. That's all I can do. Anything else, I am not interested in."

Oleg looked rattled. A couple of seconds passed, and the people in the booth behind us started talking again.

Oleg said, "Okay, okay. Yes, we are here to do business."

All I was hoping was that the watch-recorder had caught everything.

CHAPTER 13

AGENT TRUST

It didn't happen quickly, but I felt like the FBI agents were growing more comfortable with me. I kept getting little signs. One summer day when we met for breakfast at the Metro Diner on Broadway and 100th Street, they came as dressed down as I was—Ted in jeans and a short-sleeved polo shirt, Terry in chinos and a button-down with rolled-up sleeves. Maybe I was reading too much into it. Maybe they were just sick of walking around like a couple of funeral directors on a house call. But as we sat together in a back booth, some of the stiffness seemed to evaporate from our interaction. It didn't feel so much like I was reporting in to them or they were directing me. It was more like we were talking and trading ideas and giving each other shit.

"You know that guy on *Lost*?" Ted asked me. The plane-crash TV show had just finished its third season. "That dude who plays the Iraqi guy? He could play you in a movie."

"That's racist, Ted," I told him, trying to look offended. "You're Irish. What if I told you Colin Farrell has to play you? Or Mickey Rooney? Or even worse, Mickey Rourke?"

In the short time I'd known Randi, everything had been so businesslike with her. Even when she and Terry were teasing, she was a straight arrow with me. But over time, with Terry and Ted as my team, the tone between us loosened up. We often talked the way I talked with my friends. "Seriously, dude," I said to Terry at the end of the meal, motioning at his plate of neatly piled and completely untouched potatoes, "how are you still alive? Remind me, what is it that you *do* eat?"

Every single time I had been in a restaurant with Terry, he had done exactly what Randi had accused him of, refusing to consume fruits, vegetables, or anything that didn't owe its very existence to a chemistry lab.

"I am a finely tuned machine," he declared with total seriousness as he moved the uneatables around the plate.

"Of processed food!" Ted jumped in.

I looked at my breakfast omelet. "So wait. Do you eat cheese?"

"Yes," Terry said. "Yellow cheese."

"No, man," I objected. "That doesn't count. That's not *real* cheese. It's as fake as Oleg's cover story."

We all laughed. But Terry still didn't eat his potatoes.

When there was a lull in the laughter, I decided it was time to come clean about something that had been bothering me. "Look, guys," I said, "there's something I need to, um, admit to you. I've been carrying around this secret for a while now."

Ted and Terry glanced at each other nervously. I noticed Terry fidgeting in his seat.

"You guys really fucked me over in a big way," I told them. "Not you, Ted. You weren't here yet. But Terry was." I told them about the day that Ava had uncovered the bright yellow maxi-pad wrapper in our apartment.

As I finished telling the story, Ted had a shit-eating grin on his face. Terry's mouth was just hanging open.

"Really," I said, "it wasn't funny. It almost cost me my damn marriage, guys. That was not an easy thing to explain to Ava. Keeping secrets from her is hard, and right now I don't have a lot of people to talk to."

"I have an idea," Ted said, handing me a business card and telling Terry to do the same. "We totally get that this is stressful. If Ava has any questions, anything you think she should hear from us, we would be happy to sit down with her. It's no problem. We understand the need for the support of your wife. Please, give her our cards."

"Thanks, I really appreciate it. You probably have a second career in marriage counseling."

"No problem. And Terry and I promise not to leave our lip gloss and nail polish at your place."

We had an easy rapport. They were professionals, experienced at working with assets. But I think it was more than that. Maybe this sounds like I'm bragging, but I really do think they got a kick out of me. I was a little different from most of the sources they worked with on the Russian counterintelligence beat. More attuned to pop culture. Perhaps more educated. More Americanized. More like them.

At the same time, I recognized Ted and Terry weren't *really* my friends. Even though we were laughing and goofing around and genuinely enjoying each other's company, they weren't hanging out with me because they liked my witty banter and cocky attitude. This was fundamentally a professional relationship. Each had something the other wanted. Our partnership would continue as long as it was useful. They wouldn't hesitate to drop me the minute I did something they didn't like or if they decided I was more trouble than I was worth. We'd never have another diner meet-up again. If I did something really bad, I assumed they'd arrest me or do something even worse.

The truth is, I had enormous respect for both of them. They cared about doing quality work. They took the rules of the game very seriously. Actually, despite all the strategizing and maneuvering, they never considered it a game. They were working counterintelligence for the FBI, and I never saw them face that responsibility with anything less than the utmost of care. They followed the rules, even those governing how they could treat the Russians. When I asked why they didn't just throw classified documents at Oleg and then arrest him, Ted replied: "There is a difference between them and us. We don't manufacture evidence. We do things cleanly."

"What are you worried about, entrapping him?" I asked.

That was my word, not theirs. But that seemed to be the point. "There are rules we have to follow," Ted said. "It has to be clean." That was the word they kept using, *clean*. It was clear to me they wanted to do this the right way. I was still learning the rules. But for me, this meant no shortcuts.

Still, something seemed out of balance. I spent a lot of time thinking about the foreign spies working in my country to undermine, subvert, and attack America. They ignored our laws and international law. But from what I was able to tell, we were constrained by our laws in the methods we could use to combat the people who didn't play by any rules. We couldn't fight fire with fire. We had to rely on careful planning and street smarts to outwit and outmaneuver them. As maddening as this felt at times, I also understood that if the agents could have made things up without any evidence, I would have been out of a job.

I watched their investigative moves carefully, constantly learning from them. It was mostly little things. When we were sitting in a diner and the waitress would come over, for example, Ted and Terry would reflexively turn all their papers upside down. Ted kept his driver's license backward in his wallet. They were always keenly aware of their surroundings, constantly checking: *Who is behind us? What can people hear? Do they stop talking when we start talking, as if they're listening in?* And they had certain ways of dealing with me. When we met, they liked for us to come and go separately so fewer people would see us together. And very often, I observed, after I sat with both agents in a restaurant, one of them would excuse himself and go to the bathroom. What was that about? Did they really have to pee that badly? Or was one of the agents going into the bathroom to turn on a recording device of some sort? I wasn't sure. Maybe I'd read too many spy novels. Or maybe I was getting good at recognizing how this business worked. When I joked about it, Ted and Terry just smiled.

Given what the three of us were trying to do together, paranoia was warranted. The agents were constantly cautious in ways I thought I needed to be as well. Unfortunately, I'd always been an out-there kind of person. Caution didn't come so naturally to me.

As Ted, Terry, and I talked in the booth that day, a woman came up to the table—not the waitress—and asked for money. She was persistent. She just kept standing there. Ted had already flipped the papers over. I watched the woman and watched the agents. Terry said no for the second or third time, and the woman still didn't leave.

As the senior agent, Ted seemed to feel like it was his place in the hierarchy to exude confidence and leadership and, even if this was just an unexpected annoyance, be the big FBI man. I guess he could have flashed his badge or subtly shown his gun. He didn't need to. Sitting there being badgered by this woman, Ted didn't even raise his voice. For a moment I thought he'd stare the woman down. Instead, he growled at her. Literally. And then again, louder. Even I was intimidated by Ted's roar. And the woman backed away quickly.

I looked at him, a little shocked and a little amused. But I had to admit, he'd demonstrated that sometimes doing the unexpected gets results.

Ted looked thoroughly satisfied with himself. "Hey," he said, "did it work?"

This is a man I have to trust, I thought. And truthfully, I did.

⋆   ⋆   ⋆

Establishing rapport helped me acclimate to this new world. The agents and I also had some serious issues to sort through. I was certain we'd arrived at a key moment in the operation. I didn't want to let it slip past us.

"I think it's fair to say we have Oleg's attention now," I told Ted and Terry that day in the Metro Diner. "So how are we going to hold it? And what are we going to do with him?" Before they could answer, I went on, "It's all about the information."

I don't think they knew what I meant. I was thinking about what Cosmo, Ben Kingsley's computer-hacking mobster character, says in *Sneakers,* the first major Hollywood movie to focus on the National Security Administration: "There's a war out there, old friend. A world war. And it's not about who's got the most bullets. It's about who controls the information. What we see and hear, how we work, what we think . . . it's all about the information!"

I smiled to myself. It didn't matter that the agents didn't know where I was getting my ideas. "What information do we offer him—and how?"

The way I read our challenge, we had to promise Oleg something juicy enough to maintain his interest without actually handing him any genuinely damaging military secrets. The last thing I wanted to do was compromise U.S. national security. I didn't think the agents would let me even if I tried.

"So how do we strike a balance?" I asked the agents. "How do we narrow the focus of what we're doing?"

For months, I had been dropping hints to Oleg about all the new projects the company had been taking on and my resulting access to cool stuff. We were advising the National Defense University on transferring from paper to digital. We were doing a retrospective conversion project for the Department of the Interior. We'd been getting queries from everyone from the Joint Special Operations Command to the U.S. Navy SEALs.

"But everything I've told him has been pretty vague," I said to the agents. "If we leave it undefined, you know he'll start asking for things we can't get him or wouldn't want to. We don't want him dreaming up stuff on his own. That's dangerous. We have to deceive him into believing that something fake is real."

The agents nodded.

"Did you ever hear how the Allies in World War II used thousands of inflatable tanks to convince the Germans that the D-day invasion was not about to happen in Normandy?" I asked. Ted looked at me and shook his head. I continued, "The Allies built this massive fake army that looked real when the Nazis flew over at thirty thousand feet. It wasn't perfect. But it was real enough to fool them from their vantage point. We need something deceptive like that. Something that fits in with what I've told Oleg so far. Something, based on what I've fed him, that he thinks might be possible."

Terry stared at his plate and looked up. "A project that looks real but isn't, a project that can't easily be checked on," he said.

"Exactly, but what are the rules?" I asked. "What can I do? How far can I go in enticing him?"

Terry stopped me. He had his serious face on. "Everything has to come from him," he said. "It can't come from us. It can't come from you. I'd rather have him say 'I want you to get that for me' than you saying 'Let me get it for you.' We have to create an environment where he's the one who's doing the asking."

"But don't we have to focus him?" I asked. "God knows what he might ask for."

Ted stepped in. "If you're going to dangle something in front of him, it has to be bright but not too bright. It has to be good without being Holy Grail good. They want information only slightly more than they want to control everything."

I wasn't sure what that meant in practical terms. I sipped my coffee, and for a moment I didn't say anything. *Great,* I thought. *I need to get this guy interested without entrapping him and do that before he loses interest and decides to walk. Good luck.*

Making him believe I had something valuable for him without entrapping him. That could be a subtle distinction. I had to be careful about offering something while giving him enough information so that he'd request it. Where was the line? It was a distinction that Ted and Terry kept harping on. We could dangle things, but it was up to Oleg to take the assertive steps forward.

"Whatever we put out there," I asked, "does it have to be real? A project I'm actually working on?"

Ted thought. "Not necessarily," he said. "Just don't offer anything you can't deliver." He said he had tremendous professional respect for Oleg. "They're warriors just like us, devoted to their country. They have their own command-and-control structure. They live under many of the same pressures we do. And they have their own resources."

Although I hadn't thought much about it, what Ted said was true. Oleg had to brief a boss who, in turn, had to brief another boss and so on. All of them, straight up the line, would most likely look to validate anything I told Oleg. And they had time on their side. They were setting the meeting schedule. They were establishing the pace. They could hold off on meeting with me till they could check out everything I said. I knew that convincing Oleg was part of the battle. But getting past the sniff test in Moscow was the victory that mattered.

Now, at least, I felt we'd agreed on the makings of a plan. I could continue to use my company as a cover and an explanation for why I had access to things Oleg might want. I had proved to him that I was real. The trap was set. Now we just had to bait it.

I recalled how eager Oleg was to get the reports from the net-workcentric warfare conference and how much effort the agents had to put in to reconstruct all that data. "Maybe I could attend some conferences for him," I suggested. "Instead of struggling to get the minutes of months-old conferences, wouldn't it be easier to have me go? I could take notes on the major presentation and scoop up every handout in the room. You guys could vet them and make sure I'm not giving away anything damaging. Or we could throw in some purposeful misinformation and mess with him."

I thought that was clever, actually. It would also be another way of increasing my involvement, and it sounded like it might be fun. "Wouldn't that be easier than reconstructing later?" I asked. The agents nodded, but more in a yeah-we-can-consider-it way.

That wasn't my only idea. In fact, it wasn't my best idea, even if it was the only one that would *force* me to go to places like Finland, Portugal, and Australia. Closer to home, I'd been thinking of the possibility of dealing through a government contractor instead of the government itself. From my years of working with so many of them from around the country, I knew that private companies had a much easier time keeping secrets than the government did. I had some government contracts with me that day that helped prove the point.

I handed one to Ted and one to Terry. "The problem with government contracts," I said, "is that records exist. They are public. Many of them are indexed by Google. If we made up something that supposedly the government produced, the Russians could check pretty easily. It wouldn't take more than a cursory look before they'd see that what I was offering them was phony.

"But," I continued, "what if we're dealing with private company records? There wouldn't be traceable public records." I paused to let that sink in. "So maybe we should be thinking business-to-business instead of business-to-government. It limits the need for theatrics."

This was something I knew about. Because many of our customers were agencies of the federal government, those contracts were available for anyone to see. If we wanted to operate in the shadows with Oleg, it would have to be work we were doing for a private entity—real or imagined—something he and the people in Moscow couldn't easily confirm.

The waitress came over to top off our coffees. Ted yawned and held his papers up to cover his mouth, while Terry slid his stack of papers into his lap and smoothly reached with his other hand for his toast. I began shuffling the papers in front of me, pretending to look for something. The minute the waitress left, the papers were out and our conversation continued. We didn't skip a beat.

It was Terry who first mentioned Northrop Grumman. The large defense contractor was headquartered outside Washington, D.C., but had a good-sized engineering and manufacturing operation on Long Island. "They keep archives," he said. "Maybe you could be working on something like that."

Now, that made sense to me.

CHAPTER 14

SECOND TRY

As I got deeper with Oleg and the FBI, I wanted to make sure I didn't forget the reason I was there in the first place—one of the main reasons, anyway. I wanted to join the navy. I had mentioned that to the agents a few times but had never dwelled on it or extracted their promise to help. That ambition just lingered in the background, mostly in my head. But time was passing quickly. I was trusting the agents more, enough to be open with them about my ambition to join the navy and my failed first attempt. As much as I was enjoying my role as a double agent, I understood that freelance spying wasn't a grown-up career path. Espionage agents don't normally get pensions and dental plans or regular paychecks unless they're employed by someone. I liked my furtive maneuvers with the FBI, but what I really wanted was to be on the inside of something important all the time, to live behind the giant curtain, to learn what was really going on. I was eager to do something more meaningful than running the family business. I also wanted to support myself, have a family, drive nice cars, and afford a couple of movie tickets in Manhattan. The best idea I'd come up with—and it was an excellent one, I was convinced—was to join the military as a reserve intelligence officer.

When I tried again, it would be different. It had to be. I was at the center of a real-life counterespionage operation against Russian military intelligence. I was the star of my own story, living a real-life undercover spy drama. Couldn't this be the practical experience the navy had said I lacked? Fooling a senior GRU intelligence officer had to count for something. And didn't I have the FBI on my side?

When I brought this up with Ted and Terry, they said three things to me. One, it might not be easy. Two, they could not guarantee results or subvert the navy's procedures. And three, they would try to be as helpful as they could without divulging any more than they were allowed to. The whole process seemed shrouded in mystery. "It's just one of those difficult situations," Ted said vaguely. Still, he and Terry vowed to try. And they did.

Just before Thanksgiving 2007, Ted gave me the business card of a recruiter in New York who handled direct commission applicants. Her name was Lieutenant Juli Schmidt. She was, more or less, the New York Lino. Ted said she came from the south shore of Long Island and had attended the Naval Academy in Annapolis, Maryland. She had an office in the same lower Manhattan building as the FBI office, 26 Federal Plaza.

"Hello, Lieutenant," I said when I got the recruiter on the phone. "My name is Naveed Jamali. I was told to give you a call."

"Hi," she said. "I'm glad you called."

She was friendly and willing to help. She seemed very bright, I could tell that immediately. Annapolis didn't accept too many idiots.

She never said how much she knew about my recent adventures with the FBI and the Russians, although the agents told me they had met with her and presumably shared some information. She clearly knew I was an FBI referral. I gave her a bare-bones rundown of the navy and me. "I applied to the direct commission program in 2003 and didn't get in," I told her. "And I'd like to try again."

Ever the double agent, I didn't broach my involvement with the FBI's counterespionage operation, and she didn't ask about it. I just mentioned what I'd accomplished since I had last applied to the navy: I was running a $2-million-a-year business, dealing routinely with high-level federal officials on their complex research needs. That should pump up my résumé, I thought.

"Very interesting," the recruiter said, sounding like she meant it.

But in the vein of nothing worth having ever comes easily, four years had passed since I'd gotten rejected, so I would have to submit a whole new application and go through all the interviews and tests again. "If you're up for that, we might as well get started," she said.

"Let's go," I said.

She said I should begin with the navy's basic ASTB, the Aviation Selection Test Battery. I didn't want to blow it. It had been a few years since I'd had much practice at test-taking. So while the agents and I prepared for my next meet-up with Oleg, I bought a fat test-prep book and crammed like I hadn't since eighth-grade history class.

The Friday before Christmas, I went down to the recruiting office and took the test on a computer. It was like the dreaded SATs and GREs, except that all the questions now had an aviation and maritime focus. There were drawings of planes at different angles: "Is this plane turning toward you or turning away from you?"

That wasn't hard. It was impossible! You had to tell the orientation of a plane in a two-dimensional drawing without the benefit of any frame of reference. There was no way to prepare for those types of questions. I was guessing so I wouldn't run out of time. I felt better prepared for the questions that required math or memorization. Convert knots into miles an hour? That I could do. Name the different parts of the ship—"Which is the starboard side? What's a foc'sle?"—piece of cake.

As I was clicking away on my starboard and foc'sle, a loud burst of yelling erupted a few feet from me. Terry King, the office coordinator, was on a conference call with recruiting headquarters, and someone was furious that people weren't joining the call on time. I couldn't understand why the person was so angry, but I found his shouts a little distracting as I tried to decide whether yet another fighter jet was banking toward or away from me.

I finished my test and took a deep breath. I wasn't sure if I had made the cutoff. I walked into King's office and tried to chat him up. "What was up with that call? That guy sounded pissed. What did the navy do to that poor man?" I teased.

"Do to *him?*" King asked. "Listen, some people just don't do well under stressful situations. But there is a way to treat people, and I'm pretty sure he's doing it all wrong."

He computed the scores and checked them against the required grades. Those few seconds were agonizing. Finally, he threw me a lifeline: "It looks like you did just fine, just fine."

King seemed relieved that I had made the cutoff. That made two of us. As he filled out paperwork, he told me that some people have a tough time with the ASTB. He mentioned one woman who'd recently started the test on the same computer I had. "We went to check on her, and she was just gone," he said. "Gone. She'd completed the test, must've known she bombed it, and decided, 'This isn't for me'—and then she bolted. We never heard from her again. But you don't have to worry about that. You did fine."

I wasn't sure what the ASTB had to do with being an intelligence officer in the navy, except that I had to get past it, and there were about six thousand other tests to go. This was going to be a long, drawn-out process. I went to Navy Operational Support Center, in the Bronx, for my medical screening. I had to do follow-up blood work on Long Island, then back to the Bronx for a hearing test.

The biggest challenge seemed to be finding out what the steps were and getting them scheduled. Invariably, there were cancellations and follow-ups and procedures I hadn't heard of. If they had a test and it had an acronym, I took it. There was an air of random tediousness to everything. Luckily, Juli seemed to be plugged in to the right people and knew how to keep the process moving.

I was one busy guy. I had a business I was running and all the difficulties that came with that. I had a wife. We were still starting our life together. There were the cars. I couldn't ignore them. And Oleg, of course. That meant keeping sharp with the split personality. On top of all that, I was applying to the navy again. Some days, I didn't know where my head was supposed to be and which hat I was supposed to be wearing. Was I the boss? The double agent? The husband? The recruit? The young, fun-loving fast-car enthusiast? Each role demanded something different from me.

To make things even more complicated, although the navy and the FBI were both government entities, they were two totally different worlds. Everything about the navy was highly bureaucratic, with thousands of rules and requirements and endless layers of supervision and no clear answer to anything. By contrast, no one ever told me to study an FBI manual, Chapter 15, Section 10, Paragraph 25, so I would know how to cut my hair or speak to Russians. The agents and I had freedom to maneuver as we saw fit, and nobody was looking over our shoulders, it seemed. Here was the best part: So far, we'd been wildly successful.

While I kept inching my way through Juli's process, Ted and Terry went off in hunt of some high-ranking allies to help my cause. Ted got me a meeting with naval commander Jeffrey Jones. The commander wasn't part of the normal recruiting process. He reported directly to a three-star admiral at the Pentagon. I don't believe he'd ever conducted a reserves-recruiting interview. He was an attaché to the U.S. Mission to the United Nations whose office was at the UN, but he agreed to see me at the recruiting office downtown.

The moment I met him, I understood this was one smooth professional, and it wasn't just the strong jaw, penetrating eyes, and beautifully tailored dark gray suit. He was scary smart, totally low-key, and as deadpan as the flat-toned comedian Steven Wright.

"I like to get up early," he announced as soon as I sat down across the desk from him. "Most people get up at five in the morning to make love to their wives. I'm on the road to the office by then."

He spoke without an ounce of intonation, then waited to see how I would react. I didn't. This man meant business.

He asked me about my background, my family, where I grew up, where I'd gone to college, what I'd been doing lately, almost everything except what I had done with Ted and Terry. At the same time, I had the feeling that he knew a lot more than he was letting on.

He seemed eager to sell me on the idea of becoming a military diplomat. "You'd be perfect as an attaché," he told me. "They'll send you to school. Since you have a French mother and you've spoken French your whole life"—thanks, Mom—"you would probably end up in some African country. It's great. You bring your family. They give you a driver. They'll pay for school."

I must have been smiling.

"It isn't easy to find suitable people for these positions," the commander continued. "When I go on leave, we have someone fill in for me. He's a lawyer. Most of the people we have filling in—lawyers, investment bankers, other professionals—are very polished, very cosmopolitan. But they have little idea what it is to do real intel collection, to live in this world. There is a shift in the navy to find people for these roles who are more diverse and more well rounded. You are very polished. I could really see you doing this."

He said he was set to retire in the next few months and was keen to get his report on me to his admiral before he left: He was driving down to the Pentagon soon and would make his feelings known.

I told him this all sounded amazing to me. "Anything I should be doing now?"

"You can't apply right out of the gate," he warned me, trying to reel in some of my let's-do-this-now enthusiasm. "You have to get into the navy first. But you might look at taking some courses now. You'd find them interesting, I think, and they'd set you up well for the future."

He told me I should check out the State Department's Foreign Service Institute. I promised him I would. I told him how much I'd enjoyed meeting him and thanked him for his time.

After I left the office, there was no dampening my excitement. I got Ted on the phone immediately. "My bags are packed!" I announced. "He was trying to sell me on the military attaché program. I would totally be into that. When can I start? He made it all sound so exciting, so cool. Commander Jeff Jones—even the guy's name sounds cool."

"Sure," Ted said noncommittally. Then he steered the conversation back to Oleg.

CHAPTER 15

WORTHY ADVERSARIES

"You up for lunch?" Terry asked me.

"Sure," I said. "Where do you want to go?"

"Don't worry about it," he said.

Ever since Oleg and I first left the office together, I'd been laughing with Ted and Terry about the Russian's taste in restaurants. Oleg had the entire New York metropolitan area to choose from. He had a Russian Federation expense account. And yet he always seemed to find his way to the blandest American chains. Someone back in Moscow must have told him, "Cardboard-flavored foodstuffs are what New Yorkers really love!" I'd hoped Ted and Terry would start springing for some first-class New York dining establishments. They had expense accounts, too. Though that never happened, they had shown a knack for finding their way to tasty local joints.

As we drove east from the city in Terry's Ford Taurus, he and Ted were oddly vague about where we were headed and the purpose of the lunch. "Just a couple of guys you should meet," Ted said when I pressed him for more details. "You'll just tell them a little about what you've been up to. Maybe they can be helpful somehow, I don't know. They just want to meet you, that's all."

Did this have to do with the Russian operation? Or getting me into the navy? Or were these people relatives of Ted's and Terry's who'd always wanted to meet a Pakistani-French-American who liked fast cars? I had no idea. I assumed we weren't running a random meet-and-greet campaign. We were trying to keep our activities on the down-low. Whatever. I'd taken another day away from my office and was already in the car. I didn't feel like I had much choice. Plus, it was almost noon, and I was hungry.

Given all the talk about Oleg's tacky taste in restaurants, I was more than a little surprised when Ted, Terry, and I pulled in to a Chili's off the Seaford–Oyster Bay Expressway in Bethpage, Long Island. Had the agents gotten their hands on a copy of *The Russian Diplomat's Dining Guide to New York*? I knew this couldn't be the pinnacle of Long Island cuisine.

Waiting at the table for us was an agent from the Naval Criminal Investigative Service. The NCIS has a big job to do, investigating and defeating criminal, terrorist, and foreign-intelligence threats to the U.S. Navy and Marine Corps. "On land, on sea, and in cyberspace," as the NCIS agents like to boast. Oh, and on TV, too. Most people knew the organization's name only as the title of a long-running CBS television program starring Mark Harmon as Special Agent Leroy Jethro Gibbs. The real NCIS agent brought along a former marine pilot who now worked for Northrop Grumman, the defense contractor Terry had mentioned. I knew they had a big facility in Bethpage.

It was a very weird lunch.

After we got our Tex-Mex orders in, the NCIS dude went on for about forty minutes about his diet and exercise regime. "I haven't had sugar or flour in five years," he declared proudly. Really, he and Terry should have had a bizarre-eating habits throwdown: Processed mystery meat versus shredded lettuce! May the strangest diet win!

The man went on to recount how much weight he'd lost, how low his body-fat was, and what great shape he was in, physically and mentally. He did look lean and healthy, but no sugar or flour, how could it possibly be worth it? Obviously, he had no plans to dive into a Southwest quesadilla—another reason to question why, of all places, we were eating here. I was waiting to see if he scraped all the cheese out of the skillet queso dip when it arrived.

Somewhere along the way, the marine pilot, a pleasant enough guy in his late thirties, got to squeeze in a couple of quick battlefield anecdotes about ditching his helicopter over water and getting picked up by "Pedro, the rescue bird." If he'd had time to tell the story properly, it might have been interesting. He explained quickly that he went to work for the defense contractor after leaving the marine corps.

Sitting there, I felt trapped in a scene from *Dogfight,* the River Phoenix movie about the group of marines and their fervent competition to bring the ugliest girl out to dinner: Whoever has the homeliest date wins. The marine pilot was brought by the NCIS agent. I was brought by the FBI. We sat there looking at each other politely and not saying much. Finally, the pilot handed me his business card and said quietly, "You can give that to your friend." I was more than a little surprised when the FBI agents nodded. That smelled like trouble immediately.

It was the first time I'd seen the FBI involve anyone outside the Bureau or my family—any outsider at all—in what we'd all agreed was a highly secretive relationship between me and my Russian spy. It was also the first I was hearing about me playing human conduit between the Russians and anybody else. Wasn't the whole idea of a business card to deliver your contact information so that somebody could—oh, I don't know—contact you? In other words, once I handed Oleg this card, he could reach out directly to Mr. Attack Helicopter Pilot, his badass self. After all my conniving and groundwork, was our active operation moving in a whole new direction—without me?

I didn't make any promises either way. And since the NCIS agent seemed to have completed his diet-and-fitness lecture, we were all free to leave. We climbed into Ted's car. They weren't any more charmed by the NCIS guy than I was. "What a fuckin' asshole," Ted said. "We drove all the way out here to hear Mr. Jenny Craig?"

"He only eats the things that I don't eat, and I don't eat anything that he does," Terry said. "Why did we meet him again?"

As far as I could tell—and as far as Ted and Terry were willing to hint—the NCIS agent was maybe going to connect the agents to the navy for me, and the marine pilot was some sort of contact for us at Northrop Grumman. It would have been nice if Ted and Terry had mentioned that to me going in. Weren't we working together? Was something bigger at play?

"Why should I give that card to Oleg?" I asked. "Am I the cutout here?"

The agents looked a little startled by my question. "The cutout?" Terry asked.

"I can see how this goes," I said. "I give the card to Oleg. The two of them start talking. He becomes Oleg's new connection. Oleg goes with this guy. They don't need me anymore. I am left high and dry, cut out of the entire operation. What value does any of that have to me?"

"That's not anyone's intention," Ted answered. "The marine is just a contact for us at Northrop Grumman. He might help us get some stuff if we need it."

"Why should I do this?" I said. "You told the NCIS guy we need to get in to Northrop Grumman, and he decides to send in some military guy who's already on the inside, and squeeze me out. Suddenly, I'm yesterday's news."

The more I talked about it, the more concerned I got. I was slowly convincing myself that the FBI no longer had any use for me. The conversation went on awhile. There was a lot of traffic. We still weren't done by the time we got back to New York. Neither Ted nor

Terry had said anything to make me feel better about adding two strangers to the mix and making me the card-passing conduit.

I was still pissed a couple of days later when I met with the agents at the Metro Diner. I came prepared with a detailed brief for them, an official-looking line chart of our effort and its return.

"Very impressive," Ted said when he saw my chart. "You did that on your computer?"

"Look," I said, "this is the level of effort I have to commit to. The business has a commitment, too. There is a cost to my company. It is not my money I am diverting. Now you want me to bring someone else in here? It definitely feels like I'm being pushed out after doing all the heavy lifting."

"No," Ted said. "These are just people who might be helpful."

"Then why am I supposed to give the pilot's card to Oleg?"

"No one said you had to give him the card. Just hold it. Maybe it'll be something you can use, maybe not."

I wasn't completely satisfied. There was clearly lots going on without my knowledge or involvement, and that put me in a bad position from every angle. I complained some more about the way the entire lunch had been set up and conducted. Ted clearly didn't love the NCIS agent, I knew I had that on my side. "I'm not defending the guy," he said. "Let's just see if he turns out to be useful."

"If you'd just told me we were meeting some guys who could help us get in to Northrop Grumman, I wouldn't feel like I was being set up," I said. "Besides, that NCIS guy was a clown. He's useless to us."

"You're really worried about this?" Ted asked me. "There is no need to be. Nobody wants to replace you. I can assure you that won't be happening."

"Good," I said without much confidence. Now more than ever, I was eager to enhance my value as an asset the agents wouldn't want to lose. Thankfully, I had an idea: "The future is DTIC."

For months, something had been nagging at me. All this material the Russians had been requesting over the years, how did they know what to ask for? How did they even know it existed? I asked Ted and Terry: "Have you guys ever looked into how they know the exact titles of things to ask for? It doesn't make sense. The Russians somehow know this stuff exists, but they can't get it? Isn't that a little strange? It's not like most of this information is ever publicized."

The agents seemed intrigued.

"I went poking around on my own," I told them. "I was looking for commonalities in the documents that the Russians asked for. The reports came from different agencies. They were written at different times. Some, though not all, were available for purchase through the Government Printing Office. So what one thing did they all have in common? It took some investigation, but I think I've found the link."

All this information and more, I told Ted and Terry, could be retrieved through a proprietary government database run by the Defense Technical Information Center. "This DTIC system is like an in-house Google for reports," I said. "It's a way of quickly combing through millions of ridiculously obscure military-technology titles and, if you have access, getting the actual reports." Then I leaned forward for dramatic effect and lowered my voice to a whisper: "As far as I can tell, every report the Russians have ever asked for is housed in DTIC. We have to leverage DTIC with Oleg."

This didn't have to slow our progress on Northrop Grumman. I made that clear. We should proceed with whatever we could get from the defense contractor and offer it to Oleg. In fact, Northrop Grumman would be a good test run for my DTIC approach. "But the real prize, that comes next," I said. "From here on out, we have to be the ones defining the options. We have to offer him what amounts to a catalog. This is how we get away from him ordering stuff. This is how we're the ones who are in control."

The agents seemed receptive. They agreed to discuss it with their superiors and get back to me. So we ended on a positive note, but what an emotional journey to get there. Sometimes Ted and Terry could really frustrate me. I understood that we were all operating on complicated terrain. But everything seemed so maddeningly slow and obfuscated. And these unexpected sideshows kept popping up. No bullshit.

I finally blurted out, "God, that was exhausting! Ted, you are a worthy adversary! Don't let anyone tell you otherwise."

He seemed taken aback by that. "A worthy adversary," he said, letting the phrase hang in the air. "That's a very interesting choice of words."

CHAPTER 16

EL DORADO

His face was badly swollen. His cheeks looked almost rubbery. He was slurring even his precise Russian-English words. I knew dental pain when I saw it, and Oleg had a mouthful. As we sat in a booth of the El Dorado Diner on Central Avenue that sullen October morning, I actually felt sorry for him.

"Did you get punched?" I asked him.

I don't think he found the question amusing. "I punch," he said without cracking a smile, not that he could have. "I do not get punched."

"Except by dentists," I added, unwilling to allow the Russian the final jab in a back-and-forth.

He'd had an abscess, he explained. The dentist had to yank out the tooth. I wondered if he'd been expecting some vodka anesthesia. Back at the GRU Academy on Narodnogo Opolchenia Street in Moscow, Oleg might or might not have received instruction on the tongue-loosening power of tooth-extraction pain, but he had absorbed the lessons on stoicism. Admitting pain, I suppose, was as unthinkable to

Oleg as admitting weakness. He swore he was feeling okay. His GRU trainers would have been proud.

I pitied the poor FBI transcriber who had to transcribe this conversation from the recorder-watch. Subject: Rotten Russian Teeth!

This was my first meeting with Oleg since I'd pitched DTIC to Ted and Terry. There hadn't been any changes to our operation. No one had told me not to meet with the Russian. I hadn't gotten any directions to pass him off to the marine pilot or to anyone else. In fact, things seemed to have settled back into a state of normalcy.

I did my best to ignore the dental issues and focus on the business at hand. "I have some news," I told Oleg. "I might be joining the navy."

"The United States Navy?" he asked.

What other navy would I join? "There is a special program," I said. "It's called direct commission. It is very selective. But if you are accepted, they bring you on as officer immediately."

A small grin swept across Oleg's pained face. I'd known he would like the sound of that. He was a captain in the Russian Navy, still on duty, assigned to diplomatic responsibilities in New York, also known as spying.

I explained a little more about the direct commission program. It was for the reserves, I told him, so I could keep my day job. "Things wouldn't have to change for you and me," I said.

"They might even get better," Oleg answered. "We may have something new to celebrate."

I moved things on quickly. "I also want to tell you about the Northrop Grumman project. It will be a large project. It hasn't happened yet, but it will at some point. They'll be sending us paper documents. We'll digitize those, then send them back to the company. I'll only have a small time frame. I need to know whether you're interested."

"I am interested," he said. "It will depend on what the documents are."

"Of course," I said. I handed him the card from the marine pilot.

"He's my contact there." Oleg slid the card into his pocket and handed me his own stack of papers with two items highlighted. In the margin next to one of them, he had written: "Find out the price."

I told him I would check. This seemed like the perfect moment to weave DTIC into our conversation. "If I could get you access to a federal database with a wide variety of defense-technology information, including the titles you just asked for, is that something that might be useful to you?" I asked. "If so, that is something we can certainly discuss."

He lit up. "Yes," he said, "I would be interested."

"What I would like to be able to do," I told him, "is show you a list of documents—maybe a long list—that I might be able to get for you. You can tell me which ones you might want, and I can tell you how much you'll have to pay for those."

"You will show me the list, and I will tell you what I am interested in?"

"Exactly," I said.

"I would be interested in that."

"We'll have to work out the money," I said. "But I think we can do that."

This was perfect. I'd just offered Oleg the possibility of access to the database that I believed his bosses had been trying to break into for years. He'd be a hero. For both of us, it was very hard not to smile.

He wanted to know more, his gaze told me that much. But it was time to leave that topic and return to the reason I was there. "What I can do with Northrop Grumman is just a small example of what I can get for you." I don't know how disappointed he was that I'd taken a step back from the bigger get, but I needed to show that I was in control. "Northrop Grumman, it's just a start," I said.

"Just a start," he said, carefully repeating my words.

★   ★   ★

In the diner that day, it wasn't all about databases. Oleg and I caught up on a few other things. He had his own agenda, too. He mentioned France again. "French is such a beautiful language," he said. "You are lucky to have a mother who is French." What was it with Oleg and France? Clearly, he was greasing me up for something. I just didn't know what. He obviously agreed with my mother, who had told me since I was a boy, "Naveed, travel is broadening." She and Oleg hadn't clicked so well in their brief business relationship, but they'd definitely agree on that.

"You like to travel?" he asked. "Do you like to travel abroad?"

His grasp of small talk was either very poor or very transparent. Who doesn't like to travel? What was he getting at? "Sure," I said. "I like to travel. It's a little harder now that I have a company to run. But I like it, of course."

"Are there places you have always wanted to visit?" he asked.

I knew this was dumb the second I answered. I blurted out, "Mexico."

I couldn't believe I'd said that. But for some reason, as he was questioning me, I was thinking about *The Falcon and the Snowman*, the Sean Penn and Timothy Hutton movie about a couple of well-off California kids who sell classified documents to the Soviet Union in the 1970s. Their exploits take them to Mexico, where bad things occur.

"Ah, Mexico," Oleg said excitedly. "Mexico is a wonderful country. We should visit there sometime." Great! Had he seen the movie?

Did I really want to go to Mexico with Oleg? There I was, looking at the puffy aftereffects of his dental procedure and imagining what Russian intelligence officers might do with me off American soil: I was in a dusty Mexican village. A hulking man was wiping his hands with a towel after extracting the first two of my teeth, trying to get me to talk. I'd stumbled blindly into my own imagined version of *Spies Like Us*, where the Russian interrogator, played by James Daughton, is questioning Chevy Chase's suspected spy Emmett Fitz-Hume. "Every minute you don't tell us why you are here, I cut off a finger," the interrogator declares.

"Mine or yours?" the Chevy character asks.

"Yours."

"Damn!"

I still couldn't believe I'd suggested Mexico.

"Yeah, yeah," I said dismissively of Oleg's perked-up interest. "Next time we meet," I said, steering as far away as possible from any visits south of the border, "perhaps we can talk more about DTIC. And we'll see what happened with Northrop Grumman."

"Yes, good idea," Oleg said.

After we finished and he paid the bill—in cash, as always—we walked outside together to the diner parking lot. That was when he got his first glimpse at my new Corvette.

"Look," he said excitedly. "You got a new car. A beautiful Mustang."

He might as well have yanked a molar out of my mouth with a pair of rusty pliers and no Novocain right there in the parking lot.

"A Mustang?" My voice dripped with revulsion. "Did you say a Mustang?"

His eyes widened and his jaw dropped. He had no idea what he had said that was wrong.

"Do I look like somebody who dates his sister?" I asked him. "It's a Corvette, Oleg. Don't insult me like that. A Corvette."

"Yes," Oleg said. "Obviously. A Corvette. I like it very much."

"It's a Corvette," I said again. "A Corvette. Not a Mustang."

"A Corvette," Oleg said.

When I met with Ted and Terry later that afternoon, they loved the Corvette bit. Especially Terry, who had his own Corvette. "Good for you," he said. "You told him. Who the hell confuses a Mustang with a 'vette? It's a Corvette."

"Yeah, fuck him!" Ted said.

The agents were not as happy about Mexico. When I recounted that part of the conversation, they got serious.

"Whose idea was Mexico?" Ted asked. "Yours or his?"

"It was mine," I admitted. "But couldn't you guys come with me? If you can't come, can't you assign an agent to protect me while I'm down there?"

"What is wrong with you?" Terry shot back.

Time to break the tension with humor, I thought. "You could send a female agent to pretend to be my wife," I said, "like Linda Hamilton in *Terminator 2.*"

"I'll have to check," Terry deadpanned. "But I think we're using her with someone else." Ted just shook his head.

The agents made clear that under no circumstances would I be leaving the country with Oleg, especially not to Mexico. For one thing, the FBI's jurisdiction in a case like this one was carefully limited to the United States. "Just imagine," Terry said, "if the Russians have some suspicion that you're working with the FBI. This is their plan. The first thing they'll want to do is move you out of the country. Away from the Bureau's protection. Where no one is watching you. Out of our reach."

Now I had something new to worry about. Was that why Oleg had brought it up?

"Oh, yeah," Ted said to Terry. "It'll be great. We'll just turn him over to the 'Christian Inaction Agency.' "

I had never heard that nickname for the CIA, though I was sure it carried decades of bureaucratic rivalry.

"Trust me," Ted said. "You don't want to work with those guys."

CHAPTER 17

EASY LIES

Ted and Terry said hardly anything in the car.

Two weeks before Christmas, the three of us were heading east again in Terry's Ford Taurus, on our way to Northrop Grumman. Something about the Long Island Expressway seemed to strike these agents mum. The agents mentioned that we'd be stopping first at a nearby motel, where we could map out an action plan.

An action plan?

"So what's this all about?" I pressed as we sat in heavy traffic somewhere in eastern Queens.

"We'll discuss it when we get to the motel," Terry said firmly. Then he quickly changed the subject, describing how he'd gotten his car cleaned that morning, inside and out. "I even went for the Armor All."

"Good for you," I mumbled. Nothing he did would ever make a Taurus look good.

I was feeling nervous about our little field trip. I had a sense the agents might be nervous, too. By now they had to know I did not like surprises.

The Meadowbrook Motor Lodge billed itself "Long Island's premier property for budget-conscious travelers." I'd say the emphasis was more on "budget" than "premier." Ted went into the office and got the room key. Then he, Terry, and I went inside. Terry and I both grabbed chairs. Ted sat on the edge of the bed.

"So here's what's gonna happen," Ted said. "We'll drive over to Northrop Grumman and drop you off at the building where they have their archives. It's just like a library. People are there to help you. You go in and get whatever it is you get."

This was not calming me down. I had no idea where I was going once I got inside, who I was going to meet, what I was going to ask for, or even what I was going in to get. When I realized Ted was finished laying out his "action plan," I asked, "What am I getting there?"

"I don't know," Ted said. "That's up to you."

Why did they always answer like that? Maybe they didn't know any more than I did. So much for having our marine on the inside.

"So I'm just going to walk into this place and ask for stuff? What stuff? Why do I say I'm there? Do I tell them I'm with the Literacy Board and I'm there to check for dangling participles?" Okay, that was dumb. But I did feel like I was flying blind. "Can you at least tell me if they're expecting me?"

"They know that somebody may be coming by," Terry said. "Just do what you do well. Tell them a story about research and digitizing and needing some technical manuals."

I was starting to think I might need my own plan—for getting safely out of there. I remembered what Sam, the Robert De Niro character in *Ronin*, said after stashing his gun in an alley behind a mobbed-up restaurant: "Lady, I never walk into a place I don't know how to walk out of." Was I about to violate the *Ronin* rule? I was glad I had two hundred dollars in my back pants pocket and 666-6666, the number for Carmel Car Service, programmed into my phone.

I knew how the agents felt about keeping these interactions

organic. Like me, they were reluctant to be nailed down by detailed scripts. But how about a little guidance here, guys? "I'm guessing that I can't mention why I'm really there, right?"

"That would be a correct assumption," Terry replied.

I looked at Ted. The way he was sitting on the edge of the bed, his left foot was on the floor, and his right leg was resting on the bed. I had a perfect dead-on view of his nine-millimeter Glock model 20 semiautomatic handgun poking out of the bottom of a leather hol-ster—angled straight at me. I knew that was the gun he carried. I'd just never had such a clear, down-the-barrel view.

I'm sure that was an accident—right?

"Look, Naveed, this is totally voluntary," Ted said. "You should only do what you feel comfortable doing. We don't want you to feel this is something being forced on you."

I didn't acknowledge the gun, though I could have sworn Ted had a twinkle in his eye. "Voluntary? So I could voluntarily get up and walk out of here?"

Ted's eyes stopped smiling.

"What happens if somebody starts asking questions about why a random guy is walking in and walking out with a pile of company documents?" I asked. "What happens if they call security?"

Terry said, "We'll be waiting in the parking lot."

I thought about it for another second. So I was expected to walk into a place where the people were, at best, vaguely expecting some-one but not me specifically. I would then sweet-talk my way into get-ting something—I had no idea what—we could use for the op. Once again, the FBI didn't want their fingerprints on any of this. It was command-and-control from thirty thousand feet—or at least a hun-dred yards into the parking lot. On the flip side, I was pretty sure that if things went south, Ted and Terry wouldn't let me rot in jail. They were the FBI. They must have friends in law enforcement, even on Long Island.

So I agreed. Despite my misgivings, I trusted myself. And I trusted the agents. I wasn't willing to give up on Oleg yet.

I smiled and got up from the motel-room chair. "Okay," I said. "Let's go shopping."

Terry drove to the parking lot. As we stopped, he pointed out the building where the archives were. Ted turned around to look me straight in the face. "We trust you and your judgment," he said. "Just be careful. These little guys can talk. If you're not careful, you'll be in there for hours."

"Yeah," Terry added, "they're mostly retirees in there. Volunteers. They have plenty of time on their hands."

Great. Now I had to look out for elderly rambling conversationalists. I got out of the car and went inside.

I introduced myself using my real name, not knowing if that would help smooth the way or not. Then I gave them a story that, like most good ruses, was rounded partially in truth. I told them I worked for Books & Research, a government contractor and information firm. We were working on a digitizing project and needed some research material that we could test the system on.

"Do you have any material we could scan?" I asked the helpful clerk.

"I'm sure we do. What do you want?"

I knew that Northrop Grumman had built some of the leading jet aircraft in the U.S. arsenal. Back in the 1960s, they'd even built the Apollo lunar-landing module. Despite the heated U.S.-Soviet space race that had come to symbolize the Cold War era, I didn't think Oleg had much interest in space travel.

But there were plenty of other items in the Northrop Grumman catalog to choose from. "Some of the military aircraft the company is so respected for?" I suggested with a small note of flattery.

The clerk didn't hesitate. He mentioned several jet fighters I had heard of, the F-14 being one of them. "Okay," I said. "Let's see those."

It went on like that, with the clerk proudly throwing out names of Northrop Grumman product lines and me saying, "Can I see those, too?"

I didn't sign for anything. I didn't show any ID. I didn't promise to return anything. I did give them my business card, which said "Books & Research," but anyone could have printed that up at Kinkos. No one mentioned they'd been expecting me. No one said anything about the marine pilot I had met or whether he had somehow vouched for me. No one mentioned the FBI. I truly got no indication one way or the other whether the FBI had greased the way for me.

Either way, I left Northrop Grumman with a shopping list of enticing documents about America's frontline military aircraft, enough to fill a large cardboard box and, I hoped, to catch a Russian spy. I walked back out to Ted and Terry, who were right where I had left them in the defense contractor's parking lot. It would now be the agents' job to fill my order.

Driving back on the LIE, traffic was terrible. I reviewed the material I had received. It all looked pretty impressive, I had to say.

Traffic was in a choke hold at the Queensboro Bridge. "Fuck this traffic," I said to Ted and Terry. "Can't you turn on a siren or something?"

The car was at a standstill. They both turned around and looked at me.

"We can't," Terry said.

"What do you mean, you can't? You're the FBI. Why can't you? Who's gonna know?"

"We'd know," Ted said.

I didn't think he was joking. He didn't crack a smile.

When we finally reached my street, Ted pulled up to the curb in front of a fire hydrant. The plan was to leave the box of manuals with the agents for now. Before I could get out of the car, Ted stopped me, saying we had some paperwork to take care of. "Why don't you give it to him," he said to Terry.

It was a three-page typewritten document. "Code of Conduct," the page on top said. The document was fairly detailed. It included a long list of items I was expected to agree to. Promising I wouldn't represent myself as an agent of the FBI. Acknowledging I was subject to all federal, state, and local laws. Saying that anything that I received in the course of the investigation would be turned over promptly to the FBI.

There was more, but Ted didn't wait for me to finish. "Okay," he said, "there's a place to sign at the end."

I flipped the pages, looking for the signature block.

"You're not gonna use your real name," Terry said.

This was new. I'd used Naveed Jamali since we'd begun the operation. "Okay."

"You're gonna sign it like this," Ted said. "Green Kryptonite."

"Green Kryptonite?" I asked him. "What the fuck is that?" Had I just gotten a code name?

"Yeah. It's a pretty fuckin' cool name," Ted said proudly. "I checked. It wasn't taken yet."

I guessed they had a no-doubling-up-on-code-names rule in the FBI. I knew Ted was a fan of superhero comics. I was sure he hadn't stumbled onto this one by accident. I knew enough about kryptonite: In its presence, Superman turned weak and nauseated. His veins popped out and his skin grew dark. He lost his superpowers and even risked death. That kryptonite was one powerful substance!

"So Wonder Woman and My Little Pony were already taken?" I teased. "I know you're looking to evoke fear in the hearts of our enemies. But Superman? This sounds like a name that was chosen by some forty-year-old guy who lives in his mom's basement and plays a lot of World of Warcraft. You wouldn't know anything about that, would you?"

Ted groaned. But the truth was, I couldn't stop smiling now that I'd been given my very own FBI identifier.

Wow, I thought. *A code name.* That was pretty cool. I totally forgot about all the concerns I'd been feeling earlier. Who cared about danger and threateningly pointed Glocks and grabbing secret documents from a government contractor? I was a grown man, and I had a code name. If only my six-year-old self could see me now!

And though I would never admit it to Ted, he'd made a pretty awesome choice. Green Kryptonite sounded thoroughly badass to me.

CHAPTER 18

SPEEDING UP

Oleg and I had agreed to continue our Westchester County lunch tour at the Fountain Diner in Hartsdale. He was already in the booth when I walked in that late December morning. After we said hello, he immediately excused himself to use the men's room.

What was it with these espionage guys and their constant bathroom visits? The agents, Oleg—there wasn't a normal-size bladder on either side of the post–Cold War. I'd hate to take a cross-country road trip with any of these people. We'd be pulling in to every second rest stop from the New Jersey Turnpike to the Santa Monica Freeway. It would be like traveling with a carload of six-year-olds. We'd die of old age before we ever saw the Pacific.

I picked up the lengthy menu and watched him make his way quickly to the men's room. If Oleg was wearing a hidden recorder like I was, why run to the men's room? Couldn't he press *record* in the parking lot?

When he got back to the booth, I got right down to business: "I looked for your articles. I have a good idea where to get them. But that's just two articles. That's nothing. As I mentioned last time, I think I have a better solution for you."

Oleg looked at me, but he didn't look happy. Did he think I was stalling?

"The federal government has a lot of databases. Some are far more interesting than others. They focus on all kinds of different things. One of them, the one I mentioned last time, is called DTIC. It covers some areas I think you are very interested in." With that, I handed over the coup de grâce: a neatly formatted twenty-page bibliography of articles about the Tomahawk cruise missile.

I gave him a minute to turn through the pages and fully appreciate what he was looking at. "I can get access, but it won't be cheap," I warned him. "I don't know how much, exactly. But for that fee, you will get everything."

"Everything?" he asked.

"A lot," I said. "You might find that would be a highly favorable return on your investment." I might as well talk in business terms.

"Okay," Oleg said, nodding slowly. "I like that."

"Say, for instance, you are interested in Tomahawk missiles," I said. "You tell me, 'Tomahawk missiles.' And I can give you a long list like this one. You look at the list and tell me which titles you are interested in. I will get you those. It's like ordering off the menu at the Russian Samovar. You want the blini or the caviar?"

"Like what?"

"Never mind," I said.

He was grasping the idea slowly. "You will show me the list," he said, "and I will tell you what I am interested in?"

"Exactly," I said.

"I would be interested in that. Yes. I would be interested. Let's do this."

I told him I thought the registration cost would be around ten thousand dollars, and then there would be a fee every few months.

He didn't have that much with him, but he said he would give me what he had, twenty-five hundred, with a promise to pay the balance the next time we met.

That was an important milestone. Not the money. I'd gotten money from him before. But he took a step forward without getting prior approval from his bosses in Moscow. He showed his own ego and decisiveness. I gave him credit for his willingness to say yes.

Some of this could take a while, I warned him. First I had to register for the database and get accepted. He had to get me the money for the registration fee. "In the meantime," I said, hinting at my haul from the trip to Long Island, "I might have something interesting for you from the Northrop Grumman project."

"Yes?"

"It has to do with fighter jets," I told him.

Damn, I was getting good at this! I knew just what buttons to push.

When the waitress dropped off our food and had moved far enough away for me to continue, I told Oleg, "We have to be ready to act quickly."

I wasn't in any big hurry. I was still waiting for the FBI to get me the Northrop Grumman material. But while I was cooling my heels, I wanted more control over the pace. I didn't want Oleg constantly snapping his fingers every time he was ready for me to jump. "When I get the material from Northrop Grumman, I can't wait another month or two for you to call. The window is too short for that. I'll have to reach out to you."

This was something that had pissed me off for a long time, this whole idea of one-way communication. With the power of phony urgency on my side, maybe I had a chance to build a genuine two-way street. "I need a way to contact you," I told him. "And I don't mean email. I am not using email. Too many traces. I have another idea."

I told him that when I needed to reach him, I would be sending a signal that I wanted him to call me. "We'll use the Denver Craigslist, the lost-and-found section. I'll put up an ad saying I've lost a black North Face jacket. That will be the signal for you to contact me. Keep checking Craigslist. When you see that, you'll know I'm ready to meet."

To make sure Oleg understood, I gave him a Craigslist cheat sheet, a step-by-step explanation of where to look and what to look for. He seemed to think he could follow that.

Before we said goodbye, Oleg told me he was going home to Russia for the holidays. "But," he added cheerfully, "I look forward to seeing you in the New Year."

He left the diner with a bounce in his step.

In late January, I put a message on Craigslist Denver, saying I'd lost a black North Face jacket and I was offering a reward. For a couple of days, I heard nothing. Then Oleg called.

When my cell phone rang, Ava and I and several friends were having dinner at a popular restaurant underneath the West Side Highway called Dinosaur Bar-B-Que. Oleg was calling from a 718 number I didn't recognize. I had a feeling it might be him, so I answered.

"I saw the message on the Internet, but I can't meet you," he said.

It was loud in the restaurant. I couldn't hear everything he said. I asked him to hold a second and walked to a spot that was a little quieter, but it was still hard to hear.

"I am sorry," he said. "It is not possible. I will be calling you again when I can meet."

What could I do? I said "okay" and then "goodbye." But I was not happy at all. I thought I'd made it clear that any attempt on my part to reach him meant I was operating within a small window of opportunity. I'd stressed the urgency several times. And Oleg was blowing me off? Not cool.

Before I returned to the table, I went out to the sidewalk where I could hear, and I called the 718 number. Oleg didn't answer. Instead, I found myself speaking to a different man with a strong Russian accent. Make that *trying* to speak. It was a short phone call.

I asked for Oleg. The man knew enough English to respond, "He left."

When I thought about it later, I concluded that the whole idea of my being able to summon Oleg must have been deeply troubling for the Russians. It gave Oleg no time to alert his bosses in Moscow. It gave them no time to prepare Oleg to meet with me. No time for them to decide how far he could go. No time for whatever their pre-meeting protocols were. If I started calling audibles, I'd be taking away any advantage they thought they had.

Much as I hated it, we were back to snap, jump, meet.

You do this kind of work long enough, you go a little crazy. That's what I was finding, anyway. It's a fact of the double-agent life.

I couldn't tell anyone what I was up to. I certainly couldn't expect my friends to keep a secret as juicy as this. By the time I blabbed anything about my secret life to the second and third person, 33—and then 333 more—people would also know. And one of them would surely have a Russian friend.

I told exactly one person about my counterespionage activities. Ava. Even my parents I kept mainly in the dark. They didn't ask much, and I didn't say much. From time to time, they asked in the vaguest terms: "Everything okay at the office?" or sometimes "Still hearing from the Russians?" I answered with similar vagueness: "All good." "Same as usual." "You know the Russians." That seemed to satisfy everyone.

But thank God for Ava. She was my outlet, my confidante, the one person I could discuss my fears and frustrations with. As close as I'd grown to Ted and Terry, we mostly talked about tactical and operational matters. We were always jockeying for position, struggling for operational control. Neither party would admit a weakness to the other, that's for sure. Ava was the only one I could do that with. I always knew I could trust her. But as important as she was to me when it came to admitting doubts or fears, she was also the only one I could afford to be open with about how exciting it was, how proud I was. There were more than a few times when I just wanted to stand up and scream out loud, "Here I am! Look at me! I'm a total fuckin' amazing espionage badass!" I wanted badly to make a public pronouncement of some sort, roll down the window of my 'vette, and shout it out for the world to hear.

Instead, I got a tattoo.

I felt like I had to do something to prove this whole double-agent thing existed—prove it to myself most of all. Something actual. Something physical. Something undeniably real. Something that connected me to this long, secret journey I was on. It wasn't like I was going to keep a coffee-table scrapbook of my secret meetings with Oleg or the FBI. It would all be over one day, and what proof would I have?

So on the morning of March 22, as I was starting to prep for my next meeting with Oleg, I pulled on a T-shirt that said "NY DOESN'T LOVE YOU." Then Ava and I made a trip to Red Rocket Tattoos. I'd never gotten a tattoo. The brightly lit shop was in midtown, on the second floor of a Garment District building around the corner from Macy's. I told the heavyset biker-looking dude that I wanted the words *Green Kryptonite* in Morse code on the inside of my right forearm.

"Green Kryptonite?" he asked. "What are you, some kind of superhero?"

"No," I told him, "although I am thinking of starting a line of capes."

"What?"

"Nothing."

He looked at me a little quizzically. But from what I'd seen on bulging biceps, beefy necks, and hairy backs around New York, people made all kinds of strange requests at local tattoo parlors.

"All right," he said, "I can do that."

I didn't know Morse code. And I didn't expect the tattoo guy to know it, either. So the night before, I'd gone online and found a Morse-code chart and carefully mapped the letters out: dash-dash-dot for G, dot-dash-dot for R, dot for E, dot for the second E, dash-dot for N, and so on.

He bandaged my arm, and Ava and I headed home.

On the way back, she asked me, "Did you think this through, Naveed?"

I just looked at her and answered, "Do I ever?"

I said nothing to the agents about my new tattoo. I hadn't asked Ted and Terry for permission beforehand. They would have objected. As far as I was concerned, they weren't going to tell me what I could put on my body. And I had to admit, keeping a secret from them felt good.

I'd have to be doubly careful around Oleg. Long-sleeve shirts from now on at Pizzeria Uno! My first bet was that he wouldn't recognize the dots and dashes for what they were, even if he had learned Morse code in his school days. And what if he did crack my tattoo code? I could only imagine the questions the Russian might ask: *What is this Green Kryptonite? Why is the kryptonite green? Are you Superman?* There I'd be, trying to explain to him how Green Kryptonite was my nickname in college or that his mom and I got matching tattoos.

Call me immature if you want to. Call me impetuous. I'll plead guilty. I even went on Facebook and threw up a picture of my freshly tattooed arm with the obnoxious caption "Getting inked up, yo!," provoking my friend Benjamin Dash to comment: "You what? You got a tattoo? I hope you spelled my name right."

I had done my share of boneheaded things in my life, but I'm not sure that anything was quite the equal of getting my secret FBI code name tattooed onto my arm, then bragging about it on Facebook—with photographic proof!

But that's where my head was. That tattoo was my little F-U to everyone. It was like I was rebelling against my parents all over again. *You can't tell anyone, you can't tell anyone, you can't tell anyone*—after a while, you almost have to tell someone, even it's a biker-looking guy at a New York tattoo parlor who doesn't understand what any of it means. I think that's a normal human response to stress. It was my response, anyway.

Ava hadn't said she thought getting a tattoo of my secret code name was a great idea. But she hadn't fought me, either. She knew almost everything. After the maxi-pad incident, keeping secrets from her seemed almost as dangerous as Oleg figuring out what I was up to.

I did wonder what my parents would think of their Harvard-dropout son getting a tattoo. But they'd never connect my dots and dashes to what they'd started so long ago with the Russians. They had inklings, I'm sure, that my relationships with both the agents and the Russians had gone far beyond those they'd had. But they never asked me to tell them how far. I didn't think they really wanted to know. I didn't want to involve them. But that also left me feeling very much isolated and invisible.

I'm not complaining. But it can be more than a little rattling, living inside a compartmentalized cone of silence—hiding so much from friends and family, putting in the hours of painstaking prep, avoiding the inevitable questions about my peripatetic whereabouts, strictly maintaining my triple identity. Triple because it wasn't just my double-agent double identity I was expected to keep straight.

I was one person with Oleg. I was another person with the FBI. And I was yet another person with everyone else in my life. Sometimes I had a little trouble remembering what was real and who was me. If you think that isn't disorienting, you try it sometime.

I had my Green Kryptonite tattoo. I was hoping I would never need one that said "Naveed Jamali."

CHAPTER 19

PARKING GARAGE

I certainly wore long sleeves for when I met Oleg again. The last thing I wanted was Oleg eying my Morse-code tattoo as I handed over the Northrop Grumman cockpit manuals.

It was the early part of April—two months since our last short phone call—and he seemed unusually skittish. Oleg liked to control things. I understood that. But my Craigslist suggestion seemed to have rattled him far more than I'd anticipated. I told the FBI agents that I thought I'd scared him off completely. Really, Craigslist was just a way for me to reach him in a hurry, but he seemed to have interpreted it as my setting him up.

Whatever he was thinking, it didn't keep him away from the bundle of goodies I'd been promising. He came back to me with his own new idea.

Instead of getting together at a restaurant or a coffee shop like we usually did, this time he said he would leave his car in the city and take the train to Westchester. That was fine with me. I didn't care how he arrived, just so he came. The FBI had completed their meticulous examination of the Northrop Grumman NATOPS cockpit manuals and delivered the blue binders to me. I was itching to make the long-awaited handoff. I suggested to Oleg that he get off at the Metro-North station at Hastings-on-Hudson. I would pick him up there, I said, being doubly cautious about how I handed the manuals to him.

"It's always good to be careful," he said.

I had traded in a black 2007 Acura RDX, which I hated, for a 2008 Jeep Cherokee. Six months with the four-cylinder Acura had made me hunger for the four-door version of a muscle car.

The picturesque train station offered water views but little privacy. Instead of bringing the fat blue binders in the Jeep with me, I decided I would stash them in an out-of-the-way location and bring the Russian there. I'd let him inspect the binders, then hand him a tiny black thumb drive that contained the same material and would be a whole lot easier to carry back to the city. For our rendezvous, I chose an auto-storage warehouse on the east bank of the Hudson, barely a two-minute drive from the train station. I knew the place because I had stored my cars there. I figured I'd park the Corvette inside, leave the binders in the trunk, and pick Oleg up at the train in the Jeep. Then we'd drive to the warehouse, a giant brick garage without much in-and-out traffic, a perfectly discreet spot to hand everything over.

The early part of my plan went smooth as butter. We met at the train station. We drove to the garage. We easily got inside. I found my way to the parked Corvette.

Yes, there'd been a couple of bumps, literally and figuratively. The radar detector started squealing. I almost killed Oleg with the car trunk—or thought I had.

But the transfer got done, and I didn't cause him any permanent brain damage. If anything, our trust seemed to be restored by that day.

"I like the way this is developing," Oleg said to me before I dropped him back at the train station with a tiny black thumb drive in his pocket.

"Me, too," I said.

And I think both of us meant it.

My relationship with Oleg was never quite a straight line. The super-spy rush I'd be feeling would evaporate when I didn't hear a word from him for weeks or months at a time. Sometimes this drove me crazy. Before I knew it, I was channeling my inner Ronald Reagan, asserting my need to dominate him. I swear, the American red-baiters got at least one point right: You'll never get anything from the Russians if all you do is equivocate. Strength and directness are what these people understand. Oleg obviously cared about working me and keeping me cooperative. He never stopped treating our relationship like a chess match. He didn't mind having a strong opponent as long as he felt he was one move ahead and the game didn't come to a stalemate.

So what was the problem with the FBI? Why were they so poky and unfocused? Maybe I needed to be as clear and frank with the agents as I was with Oleg. I half wanted to slam my shoe on the table like Nikita Khrushchev, or dust off my best Reagan imitation: "We begin bombing in five minutes." After all the time and effort, my patience was running thin. This had to start paying dividends. And soon.

I met Ted and Terry in Riverside Park. It was early but already hot in the park. They were both dressed casually. It was the first time I'd seen Ted wearing his badge on his belt clip. Was that his way of flashing an "I'm in control" message to me?

"This is a lot of work on my end," I complained. "It's getting to the point that I'm having trouble justifying it. The returns just aren't there for me. It is expensive. It is time-consuming. I don't mind using the company to a degree. But the amount of work to process half a dozen books for Oleg is a waste of money. It's a hundred-and-fifty-percent profit, but it comes out to like a hundred bucks. People in the office are starting to wonder why we're doing this."

Those were legitimate questions. But my lament went deeper than the paltry return on my time. I'd be willing to expend the time and energy and more if we could move along reeling in the espionage prize. When were we going to dangle something huge in front of him? When was he going to take the bait? I wanted to be a bigger double agent, not a book snitch. I needed something real to pass to him. I didn't know how much longer I'd be able to hold his interest. "This all seems so piddling," I told the agents. "For what we've done, we could have left things where they were when my parents were around." I wanted some sort of conclusion, or at least some sort of action. I knew the famous John le Carré quote from *The Russia House*: "Spying is waiting," the narrator Harry de Palfrey says. But all this waiting was getting to me.

The agents took an understanding tone. "Of course," Ted said. "It's a lot of work. It's totally understandable the stress this puts on you and puts on the business. I am very grateful for that. We're very grateful.

"These things take time," he went on, as if it were the first time I'd heard this sales pitch. "If you rush it, their suspicions will be raised. They'll wonder why you're so desperate to help them. We've been pacing it just about right, I think. It's important that they be the ones who are driving this. It'll happen. It usually does."

I appreciated the acknowledgment. It sounded genuine. But while Ted counseled patience, as he'd done countless times before, I was running out.

"Look," I said, "I get that. I want to help you guys. I understand nothing happens instantly. But there are limits. You have to be respectful of my time. You are expecting me to be here and do this no matter how long it takes. I want to do that, I want to be involved, but I feel like it isn't taking the course I expected."

From what I read, I had the impression that things were escalating between the United States and the Russians, and I was sitting off to the side. "It's like the Russians keep messing with us," I said. "Did you see that story in the *New York Times*?" I had printed it out: "Factory Visit Tied to Ouster of Attachés from Russia," by C. J. Chivers. I handed the printout to Terry.

"The Russians just threw out two American attachés," I said. "They granted them permission to travel outside Moscow. Once the attachés reached wherever it is they were going, the Russians revoked their permission to travel and threw them out of the country for traveling without permission."

Ted and Terry laughed. "These guys are bastards," Ted said. "They rarely play by the rules. When we act, we have all kinds of rules we have to follow. We don't throw you out until we've actually caught you."

I wanted to steer the agents back to the selfish part—for me. It seemed like we had almost forgotten why I had begun all of this in the first place. "It's because of the navy," I reminded them. "Whatever I do with you guys, I want to reference the work for the navy. I want us to achieve something they can look at and say, 'He did this.' Do you think we can make that happen? Maybe it's time we try to get that back in gear."

Almost on cue, two U.S. Marine attack helicopters came roaring up the Hudson with a couple of Hueys in the mix. They flew in so loud, they almost made the concrete park benches rattle. "You know," Ted said, "the military is amazing. Every now and then, it is really impressive what we can do."

"So do you think we can try to rev up the navy process? That would help me justify all this time and effort."

Ted sounded as soothing as ever and just as noncommittal. "That's possible," he said. "Let's see what we can do."

While I was waiting, I focused on the success we'd had with Northrop Grumman and the NATOPs manuals. I was still eager to make DTIC a reality. But I couldn't just walk up to a window at the Defense Department and say, "Hi, I'd like freewheeling access to all of your military, scientific, and technical information." I needed someone who would vouch for me. I discussed this with Ted and Terry. I knew the authority of the FBI could swing open that access. And it did.

"Our boss, Frank, pushed pretty hard, and we've gotten the okay," Terry told me.

Though I had heard Frank's name, I didn't know much about him other than that he was the agents' supervisor. But I liked his willingness to get behind us. To me, he was Robin Masters, the unseen authority figure on *Magnum, P.I.*

Under the Books & Research name, I signed a written contract to "provide consultation and research services to FBI Procurement in regards to trends and patterns of federal academic, research, and training institutions on such subjects as catalog management, digitization, and other related topics. The secondary objective will be to provide book and other material procurement services."

Talk about a mouthful!

Originally, I'd told Oleg I thought the Russians would have to pay me about $10,000 to register on DTIC. It was actually $16,800, and it was paid with a check from the GSA, the United States Government Services Administration. By going this route, I didn't have to rely on funds from the company or my personal checking account. And I didn't have to wait for notoriously slow-paying Oleg. As far as he'd know, he owed me a big wad of cash.

Now I had the contract. More important, I had the documentation to prove to Oleg that I had online access to DTIC. An amazing cache of material was waiting for me. There were plenty of mundane charts and memos and reports, but also plenty of files that would have Russian mouths watering.

"Under no circumstances are you ever to give the Russians your DTIC credentials," Ted warned me. I thought that was a given. I assured him I wouldn't.

I thought incessantly about how I should present the details to Oleg. Night and day, I asked myself if I were a real traitor, how would I offer something like this? Very carefully, I concluded, focusing obsessively on not getting caught.

I had credentials and permission. I had a license from the FBI, who had paid my ticket aboard. And I had a clever answer when Oleg inevitably asked how I would avoid detection. I knew exactly what to do: I would bury the Russian requests in a batch of innocuous searches. I'd employ the same distraction technique we'd used for buying beer in high school. I would slip it past 'em, hiding my nefarious queries right in plain sight.

I decided to tell Oleg that the documents had to be retrieved in a specific manner, time, and place to avoid detection. That would sound reasonable. It would also protect me from any insistence that I deliver huge armloads of data at a time or hand over my log-in and password.

I discussed all this with Ted and Terry, who reported back to their superiors. There was a real feeling of excitement. We were finally building one hell of a sting to catch some real bad guys.

It was startling how much I had access to, a massive trove of government-funded research. Some of these studies had taken years to complete with seven-figure budgets. The data in any one of them could be genuinely damaging to United States security. None of this was intended for hostile foreign eyes. With this new access, even the most technical detail seemed potentially powerful.

★   ★   ★

On May 29, 2008, I had an eleven-thirty a.m. appointment in Ami-tyville, Long Island, with David Harris. Like Jeff Jones, he was a commander in the navy. Harris was the officer in charge of the New England region for the intelligence reserves. Through some strange quirk of military geography, that region included New York. I'd had to remind Ted about my navy agenda. But he had come through for me and set this meeting up.

One hour before I arrived at the second-floor office, Ted and Terry had already been there and left. When I showed up, the first thing the navy commander said to me was this: "So these guys with suits came in right before you did, saying, 'We can't tell you what he is working on. We can't tell you anything about it. But we can say he's a very intelligent and bright person.' I'm sitting here thinking, 'Now, what I am supposed to make out of that?'"

I said nothing. I didn't have to. Harris continued, "I'm just a sim-ple sailor who spent the majority of his career chasing Chinese and Russian subs. It's all very interesting, isn't it?"

I nodded and agreed that it was.

The two commanders I met could not have been more different. As much as Commander Jones was understated, that's how bom-bastic Commander Harris was. They even dressed differently. Harris wore a khaki navy uniform, while Jones had come to our meeting in a pressed gray suit.

Listening to the commander, I had the sense that this was a strange way for a top official to start an important meeting. The commander had said his piece in a matter-of-fact manner. He didn't follow it with any questions or seek additional clarification. He'd just described his exchange with Ted and Terry and left it hanging, as if repeating an annoying comment he'd overheard that morning in Starbucks—although I couldn't imagine Harris in a Starbucks. He was definitely more the ship-mess-deck type.

So far I hadn't been asked to say a thing. This was, I thought dejectedly, less about meeting with a highly decorated navy man than sitting in an office listening to someone talk about me.

I knew Ted and Terry had tried to help, but they'd been so cryptic with the commander that their visit had raised more questions than it had answered and would only raise suspicions about me. I was sure Harris thought the person he was meeting had to be some kind of criminal. Aren't those the people who end up cooperating with the FBI? People desperate to get out of jams of their own and strike a deal? I wished that Ted and Terry had made clear that I was never in any trouble, that there was a whole operation and it had been my doing, that I'd been the one to take the initiative with Oleg and the FBI and that even pursuing an appointment to the navy was something I'd started on my own. It seemed I'd wasted a trip to Long Island.

But then, unexpectedly, Harris seemed to put aside the FBI intro and started talking with me. "I can see you're one of those guys who's totally into reading a lot of stuff," he said. "You like to sit back and absorb as much as you can about whatever is happening, someone who wants to understand the root cause of things. Am I right?"

Well, yes, I told him. I'd been imagining what the commander might assume about someone named Naveed Jamali interested in joining the ranks of navy intelligence. Given the odd prep and my Middle Eastern name, I was betting he thought I was tied up in terrorism. I believe I managed to dispel any of that. Whatever preconceived notions he might have started out with, I think he was pleasantly surprised to hear that I was reasonably well read and well spoken and well versed in both military and world events—and most important, after some direct questioning, he knew I had no obvious criminal or terroristic connections. As far as I could tell, he seemed to enjoy our back-and-forth.

That didn't mean I'd forgotten the awkward opening minutes. As soon as I got out of there, I had to talk to Ted. "Dude," I said, "you gotta stop showing up in suits, talking to these people in the navy, and saying cryptic things about what I'm doing for you. They're starting to think I'm a drug dealer or a criminal or a terrorist. If this is help, I don't want it."

Ted let me go on, like he often did. After a while, he said, "I get it, but I can't promise anything."

On a sunny Saturday morning in late July, I was summoned to Fort Hamilton, a joint army and navy base on the Brooklyn waterfront, for interviews with the regional selection board. I met Juli in the base parking lot. She led me into a waiting area where six other nervous-looking young men were sitting uncomfortably. These were the other intelligence finalists from the New York area. I had some impressive competition: people who'd actually done stuff. A lawyer. A couple of men with law-enforcement backgrounds. Two air marshals, one of whom had a law degree. One guy was working on his PhD. Several had prior enlisted service in the navy.

Despite the seriousness of the occasion, we had all been told not to wear suits and ties or uniforms. Only one lieutenant, who seemed to know Juli, must have missed the casual-dress memo. He was wearing his navy-issue pressed khakis with several rows of ribbons on his chest. "I told you," Juli snapped at him loud enough for the rest of us to hear, "they don't wear uniforms here."

I sat next to a finalist named Thomas. From a quick glance, I could tell that he and I were the only "ethnics" in the waiting room. He was Indian-American. We bonded instantly.

"So you here for a green-card interview, too?" I asked him.

"No," he replied without missing a beat. "I'm here to audition for terrorist number three on *24*. Is this the right place?"

"I don't know. But if you and I are seen speaking to each other for another two minutes, we could be considered coconspirators, and the LT over there can legally shoot us."

With that, we laughed and shook hands. Thomas was my age, recently married, with a young daughter. He had started at the NYPD before becoming a federal air marshal. Like me, he seemed impervious to insult. The fifteen minutes we spent BS'ing that day cemented a friendship that would last for years.

One by one, all seven of us were called into the conference room and invited to take a seat at a long oak table with shoreline views. The last time I had been at a table like this—for my board interview in Boston—I had ultimately lost out to applicants with deeper résumés, many of them boasting strong operational experience. Again, I was up against some seriously credentialed competition, but I was older now. I was running a company now. And I was an actual double agent now, even if we had to be careful in revealing some of the details.

The chairman of the regional selection board, Captain Gary Golomb, didn't ask me a lot of technical questions. He didn't want to know what a foc'sle was or show me any drawings of turning planes. He seemed interested in talking about current events. He asked for my opinion about U.S. relations with Iran. We got into a long discussion of one element of the Bush Doctrine, the notion that a nation harboring terrorists is just as guilty as the terrorists themselves and should be held just as responsible when it comes to a U.S. military response.

The Bush Doctrine wasn't really invented by George W. Bush. Similar arguments were made in the "Red October" days of the Cold War against the Soviet Union and their proxy states. But it's been a key concept in America's effort to combat asymmetrical threats since 2001—plausible deniability, WMDs, the connection between Saddam Hussein and 9/11—and it keeps coming up. Terrorists exist because states allow them to exist by not trying to stop the extremists and by providing material aid.

I love talking about that stuff, and it showed. As I expected, the board didn't ask me anything at all about my activities with the FBI and Russians.

I was thrilled. I was still in the game.

CHAPTER 20

GRILLING OLEG

That Sunday morning was especially humid, one of those days when, the minute you climb out of the shower, you are instantly sweating again. The window unit in our prewar apartment didn't have a chance. It didn't help that my throat felt scratchy. I was getting a cold. But I loaded up on Sudafed D, called Ted and Terry, and let them know I was on my way to Long Island. "I'm not feeling great," I told Terry, "but I'm going anyway."

There are no paid sick days in the espionage business.

This was June 22, the second-longest day of the year. My meeting with Oleg was scheduled for noon. This time around, he hadn't slipped me a business card. He'd given me a take-out menu. I preferred that, actually. I could give some advance thought to what I'd like to order.

We were going to Vincent's Clam Bar in Carle Place. Vincent's, I learned from the menu, was known for generous portions of baked clams and a "world-famous" tomato sauce. The place traced its roots to a family-style restaurant that opened in Manhattan's Little Italy in

1904. It had to be better than Oleg's usual diners and Pizzeria Unos. At Vincent's, I figured, they could pour that famous red sauce over everything.

I had several pressing matters to discuss with Oleg that had come up since we'd met in April. I wanted to bring him up to date on my interview with Commander Jeffrey Jones from the U.S. Mission to the UN. I knew he'd be impressed by that.

I'd asked Ted and Terry if I could show Jeff's business card to Oleg. They'd told me that would be okay. But most of all on that sticky day in June, I was eager to show the Russian the insides of DTIC and explain to him all the material I could retrieve. I knew DTIC wasn't just the best move we had. It was the only move. I was itching to dangle the database in front of Oleg and see how he responded.

I decided to drive the big black Jeep. The 'vette could get you into trouble and out of it—fast. But it wasn't happy sitting still. Even idling, that car sounded like a pounding bass drum. It was one mean-looking sports car. And people noticed it. Despite its size and profile, I knew the Jeep would attract far less attention in a Long Island suburban strip-mall parking lot than my high-idling, low-to-the-ground Corvette Z06, with its aggressive camshaft and the lights and badges all blacked out.

I brought along my laptop, a Lenovo T60, made by the Chinese company that had bought IBM's personal-computing division. I also brought a 3G wireless air card and a battery charger in case the Lenovo needed a boost. Most important, I had a big stack of papers for Oleg.

That was one of the lessons I had learned from my time in both the university and business worlds. People want stuff: papers, reports, printouts, documents, certificates, directions—almost anything. This was true of Oleg. It was also true of the FBI. I liked to bury all of them in paper. It made them feel better. Somehow, all that paper made things seem more serious. When people walk away from a meeting with something in their hands, they can review it quietly later. They can double-check their faulty memories. They can explain things to their superiors and colleagues. They have actual evidence that they were *there*.

I took the Throgs Neck Bridge to the Cross Island Parkway to the Long Island Expressway to the Northern State. That was the best and quickest route I knew to Long Island from upper Manhattan, though it was busy even on a Sunday morning. Vincent's was just across Old Country Road from the Roosevelt Field Mall, in a satellite shopping strip, between Toys "R" Us and Petco. We were a long way from Little Italy.

I pulled into the parking lot and pushed the *record* button on the watch, then climbed out of the Jeep and headed into the restaurant. The lights were low inside. The air-conditioning was humming. Oleg was waiting for me near the bar. "Hey, how are you?" he asked. "Is this okay?"

"This place looks great." I left the rest of the sentence in my head: *compared to the chain dumps you've been taking me.*

"You want to sit down?" he asked.

"Sure."

The hostess sat us dead center in the dining room. The place was two thirds full, I'd say, a pretty good crowd for noontime Sunday.

The waitress brought us a basket of focaccia and poured some olive oil onto a bread plate. We ordered our lunches—eggplant Parmesan for me, fried calamari for Oleg. Surprisingly, the focaccia was excellent, but the conversation grew tense right away.

"Shall we talk about DTIC?" I offered brightly. Even before I had a chance to explain the extensive reach of the defense-technology database, Oleg began asking questions that made me think he might be running a recorder of his own.

"Tell me what you're offering to do," he said.

"What do you want me to do?" I answered. "You want me to get you stuff, right? Things that you're interested in."

"What kinds of things can you retrieve with this?" he asked.

"It depends on what you want," I said noncommittally. This back-and-forth felt more like an exercise than a conversation. Was he trying to get me to incriminate myself without offering anything in return? I started to feel uncomfortable.

I watched Oleg's face carefully, trying to get a read, paying special attention to the Russian's eyes. What was he thinking? As I stared, I couldn't help but recall the day in 2001 when President George W. Bush said he'd looked into the eyes of Russia's president Vladimir Putin and "was able to get a sense of his soul." Bush said he'd seen the soul as "very straightforward and trustworthy."

I can't say that's what I saw in Oleg's eyes. I was more aligned with Arizona senator John McCain, who reacted to Bush's observation with a sneer: "I looked into Mr. Putin's eyes, and I saw three things—a K and a G and a B."

"I can show you the kinds of things I have access to," I said to Oleg.

KGB, SVR, GRU—it didn't matter. This was my day to outmaneuver Oleg. I pulled out my stack of papers. I showed him a copy of my registration for DTIC. I showed him a couple of screenshots of the DTIC search engine. I showed him a list of the many libraries that DTIC had access to. I kept my voice low. A crowded family restaurant wasn't the best place to conduct a full sales presentation on top-secret military data. But I didn't mind giving a small taste. I hoped he was impressed enough to recognize the value.

"I'd like to move forward," I told him. "But there are a couple of things we have to resolve first." Taking charge was the best way to mask my uneasiness. "You have to pay me. You still owe a balance. If we're going to move forward, you have to settle that."

He looked at me blankly. Was he truly confused or just negotiating? Negotiating was my bet. And that pissed me off.

"There is significant risk involved," I said sternly, not giving him the opportunity to slip in another question. "I need an understanding here. We need a business plan. There has to be a benefit for me. You have to pay for the DTIC registration fee. I'm starting to feel stiffed."

I knew the FBI would eventually get me repaid for the money I'd put out. But Oleg didn't know that. Cheap as he was, he would understand cheapness from me and assume I wouldn't want to be floating money to the Russian Federation. They were a semimajor world power. I was just a little guy in New York.

"I can pay you some money now," he said. "But I'd like to get a better sense of—"

"No better sense," I cut him off. "I put myself at risk. We had an understanding. I'd like to get compensated for my time. If you want to go forward, know this: I am not going to get into a relationship where, every time I meet you, we have to discuss whether you're gonna pay me or not."

I sounded angry. That was my intent. But Oleg wasn't backing down.

"You have to understand," he said, "we want to do business. But I need to see what kinds of things we can expect. Tell me what you're offering to do." He handed me a receipt. "And you have to sign this receipt."

That set me off even more. There'd been times when my anger had been a carefully orchestrated act, but not this time. Could he possibly be serious?

"I'm not gonna sign a fuckin' receipt," I told him louder than I intended. "You want me to sign a receipt for you saying I'm doing this? This is treasonous. You go to jail for the rest of your life for doing this shit. How do I even know who you are? How do I know you're not a cop? How do I know you're not working for the FBI?"

I caught my mistake as soon as the words slipped out. *Stupid!* But I didn't give him a second to focus on it. "It seems like you're trying to trap me," I finished.

He looked around nervously, checking to see if my outburst had attracted any unwanted attention. Clearly, he wished I wouldn't talk like that in such a public place. He was right about that part. I needed to calm down. It might be better, I thought, to lower the temperature, mine especially. I needed a minute to collect myself and think. Call it a stall if you want to. Sometimes a short stall is good. The point of this whole meeting, after all, was to show DTIC to Oleg and get us started with the federal military database. Whatever provocative things he might be saying, I didn't want to derail us. So I threw Oleg a curveball.

"Show me your ID," I demanded.

Oleg hesitated.

"I'd like to see ID that says you work for the UN," I said. "I'd like to know."

He sighed aloud and smiled like a man who'd seen the first spear of light in a dark, dense forest. This was a demand he could answer. He opened his wallet and removed two laminated plastic cards. "Of course, of course," he said. "This is my UN ID. This is my residential ID."

I looked at the identification cards. They looked legit to me, as I'd expected them to. If he hadn't been the real deal, the FBI would have known. But I'd dialed the tension back and maybe thrown him off for a moment. I handed them back to Oleg.

My cold was really kicking in. My throat was getting scratchier. I was feeling feverish. "I have to go to the bathroom," I said.

I got up from the table and walked to the men's room. When I finished at the urinal, I went to the sink and started splashing water on my face. As I toweled off, a thin man came in. He was in his forties and had sandy hair. Something seemed odd about him. He didn't say anything, so I didn't hear any accent. But he definitely looked Russian to me. The man stopped on his way to one of the stalls, turned, and stared for several seconds at me. Was I being paranoid? Why did I feel like I was being followed? Maybe I was. Without reacting at all to him, I went back to the table and sat with Oleg. Our lunches had arrived.

"When we're finished, we'll go outside," I told him. "I'll show you some things I have for you on my laptop."

We ate in silence, and although the food was good, we both wanted the meal to be over with as quickly as possible. Oleg finished his calamari first and stood to leave. I put down my fork and followed. On the way to the door, he handed the waitress several folded bills—I couldn't see how much—and said, "This should cover it," hardly slowing his stride. He and I walked out into the sauna of suburban Long Island to my even hotter black Jeep. The moment he climbed inside, I threw the air conditioner on full blast and drove out of the parking lot in search of somewhere quiet we could talk. The unpleasantness in the restaurant didn't change a thing: I was still eager to show him what we could do together with DTIC.

CHAPTER 21

THUMB DRIVE

"Why don't we go into the parking garage," Oleg said.

The garage was on the mall side of Old Country Road. After I pulled the Jeep past the entrance, Oleg said, "Drive up to the second level." From there, he directed me to an empty spot a third of the way down the left row: "Pull in here."

I glanced left, right, and behind me, as I had learned. Just making sure we were alone. I noticed a gold Buick LeSabre parked beside us. There was no one else around.

"Let me get the computer on," I said to Oleg as I turned the Jeep engine off. "The wireless card should be fine up here. What I want to do is show you all the things that are available through DTIC."

Just then, a mall cop came up the ramp toward us. Growing up in the American suburbs, I knew you never had to fear the mall cops. They might have official-looking uniforms. They might even drive cruiser-looking cars. But the square tin badges they wore carried zero legal authority. There wasn't anything a mall cop could do to you.

I'm not sure whether they had mall cops in the Soviet Union's

Moscow suburbs when Oleg was a teenager, but he looked a little spooked when the Roosevelt Field officer pulled around in his white Chevy Cavalier with flashing amber lights. "Let's just wait," Oleg whispered to me.

I shut the lid of my laptop and didn't move. The mall cop rode smoothly past us. "Goofballs," I mumbled as I opened the laptop again.

"By the way," Oleg said, reaching out his hand to me, "I brought this back for you." It was the black plastic thumb drive I'd given him in April, the one with the Northrop Grumman cockpit manuals.

I wasn't sure why he was returning a twenty-dollar thumb drive. But I took it and dropped it into the cup holder by the Jeep's gearshift and said, "Thanks," before turning back to my DTIC demonstration on the laptop.

"The nice thing," I told Oleg, setting up the sales pitch, "is we can browse through this directly. I can set it up to run automatic searches. It can store articles in a bibliography for a period of time."

I showed him the basic search function and then a list of articles. "You can do it by date range," I told him. "By a string, if you like." I showed him how each article was coded with a number and accompanied by a brief abstract. "I'm the one doing the requesting," I explained. "Here's the bibliography that it's stored on. Here's the actual article. Here's how the information in the article matches the bibliography."

I didn't call up any individual files. I showed him how the application worked. Totally at random, I slid the cursor to an article from a long list of search results. I noticed it was from DARPA, the Defense Advanced Research Projects Agency, and had something to do with linguistics. I didn't read the full title at first. But I knew it had to do with teaching foreign languages. This wasn't out of the ordinary for DTIC.

DARPA is the Pentagon office that funds research into new technologies for the U.S. military, and that can mean almost anything.

DARPA was created in 1958 in response to the Soviet Union's first Sputnik launch. President Eisenhower wanted to make sure that the U.S. military technology was more sophisticated than whatever our potential enemies had. But DARPA isn't all missiles and programming code. Many DARPA-funded technologies are now commonplace in the civilian world, including computer networking, hypertext, early versions of GUI (graphical user interface), and the latest language-training techniques.

"Can I get a copy of this?" Oleg asked.

"You want a copy?" I said. "Sure, I can get you one later."

"Can I get it now?"

"I don't have a printer here," I said. *Uh-oh!* I was stalling. I wasn't sure he knew it, but this was starting to feel like a problem to me.

I read the title more carefully: "Final Technical Report, March 2008. Robust, Rapidly Configurable Speech-to-Speech Translation for Multiple Platforms." I didn't know what that referred to, but it clearly had to do with language translations. It didn't sound like much of a beach read. *Boring* was the word that came to mind.

Oleg seemed to have chosen the article entirely at random. It was the one my cursor happened to land on. I suspected he just wanted another piece of paperwork to pitch to his superiors on the value of what he was doing for them, further evidence of his new American contact's impressive access.

I didn't dare look at him directly. From the corner of my eye, I could see that his facial expression hadn't changed. But I still had the sense he was excited—just trying not to show it.

Ted and Terry and I had discussed many scenarios as we planned for this meeting with Oleg. But we hadn't discussed my giving Oleg any actual files. Not before they'd vetted every document. The issue hadn't come up in our conversations.

"Do you mind putting it on the thumb drive? You can copy it there," Oleg said.

Oh, fuck! Oh, fuck! Oh, fuck!

What was I supposed to tell him? What was I supposed to do?

Panic was starting to rush through my veins.

The whole point of this exercise was giving Oleg access to DTIC—or making him think I was. But everything I gave him had to be approved by the FBI.

Stop. Think.

A file about linguistics—how sensitive could that be? The Defense Department equivalent of a junior high school Spanish lesson? He wasn't asking for the U.S. nuclear missile codes! Those wouldn't have been on DTIC anyway.

I didn't know what to do. I couldn't let Oleg see any hesitation. Hesitation was weakness. I had to act like his request was no big deal. If I were a real spy, I wouldn't give a shit about handing over a linguistics file. If I were a real spy, I'd be cocky, arrogant, eager to demonstrate what I could offer. I wouldn't give him my log-in and password. I wouldn't give him my PIN at the bank. But for a spy, this was a benign request. I was only establishing that I was real.

I hadn't discussed it with the agents, who had layers of protocol. I was out on a limb. Roll with it. I had to. All along, the agents and I had agreed: "There is no written script, no list of boxes to check off every time. We always want to know where we're heading, but an effective double agent has to think calmly on his feet."

Wasn't that what made me good at this?

The evidence exploded in my mind. The odd questions at Vincent's had been a clue. The seemingly innocent return of a disposable thumb drive had been another. Oleg was testing me. I didn't want to blow all the trust I'd built with him, not over a single innocuous article from DTIC. I needed an answer—now. I had Ted's voice ringing loudly in my head: "There can be no hesitation. You almost have to believe what it is you are saying. You cannot show him any doubt."

Oleg plucked the thumb drive from the cup holder. He handed it to me. I suspect he was just as nervous as I was, but he didn't show it, and I don't think I did, either. He was watching me closely. I could hear my breathing and his. He was paying careful attention to every single twitch.

I was moving on survival instinct. I was thinking, *Just make it real. Don't let on to anything. Don't blow your cover. Do what you have to. Keep the pace steady and slow.*

I took off the plastic cover and slipped the thumb drive into the USB port on the side of the laptop. I saw a tiny red light flicker on. Then a little window popped up on the laptop screen, asking what I wanted to do next:

Import Pictures and Videos?

Open Folder to View Files?

Use This Drive for Backup or Speed Up My System?

I didn't want to do any of that. So I clicked the window out.

Think three or four—not twenty—steps ahead. Stay in the moment. Be believable.

I had Windows Explorer already open. I copied the linguistics-file PDF from the DTIC directory. I dragged and dropped the file onto the thumb drive. And I clicked out of Explorer.

Just stay in control.

Casually, I reached down and slid the thumb drive out of the port. I slipped the cover back on and handed the thumb drive to Oleg.

The whole maneuver lasted maybe six seconds. Those six seconds almost ended my double-agent career.

CHAPTER 22

BLOWING IT

Neither Oleg nor I said much more that day. I was feeling even sicker than before, though now the fever was layered with a rising sense of dread. I told Oleg I would talk to him later. He said yes. He handed me a business card for our next meeting location, a Hooters in Wayne, New Jersey. Obviously, Oleg wasn't making a habit of cooked-from-scratch joints. We were heading back to the generic American chains, albeit an outlet more famous for its bold displays of female cleavage than for its burgers, beers, and chicken wings.

"You have been to this restaurant?" Oleg asked me before he climbed out of the Jeep. "People say it has a good atmosphere."

Whatever.

Oleg opened the door, got out, and climbed into the LeSabre parked next to us. I hadn't realized he'd chosen the space right next to his own car. It was the kind of car someone's dad might drive, a full-size upscale sedan. Oleg's was a 2005, the LeSabre's final year of production. Now, that was an American car!

He backed out of his space. Then I backed out of mine. I didn't like where this was heading at all.

Shit, I thought as soon I was safely out of the garage. *What happened? Did I just do something I am going to seriously regret?* I'd handed Oleg a document that had not been preapproved by anyone, done it completely on my own. Whatever my reasons, I'd broken one of the protocols I had followed from the start. *Dammit!*

I got back on the LIE and headed west. There was only one way I knew to deal with the unease I was feeling, not to mention my now-raging head cold: I drove like a crazy person. I wove through the heavy Sunday-afternoon Hamptons-to-Manhattan traffic, finding breaks between the jammed-up vehicles and squeezing in aggressively. After two or three exits of that, I pulled off somewhere in eastern Queens. I waited to be sure no one was following me, although it was hard to imagine how anyone could have. Then I called Terry.

"That's good," he said when I told him I'd pulled off at an exit. "Let a little time pass. Make sure no one's waiting for you. Then come on in."

I didn't say anything about the thumb drive or the details of my encounter with Oleg. But my discomfort was definitely intensifying. What was I thinking, handing Oleg that thumb drive? I didn't need to ask. I knew the FBI never would have approved of that. How the hell was I going to explain it to Ted and Terry? But what choice did I have? All those thoughts were rushing around in my brain.

I'd agreed to meet the agents at the Marrakech Hotel, a Moroccan-themed budget option on Broadway and 103rd Street. I'd walked by the place a thousand times. All I can say is I hope they got a federal discount.

"Something happened" was as much as I let on to Terry over the phone before I pulled back onto the highway. "I'll tell you all about it when I get there. I could really use a beer."

"Okay, sure," he said. "What do you want?"

"Something shitty," I said. "And cold."

"Got it."

I parked the Jeep in my garage at 110th Street, grabbed my laptop bag off the seat, and walked the seven short blocks to the hotel. My head was pounding with the cold, the anxiety, and the Sudafed.

The Marrakech lobby had low lighting and dark walls. The elevators were just past the desk to the right. As I breezed toward the elevators, I heard a woman's voice: "Excuse me, sir. Can I help you?"

Damn! I didn't realize the Marrakech was such a high-security location. I wasn't looking for a whole bunch of questions from a nosy desk clerk.

"Are you a guest here?" she asked.

"I'm going up to see someone," I said.

"Name of the guest, please."

I wasn't sure I wanted to answer that. "Just a friend," I said. "In 305."

"Okay, can I have your name?" She wasn't backing down. "Would you sign the register?"

I was just about to bolt for the elevator and make her come after me when the weekend day manager stepped out from an office behind the desk. "It's okay," he said to the clerk. "He's going to see someone."

I don't think the manager had any idea who I was or who I might be meeting or that FBI agents were using his hotel for a postoperation debriefing in a sensitive Russian-espionage case. Or maybe he did. Either way, I appreciated the just-in-time assist.

I pressed the third-floor button in the elevator and made the short ride up. As soon as the car stopped and the door was halfway open, I squinted into the dark hallway and found 305. I knocked. Terry let me in.

"Jesus!" I said to him and Ted. "What did you tell the desk clerk? She acted like I was coming up here for a three-way!"

"You're not?" Ted deadpanned.

Tense as I was, even I had to smile at that.

★   ★   ★

I sat in a black vinyl desk chair in the cramped hotel room. Ted handed me a can of Miller Lite. I fumbled for a place to start.

"That guy is such a fuckin' asshole," I said. "He frustrates the shit out of me! We try to get a plan together. At the very last second, he always wants to change things."

"So what happened?" Ted asked. "Tell us what happened, Naveed. Did he ask about Mexico?"

"No, no," I said, not expecting that question. "Mexico was the one thing that didn't come up." *If only the issue were Mexico!* "At a certain point," I continued, "he tried to get me to sign something. A receipt. I didn't sign it."

"A receipt?" Terry asked a little incredulously. "He wanted you to sign a receipt for committing treason? That takes balls."

"He wanted me to sign a receipt for the three thousand he paid me last time," I said. "Why didn't he just give me a self-addressed stamped envelope to send to the FBI? That would've made the whole thing easier. You guys wouldn't even need to investigate."

"When it comes to money," Ted said, "it's never quite clear with these guys. Are they padding their own pockets, or are they being directed by some idiot bureaucrats back home? The money is always tricky with them."

"Yeah," I said, only half listening as Ted tried to calm my anxiety. Obviously, I was stalling. Russian Mission accounting issues weren't what had my stomach churning. I knew the real delicate issue was waiting ahead, and I wasn't rushing to get there.

"I made him show me his ID," I told the agents. "I said, 'How do I know you're not a federal agent? How do I know you really work at the UN?' "

Both Ted and Terry laughed at that. "Good for you," Ted said. He sounded genuinely impressed that I seemed to be holding my own against an experienced Russian military officer who was a professional spy.

The compliment was at least partly warranted, and I felt proud of that. But the good feeling wouldn't last. I dropped the bomb slowly.

"Then we talked about DTIC," I said.

Ted asked, "How did that work out?"

I took another swig of Miller Lite. "Not too well," I said.

They looked up together. Neither one said anything.

"I gave him the papers in the restaurant and showed him everything we talked about," I said. "Then we walked to the Jeep and went to a parking garage. I was showing him how the searches work, and he gave me back my thumb drive from last time, and there was a document on the directory I was randomly pointing to, and he asked if he could get a copy of the document. I didn't have a printer or a CD burner in the Jeep, of course, so he said to put the document on the thumb drive, and I did and gave it back to him. Luckily, it was just a document about linguistics."

It came out like a run-on sentence. I guess I was hoping the response might be gentler if I explained in a single breath. Or maybe I hoped the part where I handed over a DTIC doc would get lost in the rush of other details.

I saw some glancing, but Ted and Terry didn't speak. They let me finish without interrupting. But their body language—they both sat up stiffly—suggested concern. Was it shock? Was it panic? I couldn't tell.

Ted broke the tension. "You know, Terry," he said calmly, "at least now Oleg knows this is all for real. He'll never doubt whether it's real or not."

Terry nodded, but he didn't smile.

"Look, guys," I said, trying to get in front of whatever was coming, "I had no choice. If this was real, I would have given it to him. I had to give it to him. What was I supposed to do?"

Terry didn't sound convinced when he said, "You could have

stalled. You could have asked for more money. You could have done anything but give it to him. We never discussed you putting his thumb drive into your computer and taking anything out. Did we?"

"Wait a second," I said. "That's bullshit. I had two heartbeats to make a decision. I went with what I thought was right. I thought it was 'Everything has to be in the moment.' That's what we've always said."

"Still," Terry said.

"Are you telling me you don't have my back with this?"

"We're gonna have to see how it plays out. I don't know what the reaction will be."

"What the fuck does that mean?"

"The reaction above us," Terry said.

"So after three years of doing this, all the hard work and respect I've earned is forgotten because of a split-second decision I had to make when I was placed in a no-win impossible situation? You're fuckin' holding me to an impossible standard. Really, dude, what was I supposed to do? If I said no, he'd walk away unconvinced—or even worse, believing he'd been set up. Luckily, the doc seemed innocent enough. Linguistics? That didn't feel like anything that could compromise national security. It really could have been so much worse."

I could tell that my explanation didn't fully ease their concerns. It didn't ease mine, either. But these agents had been with me through so much. They were as deep in this as I was—and believed in what we were doing just as strongly. At least that's what I thought, what I hoped was true.

I didn't know what else to say. Terry seemed to be struggling with his desire for strict adherence to FBI rules and standards. It was Ted who tossed me a small life preserver.

"There's a guy in our office," he said. "He's about to retire. He's one of those guys of indeterminate background. He could be Lebanese. He could be Hispanic. You just don't know. He wears open shirts down to his belly button. Chest hair hanging out. He worked under-cover for decades. He's one of the most prolific undercover guys we have. And he doesn't get drug-tested. There is an understanding—an expectation, I guess you'd call it—that at some point he might have to solidify the trust of the people he's dealing with by sampling illegal drugs. This is really not so different than that."

I appreciated Ted telling me that story. It was a comforting anal-ogy. There was an agent who would have understood why I had to give Oleg that document. I wanted to meet him before he retired. I almost wanted to hug him.

"We understand," Terry said, sounding a little calmer but no less concerned. His tone, I realized, was all business. "Listen, we're gonna do a little damage control. The first thing we need is to get the name of the document and any other details you have."

"No problem," I said. "I have everything."

"We'll have to figure out what was in there," Terry said. "We'll have to let some people know."

It was only when I went back into my laptop that I saw this printed at the bottom of the document I'd let Oleg remove: "Under 22 U.S.C. 2778, the penalty for unlawful export of items or information con-trolled under the ITAR is up to ten years imprisonment, or a fine of $1,000,000, or both. Under 50 U.S.C., Appendix 2410, the penalty for unlawful export of items or information controlled under the EAR is a fine of up to $1,000,000, or five times the value of the exports, whichever is greater. For an individual, the penalty is imprisonment of up to 10 years, or a fine of up to $250,000, or both."

I didn't know what all those statutes and penalties meant or how, if at all, they might apply to me. I'd seen language like that on plenty of government documents, many of which were totally innocuous. But in the frame of mind I was in, it was all a little rattling.

"Fuck," I told the agents, "I can't believe I gave him that document."

We finished our debrief with me handing over the watch. Ted and

Terry would take it back to the office like they usually did and download the audio. "We'll turn it around as quickly as possible," Terry said. "We'll see where things stand."

As I walked home from the Marrakech, the adrenaline of the past couple of hours was wearing off. The head cold had settled in fully. I was feeling shitty and sorry for myself. With each block north, my self-protective anger was turning more into despair.

I can't believe this, I thought. *They are trying to motherfuck me. I take all the risk. The minute there is something questionable, they're ready to throw me under the bus—then take turns backing over me.* I was Matt Damon confronting Leonardo DiCaprio in *The Departed*: "Just fuckin' kill me." I had gone from being the ally of a powerful agency to thinking the agency might turn on me. I'd gone from being livid to thinking maybe I had no one to be mad at but myself.

I walked into the apartment. I threw my stuff down. I went into the bathroom and turned on the shower, all hot. I shut the door and let the room fill with steam and lay on the floor.

A few minutes later, the door opened. Ava walked in with me on the floor and the bathroom filled with steam. "What's wrong?" she asked.

It was all I could do not to cry. "I screwed things up," I said. "I can't believe it. I fucked this up."

"Just tell me what happened," she said.

I told her all about Oleg and the thumb drive and Ted and Terry and how they'd reacted and how I was pretty sure I had ruined everything.

She just stood there, hands on her hips, looking stern. "That's it?" she finally said. "That's what you're worried about? Look, if they're gonna pull the plug, they're gonna pull the plug. You've done more than most people would have. More than most people would do in a lifetime, in a hundred lifetimes. You've had a great run. But this operation isn't real life, not our real lives."

"But I really don't want it to end yet," I said. "I'm not ready. If it's gonna end, I want it to end on my terms."

"Naveed," she said sharply. "With all the work you've done for them, do you really think they're gonna pull the plug? What would they gain by that? This may be a game to them, but it's an important game. This is all about manipulation. I'm completely confident this is not the end of the story. By the time it's over, something big is going to be achieved. I promise you. I don't know what, but it will be."

"Maybe," I said.

Ava wasn't finished. "But you have to look at this for what it is," she said. "There is no future in this. There is no career. You have to find a way to be at peace with that. You do this because you want to do it. But it will end when it will end. You won't have control over that. This doesn't define who you are as a person. This is just something that you did." Ava's voice softened, "I promise you, Naveed, this won't be the only accomplishment in your life."

I stared glumly into the steam.

Early Monday morning, while I was driving to the office in Dobbs Ferry, Ted got me on the phone. He sounded a couple of notches more serious than he had the day before.

"You know," he said, "they can do bad things with thumb drives. They could have put something on your laptop that lets them trace everything you do on there. We need your computer."

I pulled over to the side of the road. "I don't want to give you my computer," I said. "I don't understand what the problem is."

"We need your computer," Ted said again.

"I don't want to give it to you."

It was my computer. I used it for my real work. I brought it home at night. I had personal things on there. I had my mail. My banking. Personal stuff. This seemed invasive to me, to have someone looking into my life like that. I wanted to know that, if I ever wanted to walk, I could walk. This felt just like Oleg asking me to sign a receipt: *Sign here if you want to be caught doing something illegal.* From the start, I had thought of myself as the agents' civilian partner. Now I was feeling more like their target.

"Are you saying I have to? You're going to force me to?"

"Look," Ted said, "no one wants to go down that road. Let's do this the friendly way."

What was the alternative? Bright lights and rubber straps? Weren't we all on the same side? Again, I didn't feel like I was being given much of a choice.

No one threatened me directly, certainly not Ted or Terry. But I was definitely being told there were no other options. They never said explicitly what would happen if I refused to turn over my computer. But isn't the fear of the unknown always greater than the actual thing?

Finally, I agreed to give it to them. And they agreed to take it for one day, image it, and give it back to me.

I got to the office and did what every perp in history has done when he thinks someone is coming after his computer: I spent the rest of the day trying to wipe everything clean. I deleted my personal email. I removed the battery. I disconnected the laptop from my work and home networks. I formatted the hell out of the whole machine, which I knew was unlikely to make much difference but I did anyway. They're the FBI. They can retrieve anything they want to without much trouble, even data that's been theoretically deleted or overwritten. I went through the motions anyway. I had to assume the Russians had compromised the laptop. I would have preferred to trash the hard drive the second I got home.

I met Terry at Ninety-fifth Street on June 27. He gave me a piece of paper that looked like a warrant. It wasn't. It was more like a please-and-thank-you warrant.

The document was quite specific. "Agents will take possession of the computer for a period of one day," it read. "Two copies of the hard drive will be generated. There will be a review of the imaged drives. The FBI will search for any evidence of a potential computer intrusion by a foreign intelligence service."

"Voluntary surrender," the document said at the top. But none of it felt very voluntary to me.

CHAPTER 23

HOOTERS

Had one tiny thumb drive changed everything? The agents returned my laptop in twenty-four hours. They didn't seem to find anything troubling on it. But in the days that followed, no one seemed to know where anything stood—least of all Ted, Terry, or me. We were in a holding pattern of some sort. We just didn't know exactly what was being held and for how long.

"What do I do if he gets in touch with me?" I asked. "What do I say when he calls?"

No one seemed to know. Only one thing seemed to be sure. "You are not to bring the computer," Ted emphasized.

He'd said it more than once, and it was starting to feel a little insulting. After what had happened, did anyone really believe that I'd put myself back into such a risky situation? Even a child doesn't touch a hot stove twice.

I was itching to get back to whatever normal was. I hated having heard nothing from Oleg since handing him that document on my thumb drive. If he'd been testing my willingness to hand over anything he chose from DTIC, I guessed I'd passed. But then he went radio-silent. It was nerve-wracking.

Finally, he called and said he wanted to meet with me. We already had the location.

"I'm good to meet him?" I asked Terry.

"Go" was all he said.

"Okay," I said. "Well, what am I gonna show him when I see him?"

"Just don't bring your computer," Terry told me. I'd already agreed to that. "Print out some documents and show them to us first. Our people want to see anything before you give it to anyone."

I didn't appreciate the not-so-subtle reminder that I'd given away a report without authorization. I had worked with preapproved paper plenty of times in the past. If I didn't have the actual DTIC database to dangle again, at least I would have something.

I chose a shady spot in the empty parking lot behind Hooters. Even at eleven-thirty on Sunday morning, it was August-hot along the strip-mall paradise of Route 23 in Wayne, New Jersey. I took a moment in the Corvette's AC to pull myself together before meeting Oleg. I double-checked the papers I had brought along. The most important one was a fifteen-thousand-dollar invoice for the money he owed me. I pulled up the flap on my G-Shock watchband and pressed the little button to turn the recorder on. But while I was waiting for the red light to blink, I saw Oleg striding purposefully toward my car.

Oh, shit! I thought. *I'm not sure the recorder is on.*

I quickly lowered my arm to my lap, smiled, and opened the door. I was greeted by casual Oleg—jeans, a brown-and-green polo shirt, and large aviator sunglasses. He looked trimmer than he did in his boxy sport jackets. I hardly recognized him without a trench coat.

The casual attire had a reverse effect on me. I greeted him with an extra dose of formality. "Hello, Oleg. How are you?"

"It's going well," he said, big smile as usual.

I had been to Hooters once before. The chicken wings were spicy and the waitresses, too. Our server, in her orange short shorts and low-cut white tank top, gamely tolerated my asshole idiot friends. I suppose that's the whole point of Hooters.

Before heading inside for the breastaurant's world-famous hospitality and provocative views, we lingered next to my car in the steamy parking lot and talked some business. Oleg told me that his people in Moscow had finally had a chance to review the stack of Northrop Grumman documents.

"And?"

"They didn't find it of any interest," he told me. "That material has no value to them."

I knew the manuals weren't particularly hot items in and of themselves, but was Oleg messing with me? Was his response a ploy designed to undermine my confidence?

Yes and yes. I don't believe he could help himself.

"But we want to do business with DTIC," he added quickly.

"Okay," I said.

Oleg wasn't done. His friends in Moscow had given some thought to how I might be compensated for my DTIC research. "Here is how we would like to move forward," he said. "We have a proposal."

I thought we already had an understanding, if not an ironclad deal—the same one that had generated Oleg's unpaid bill. With the Russians, no deal was ever fully done. I kept learning that lesson over and over.

"This makes no sense, Oleg," I told him. "We had an agreement at the last meeting. You already owe me money. Now you're telling me we're gonna negotiate that?" Here we still were at step one, two months after I'd explained how he would have to cover the cost of registering for DTIC and how he'd compensate me for everything we got out of that database. I was feeling like a one-man collection agency, but all I could do was roll with it. "What do you have in mind?" I asked.

"You will give me the files," Oleg said. "I will bring them back. We will analyze them. We will tell you what each file is worth."

I couldn't believe he was suggesting this, although I gave him points for taking a stab at naked American-style capitalism.

"For certain files," he said, "we will pay a hundred dollars. For certain others, we will pay several thousand dollars. The files have different values. The payment will reflect what those different values are."

I didn't want to hear any more. "Are you fuckin' kidding me?" I exploded. "That is the stupidest idea I have ever heard. I give you a file and wait to hear how much you think it's worth, and then *maybe* I'll get paid? Or maybe I won't. And you'll decide how much?" I barely stopped to catch my breath. "Oleg, you don't understand the risk I'm taking. Not only do I have to maintain access to the DTIC system, I have to hide my searches. I have to embed the work I'm doing for you inside legitimate work so it can't be discovered. My costs are fixed whether I get you five files or a thousand files. The work is the same to me. The risk is the same to me. The individual files have no value to me. It is the time and risk I am taking on your behalf. Don't give me this bullshit that you'll analyze the files and tell me how much they're worth. I can't believe you'd even suggest that."

As I barreled on, the Russian looked increasingly alarmed. I wasn't sure whether this was just his next rehearsed move in a long negotiation: Propose something crazy, display concern over the hostile reaction, end up with 50 percent more than you deserve. Or maybe he'd respect me for not swallowing his first tiny dangle.

"If you want to do business, we'll do business," I finished. "If not, you're wasting my motherfuckin' time."

I really meant it. I was so pissed at him, I was ready to climb back in my car without seeing even one deep-cleavage Hooters Girl and drive straight home to New York.

Which I would have regretted immediately. I had a larger goal than maintaining my self-respect with a slippery Russian negotiator. In the big picture, it didn't matter how strong a bargain I drove with Oleg. I had to keep him talking, keep him wanting, then keep him wanting more.

I remembered what Ted had told me in our earliest conversations. "Be rough with Oleg. Threaten to leave. They have to believe if they don't treat you right, you really could walk away." Before joining the FBI, Ted had worked in the Air Force Office of Special Investigations, where he dealt with suspects and ran investigative stings. "Sometimes," he said, "you have to be belligerent. Don't always be agreeable. It's okay to walk away. If you've laid the right foundation, they will always come running after you."

I put my hand on the Corvette door and said, "What's it gonna be, Oleg? We doing business or not?" I held my breath. I was pushing harder than I'd ever pushed and, for the first time, making a deal for something I wasn't sure I could deliver.

But Ted was right. Oleg moved my way immediately. "Look, look, look," he said.

I lifted my hand from the door.

"It's okay, Naveed," he said. "Calm down. Everything is fine."

Oleg reached into his back jeans pocket and removed three envelopes. He laid them on the hood of my Corvette. They were thick. This was money, but I had no way of knowing how much. That was when I handed him the invoice.

"I want to get paid," I said. "You say this is all about trust and goodwill. You can't even settle your bar bill, and you're trying to do new things? You have my money?"

"We'll make this work," Oleg said. He opened the flap on one of the envelopes. I could see a stack of bills. He handed me that one and the other two. "Here's something to get started with. It's eight thousand dollars."

I did calm down. "Look," I told him, "you have to understand. There is a huge amount of risk I am taking here. I could go to prison. I could lose everything. This has to be worth my time."

"I understand," he said. "Why don't we go inside, where it's cool, and get something to eat."

I put the envelopes in the glove compartment. I made sure the car was locked. I walked with Oleg to the front of the building, then underneath a bright orange awning into the restaurant. Several of the waitresses were milling around the edge of the bar while a hostess in standard Hooters skimpies led us to a table in the middle of the dining room. We'd met in a lot of restaurants, but I found it a little surreal to be walking with a Hooters Girl and a Russian spy to a table. Suddenly, I remembered the scene in *Spy Game* when Nathan Muir and his protégé, Tom Bishop, are scanning a busy restaurant.

"The man reading the menu," Muir says. "Threat?"

Bishop doesn't think so. "Only to the hostess," he says.

Judging by the way Oleg's eyes stayed glued on the hostess as she returned to the front of the restaurant, I should have gotten up from the table to warn her.

"Have you ever been here?" Oleg asked me, studying my reaction like he might watch an interrogation through a two-way mirror.

"Not to this location," I said, leaving it at that.

Before we continued our conversation, I needed to make sure my watch was recording like it was supposed to. Before I could come up with an excuse to get away from Oleg's attention, the waitress arrived, introducing herself as Crystal. She was tall and blond and— does this go without saying?—massively large-breasted. She seemed nice. "What do you guys feel like today?"

She asked that in a way that wouldn't have raised an eyebrow coming out of the mouth of any diner waitress in America. But the way Crystal delivered the question seemed to carry extra layers of meaning. I ordered a Diet Coke, which, as far as I knew, carried no meaning at all beyond a Diet Coke. Oleg asked for a Sam Adams— how American can you get?—and began to study the menu.

I was feeling jumpy. The Flavor Flav watch felt heavy on my arm. I tried not to stare at it. Glancing around the restaurant, I waited for a moment when I could excuse myself. I was sweating and wanted to splash some water on my face. I also had to pee. As Crystal went to get our beverages and Oleg preoccupied himself with watching her, I excused myself and found my way to the men's room at the far end of the bar.

The restaurant was mostly empty. It wasn't even noon. The day's preseason NFL games hadn't started yet. As I crossed the room, I noticed the giant TVs were playing yesterday's baseball games.

There was no one in the men's room. I used the urinal, checked my watch, and saw that the red light was blinking like it was supposed to. I walked to the sink to wash my face and hands. Just as I turned on the cold water, the men's room door flew open and a middle-aged white man came rushing in. He was short and fat and wearing a brand-new Jets cap. I could tell the cap was new because it had a packing crease across the top.

He looked at me. I didn't look back, but I kept him in the corner of my eye. He quickly turned his head the other way and walked into one of the stalls. He didn't close the door.

Like the man I'd seen at Vincent's Clam Bar, he didn't speak, and I had no opportunity to detect an accent. But he kept glancing over his shoulder in a way that seemed odd and awkward. He looked like a man you'd see sitting on the boardwalk in Brooklyn as the sun went down on Brighton Beach. Did Oleg suspect me of slipping out to the men's room to make a phone call? Had the fat man rushed in when he realized belatedly that I'd excused myself from the table? Had he gotten the fresh Jets hat from a Russian Mission wardrobe assistant who'd assured him confidently, "This is exactly how American men dress when they go to Hooters"? Or was I being overly suspicious? I had no time to contemplate it. I had to get back to Oleg.

After I returned to the table and we gave Crystal our food orders—a plate of sliders for Oleg, a green salad with grilled chicken for me—I noticed that Oleg was staring up toward the bar. The big guy in the Jets cap was at a table near us in the dining room, facing in a different direction. Something else had caught Oleg's attention. It was one of the Hooters Girls, a petite African American.

Oleg leaned in close as if to suggest some grand new spying proposal. But he didn't mention espionage at all. "Look," he said, smiling and nodding toward the waitress. "They have black ones, too."

How was I supposed to react to that? I stifled a laugh and tried not to spit out my Diet Coke. Then I replied straight on. "Yes," I said with my best Ron Burgundy *Anchorman* sincerity. "We had the civil rights movement. People marched so pretty black women could work at Hooters."

I don't think he got it. I glanced at my menu and allowed myself one last dig. "You know, Oleg," I said, "I hear the Wayne, New Jersey, Hooters is the United Nations of Hooters. You're used to diversity, right?"

I'm no prude. I'd been to places a lot seedier. If people choose to work in a restaurant like Hooters, why would I care? If the customers want to have their chicken wings served by ersatz strippers in incredibly tight T-shirts, it's a free country, you know. But sitting there with Oleg on that Sunday afternoon, I felt physically uncomfortable—as if my boss were holding the office Christmas party in a whorehouse or my uncle were having his sixtieth birthday party at the Hustler Club.

I'm trying to conduct some international espionage here. C'mon, Oleg, stop ogling. Ewwww!

As if that weren't disturbing enough, I was recording all of it for the FBI.

The conversation didn't turn back to business the whole time we sat there. His attention was far more focused on the greasy burgers and the attentive waitstaff, with a few random grunts in my direction. It wasn't until we got back outside that Oleg was able to focus again.

"So do we have an agreement or what?" I asked him. "You're gonna pay me regardless of the documents. None of this pay-by-the-article bullshit."

Oleg sounded confident that he'd be able to make that happen. But he said he'd have to get the arrangement blessed by others. He said he'd have a firm answer for me the next time we met. Then he handed me a card for a Pizzeria Uno location across the parking lot from Hooters. Oleg's America, it seemed, was one long strip mall of bad chain restaurants. I figured I was getting close in his stack of cards to the ones that said Olive Garden or Cracker Barrel. How could we have missed Applebee's and Johnny Rockets?

Before we parted, he laid out his next round of requests. "Here is what I would like you to do," he said, handing me a sheet of paper. "I would like you to search the DTIC for several categories—general categories. Show me what you can find."

"Categories," I said. If the FBI was still on board with my DTIC idea, I could work with categories. Any category that Oleg suggested, I could plug in to the search engine, then compile for him whatever it was that DTIC sent back.

I looked at his list. I wouldn't call it bashful. One item said "Future Combat Systems," the U.S. Army's principal modernization program of the early and middle 2000s. Another was "F-22 Raptor," a fifth-generation supersonic fighter aircraft built for the U.S. Air Force by Lockheed Martin. One in particular caught my eye: "Cruise Missiles." Oleg had taken my suggestion!

"These are some very broad topics," I told him. "What I can do is generate a bibliography. That way, you will have a list of documents that should be available."

"These we would be interested in," Oleg said with some enthusiasm, though perhaps not as excitedly as he had surveyed the Hooters Girls.

After leaving Oleg, I drove straight to Manhattan. I had agreed to meet Ted and Terry for an immediate debrief at the Marrakech Hotel. This time I breezed past the desk to the elevators.

Up in the room, I told Ted I'd followed his advice and threatened to storm away unless Oleg paid his past-due bill and agreed to my compensation plan.

"He started backpedaling fast," I said.

"Good for you," Ted said. "I told you he would."

At that moment, especially, Ted's approval meant a lot to me. I trusted his experience and judgment. Ted always seemed to know what he was talking about.

I told them what had happened in the Hooters parking lot. Ted and Terry shook their heads at Oleg's half-assed we'll-tell-you-what-it's-worth proposal. They got a huge kick out of Oleg and the Hooters Girls and the awkwardness of it all for me. "He really said that about the black woman?" Ted asked. "Has he been living in a cave?"

"He said it," I assured them as they broke up laughing. Not since I'd told the agents about the Russian's book-grabbing habit had they laughed so hard at an Oleg report.

It had been a rough two months, but the briefing that day did a lot to ease the tension I still felt. Ted and Terry did a wonderful job of making me feel like I was back at the edge of genuine acceptance into an exclusive club, though I understood that I wasn't an FBI agent and therefore would never be a full-fledged insider, no matter how close I got to them.

Over time, I came to understand what a mind-fuck that can be. The FBI, the Russians, these are massive organizations with their own agendas, their own cultures, and their own clout. They will work with you or not as it suits their interests and their resources. But when you're in a position like I was, you have to look out for yourself. You're never sure who has your back—or if anybody does. You can just as easily get swallowed up by either side.

That's why Ted's departure came as such a blow to me. I got that jarring piece of news just after Labor Day. Ted was taking on a new assignment and moving with his wife to Washington. I loved Ted. He was a talented agent and a very good guy. He'd been a huge supporter of mine from the day he replaced Randi. He appreciated my drive and creativity, even when he wanted to strangle me. Despite what you might have heard about robotic, driven FBI agents, he was a human being. Ted, Terry, and I—we were a team in every sense of the word. Even when I felt totally frustrated with them, I knew we had a personal bond. And when things weren't going like I wanted, I had the impression that higher-ups were to blame. I figured Ted and Terry would always do what they could.

Ted was never one for ceremony, so we didn't have any weepy embraces or send-off meals. He just said goodbye and good luck. "I'll check on you," he said. "It's been a real pleasure, man. You'll be in very capable hands." I knew he was tired. So was I.

Those "capable hands" belonged to an agent named Lisa. She had been involved in the operation on the periphery, I learned, conducting surveillance of Oleg's wife and daughter on the days when he and I met. Soon after Ted left, Terry took me and Lisa for a get-to-know-you lunch at Harvest on Hudson, a fancy restaurant in Hastings. I tried to be open-minded.

Lisa looked like a long-distance runner. She had a short, stylish haircut and a wholesome midwestern look. She was a West Point graduate serving in the army reserves. While on active duty, she had served with the 25th Infantry Division, based in Hawaii. She was friendly and obviously smart. I couldn't think of any reason to object to her except for the fact that she wasn't Ted. I was happy Terry wasn't going anywhere.

At lunch, I expressed lingering concerns that the thumb-drive incident seemed to have changed the operation more than I was being told. I didn't like feeling out of the loop. Both Lisa and Terry tried to reassure me. Nothing would be done behind my back, they said. I'd have a chance to weigh in on everything. They emphasized how important it was for me to remain a "team player."

"Of course I will," I said. But I also remembered the scene in *Spy Game* when Nathan Muir says how much he hates being told to be a team player: "Every time my coach told me that, I knew I was about to get benched."

"I don't want be benched," I told Terry and Lisa.

"You're not being benched," Terry said.

Maybe not benched. But hadn't a new player been added to the roster? Some rules of the game had changed. Others were being reinforced as if I were a stone-cold rookie. This had to mean something, right?

CHAPTER 24

CHANGE OF PLANS

"A decision has been made—" Terry began after a couple of lame pleasantries.

That sounded ominous.

" 'A decision has been made'?" I shot back, half imitating him. "What kind of bullshit is that?"

I think Terry was startled by the intensity of my reaction. I definitely wasn't speaking with a smile.

We were sitting in a parking lot squeezed between the West Side Highway and the Hudson River at Ninety-fifth Street. At Terry's instruction, I had driven there after work one day in late September. I'd parked my black Corvette next to Terry's government-issue black Ford Fusion, which had replaced his government-issue black Ford Taurus, then I'd climbed inside with the agents.

Terry, who'd been thrown off by my interruption, got back to explaining what he meant. "A decision has been made to take Oleg down," he said. "We have decided to do it by arresting you in front of him."

The first part made perfect sense. But: "Arresting *me?*"

"*Pretending* to arrest you," Lisa clarified.

The sun was setting over the Hudson. Commuters were rushing home on the highway behind me. In front of me, people were jogging up the riverfront path. Two large sailboats were cruising back to the boat basin for the night. The sky was a rich mix of oranges and blues. But I stared glumly out the front window at the river and New Jersey beyond. Everything felt out of whack. I was getting used to working without Ted. Lisa kept taking a slightly condescending tone: "Naveed, you're a very intelligent person—we get that." Her flattery was always followed by a *but,* spoken or not. And now the plan was to "arrest" me? I seethed.

The agents in the front seat were quiet, waiting for me to absorb what they were saying. Or maybe they just wanted me to calm down.

I wondered what kind of pressure they were getting from above. In all our time together, Ted and Terry had never handed me a script. We'd sit around and piece together whatever made sense, with the agents providing guidance and oversight. But at the end of the day, I would handle Oleg in my way.

My mind went straight to the *Miami Vice* movie. Crockett and Tubbs are on to an international narcotics network with connections in Haiti, Puerto Rico, Dubai, and Geneva. But the FBI is insisting that the cops focus on some small-time local dealers. "End of story," says the risk-averse Agent Fujima. "Everything else I'm hearing is speculation masquerading as intel."

Crockett flips him a set of keys.

"What's this?" Fujima asks.

"Keys to the boat," Crockett tells him. "Go do this motherfucker yourself."

Tubbs cuts in, translating his partner's fiery words: "What he means to say is he is reluctant to abandon the penetration of a major narcotics trafficking organization."

"We're the ones doing the death-defying shit?" Crockett fumes. "And he wants us to give that up? For what? A chump-change bust so he can get his picture in the *Miami Herald* to impress the slug farm in D.C.?"

Sitting in that parking lot, gazing out over the Hudson, I was feeling like Crockett and Tubbs. Actually, more like Crockett.

I hadn't heard from the navy. I was very tense about that. After three demanding years in the double-agent business, I was ready to do something else with my life. I'd known that at some point I had to focus on my own career. But I thought we'd been aiming big and thinking long-term, longer-term than this. Out of the blue, Terry was sounding like someone's ventriloquist, giving me this decision-has-been-made crap.

I calmed myself down. Lisa must have sensed I was ready to listen and continued. "This has nothing to do with the laptop," she explained, although I hadn't asked if it did. "Oleg is leaving the country. We know he is leaving the UN, and someone new is coming in to replace him."

That was news. Oleg hadn't mentioned it to me.

"It's just part of their normal rotation at the mission," Lisa said. "But it gives us an opportunity. We don't want him to leave without taking action. Now may be our best chance."

"This is how we want to do it," Terry said.

Terry and Lisa kept saying *we* and *us*. I kept wondering: Did they really mean *they* and *them*?

"Based on the fact that Oleg is set to leave the country," he continued, "we feel this provides an opportunity to make a statement to the Russians."

I got that Oleg was leaving. I got that the Russian Mission rotation schedule was out of our control. I got that the FBI didn't want to let him leave the country without holding him responsible for repeated attempts to get sensitive information from me. But I hated the idea of moving against Oleg in a way that would put an end to my double-agent role. If I was grabbed in front of Oleg, the Russians would never trust me again as a source of information, whether they believed the arrest scam or not.

From that day forward, they'd always be worried I was working for the U.S. government, that I'd flipped in exchange for some kind of leniency deal. Wouldn't they notice that, despite my dramatic arrest for treason, my name never appeared on the docket at Manhattan Federal Court? Wouldn't they notice I wasn't on my way to a couple of decades in super-max? The Russians could read a New York tabloid as well as anyone or check the files in the clerk's office at U.S. District Court. Once we played the little theater game with Oleg, my double-agent days were done.

And what rotten timing! Just as I might be heading into the navy as a commissioned intelligence officer. Just as I could convince the Russians I was so much more valuable to them. Just as Oleg would almost certainly pass me off to his successors with a hearty hand-shake and a firm recommendation.

On the flip side, it was probably time to move on. A voice in my head—or was that Ava?—kept asking how long I wanted to live this double life. I'd been at it for three years. A lot can happen in three years, and a lot gets put on hold. Ava and I were eager to start a family. It was a time of change for all of us, the agents, too. Terry and his wife had just had their second baby. Ted was off on his new gig.

In all our time together, the FBI had never told me what the end-game was. Now someone above us had made that crucial decision. I wasn't sure Terry, Lisa, or Ted had been consulted. I was feeling like a passenger along for a very bumpy ride. I didn't like it. I needed to drive. The more I thought about it, the less I felt the FBI's decision was the right one.

Terry made the best case he could. "If Oleg believes you've been

arrested," he said, "that could be disruptive to the whole Russian espionage apparatus in New York. They won't know what happened or
why or who was compromised or who they can trust anymore. They
won't know who's on their side and who isn't."

If I had any hopes that someone wanted to hear my thoughts,
Lisa quickly dispelled them. The decision was final. The agents were
already discussing the where and how.

"We want to take you to the location as soon as possible," she
said before I climbed out of the Fusion back into my car for the short
drive back home. "We'll go through the mechanics, all the logistics
of how we're going to do it. We'll get you comfortable with everything."

This time there would be a script.

I had to clear my head.

Instead of going straight home from the parking lot, I took the
Corvette for a drive, following a route I'd taken many times, though
rarely this fast. I tore out of the parking lot at Ninety-fifth Street,
hitting the downhill slope on the southbound West Side Highway
and never looking back. That car has six speeds. Third kicks in at
110 miles an hour. I was going fast. Very fast. It was the best way I
knew to shove the swirling thoughts of anger off to the sides of my
brain. Driving that fast, I couldn't pay attention to much besides
the road. Straight south on the West Side Highway all the way to
the Battery, then back to Dyckman Street at the northern tip of
Manhattan, where I made another U-turn and turned around and
headed home.

I was rocketing well into the triple-digit speeds. I almost wanted
to get pulled over, my own fuck you to the FBI. They needed me to
do this. It wasn't what I wanted to do. Did I walk away from the whole
thing? Toss them the keys, like Crockett threatened to? Just shrug and

say, "Good luck, guys"? Or did I suck it up and follow through on what I'd started? They were playing the odds. The fact that I had done this from the start was reason enough, they believed, for me to play it out to the end—their way.

I pulled into the garage on 110th Street. That car was always hot and loud, and I was beating the crap out of it that day. The engine was so hot that by the time I stopped, it was ticking.

I walked home. I threw the keys in the bowl and walked past Ava, looking down at my shoes.

She looked up from her work. "You're home late. Everything okay?"

My answer was to order Japanese food.

"What happened?" she said.

"The FBI wants to shut everything down," I told her. "I can't believe it. After three years of all this work, and so close to getting into the navy, this is what they want to do?"

"Why do they want to do that?" she asked. "Because of the file?"

"Probably," I said.

Ava had a way of bringing me back to the basic issue in any situation. She was always good at that. "You have to make a choice here," she said. "Stop looking for their approval, or just do this and be okay with it. Either one is fine. But decide!"

I said I wasn't sure how much of a choice I really had. "Basically, the agents are saying, 'Do this.' "

Ava didn't like that. She thought I was handing over too much authority to them. "Why do you care so much?" she asked. "What difference does it make? Just walk away. Say, 'It was a nice run.' Remind yourself, 'I've got to get on with my life.' Say, 'This is too much. I have a business to run.' You don't owe them anything. You don't have to do this. You've done more than most people have ever been asked to do. It's okay to walk away from it all.

"Naveed," she added, "we've always said if it reached a certain point, you would just stop. Maybe it's reached that point."

I understood that. But I was angry. And her lack of anger toward the FBI was making me even angrier. "Don't you feel like they're fucking me over?" I asked.

Ava answered calmly. "It doesn't seem like you have much of a choice. Your choice is whether to proceed."

She was right, but I knew in my heart what my choice should be: I had made a decision to do this, and now I would see it through, even if the ending wasn't the one I had imagined. Yes, I wanted to tell them to fuck off. But I wasn't ready to walk away. I wanted to be involved in these last few moves. The way the FBI had it planned, I was done one way or another.

"Sleep on it," Ava said. She didn't say "Face facts." She didn't say "It's over."

By morning, I had decided it was better to be involved. I wasn't ready to end my espionage days cold turkey. Reluctantly, I told myself I'd be arrested in front of the Russian. I told Terry as much when he called.

That Saturday, Terry's black Fusion pulled in front of my apartment building. This was scope-out-the-scene day. He and Lisa were driving me to the Pizzeria Uno in Wayne, New Jersey, where Oleg had decided our next meeting would be.

As usual, I didn't know when Oleg would call. I just knew that when he did, I wouldn't have much advance notice. He'd want to meet with me the following day—two days later, max. So whatever planning or preparation the agents and I needed to do, we couldn't afford to wait.

Things were tense when I got into the car with Terry and Lisa, and I wasn't the only one feeling it. That morning, traffic was backed up outside the Lincoln Tunnel. We crept down Eleventh Avenue a few car lengths at a time. Just after we inched our way through the left turn onto Fortieth Street, a young woman in an NYPD uniform appeared at Terry's front passenger window and gave it two stiff taps. He ignored her. She tapped on the window again, a little more insistently.

Terry slowly lowered the window. "What?" he said more than asked.

"License and registration," the officer answered, speaking every bit as curtly as Terry had.

Terry didn't reach for anything.

"It is illegal to have tint on the front windows," she said.

By this point, the look of plain irritation on Terry's face had contorted into something far more resembling, "Are you a fuckin' idiot?" He still didn't say anything. But he grabbed the FBI parking placard sitting faceup on the dashboard ledge and thrust it toward the officer's face.

"Oh" was all she said before turning and stepping away from the car.

The air in the car was so sour that I didn't say anything. But two thoughts did go racing through my head: *What an asshole Terry was being—and I sure wished I could placard my way out of my next traffic infraction!* But his slap-back at the cop didn't seem to bring Terry any pleasure. If anything, it made him more irritable. I got the sense that he didn't like the direction we were heading any more than I did.

We made it through the tunnel eventually. Terry took Route 3, the Secaucus Bypass, weaving in and out of traffic all the way to the Willowbrook Mall and the Pizzeria Uno parking lot off Route 23. There was very little small talk in the car, but we got down to business once we were there.

Lisa and Terry showed me where I should park when I came out to meet Oleg. They'd chosen a corner space across the shopping-plaza exit road from Pizzeria Uno. We walked into the restaurant together and got a table on the far side of the dining room. Terry and Lisa already knew where they wanted me to sit. They'd clearly been to the restaurant and sorted it all out. They were counting on me to direct Oleg to a table, even if he preferred another spot, probably one with the hottest waitress.

The restaurant was mostly empty. A waitress brought us soft drinks and we ordered lunch. Then the agents laid out the scenario for me.

The idea, as I understood it, was that FBI agents would be waiting at other tables, keeping an eye on things, as Oleg and I spoke. On my signal, the agents would approach and pretend to place me under arrest. Oleg would have no idea what was happening or what it might mean. We hoped he would be thrown into some kind of panic. Then? Apparently, no one had decided for us yet. I didn't like the open-endedness of the plan.

"We want to move in while you're both sitting at the table," Terry said. "We can control the environment much better that way. It will be harder for him to move abruptly."

"Make sense?" Lisa asked cheerily.

"Absolutely not," I said, startling them. "What if somebody recognizes me? I don't want some random person I know seeing me getting arrested by the FBI, and then they hear nothing else. No way. I'm not comfortable with that. We have to come up with something better."

I felt like the agents knew the broad strokes of what we were supposed to achieve—put on a big show that would dazzle and rattle Oleg—but they were expecting to work out most of the particulars on the fly.

"Once you arrest me, what are you going to do to Oleg?" I asked Terry.

"We are waiting for guidance," he said.

"Will you arrest him?"

"Probably not," Lisa said. "He has diplomatic immunity."

"Will you be able to question him?"

"We're not sure. We're waiting to hear back on that." This wasn't making sense. Why arrest me and let Oleg go?

For the FBI and whatever other federal agencies they were coordinating with, the upcoming climax was obviously a complicated matter. Terry and Lisa made that clear. They seemed to be under a high-powered microscope. I don't think they liked it any more than I did. But the agents needed my cooperation. They needed me to follow their instructions. They needed me to play along cleverly. Unfortunately for them, I was adamantly against being fake-arrested in a crowded restaurant in front of a bunch of people I might or might not know. Would customers take pictures? Put them online? What if the Eyewitness News team happened to be grabbing a slice at the next table?

We nibbled at our lunches when they arrived. I had a grilled-chicken sandwich and green salad. Lisa had just a salad. Terry got a burger with nothing green anywhere on the plate. And then the three of us got busy concocting Plan B.

"Some things can't change. If we're going to arrest you," Terry said, "you and Oleg have to be together. It doesn't make any sense to arrest you if he isn't there to witness it."

Terry had a point there.

"So we'll have to walk outside together," I suggested. "You'll do it in the parking lot." I couldn't have Oleg wandering out of the restaurant before or after me, like he often did in his own version of FBI-surveillance caution. That would be like showing up for a Broadway play on a dark Monday night. He'd miss the show. I figured I would use the same strategy I had used at Vincent's, when I'd lured him to my Jeep to talk about DTIC.

"I have to tell him I have something in the car that he will find very enticing," I told Lisa and Terry. "That's the only way this will work. It's gotta be something pretty good. I'll have to make him want it badly."

Both the agents seemed to like that.

"So you'll get him out to the car," Terry said. "We'll have agents inside and in the parking lot. You'll give us some kind of signal. We'll move in."

"What kind of signal?" I asked.

"I don't know. You'll have a cap on. You'll take your cap off. You think you can do that? You can remember to take your cap off?"

For the first time all day, Terry was loosening up, enough to try to mess with me. That was a language I understood far better than script-reading.

"Fuck you," I said. "Yeah, I'll take my cap off. I'm just not doing it inside."

Oleg called my cell phone on Friday afternoon, October 10. He had a time he wanted to meet with me. "Sunday noon," he said.

Finally, the show was about to begin.

Since we'd already done our Uno's walk-through, Terry and Lisa decided we didn't need to meet again. But all day Saturday, the agents and I were on the phone, reviewing everything. Then, at dinnertime on Saturday, something changed. I got another call from Terry.

"Don't go tomorrow," he said.

"Don't go?"

"Don't go," he said. "We're putting it off. Tomorrow is off. Don't go."

He didn't give me a clear explanation. Just that a decision had been made—*that again!*—that I shouldn't meet Oleg on Sunday as he had asked me to. Maybe the FBI wanted to make Oleg sweat a little. The only thing Terry was clear on was that I must not—*must not!*—go to Uno's as planned.

Instead, he told me to meet him and Lisa at ten-thirty the next morning, just when I would have been driving to Jersey, in the parking lot of the Fairway supermarket in Harlem at Twelfth Avenue and

132nd Street. I guess they wanted to be certain I didn't take a one-man joyride out to Wayne.

Sunday morning was beautiful. We had a fine view of the Hudson River from the Fairway parking lot. The day seemed bright and clean. But I was feeling more like a churning thunderstorm.

"This is awful," I told Terry and Lisa. "I want it over with. I don't understand why we can't just do it. Can't you guys get your act together?"

We sat there. The time ticked on. I could easily imagine Oleg cooling his heels at the restaurant, surveying the other tables, glancing out at the parking lot, wondering where the hell I was and what my absence might mean. There was no way for me to call him. That was never how we did things. We both knew: If one of us couldn't make an appointment, we'd go on as usual, and I'd wait for Oleg to be in touch.

With the sit-down off, there didn't seem to be much point in my spending hours with the agents except for them to be sure I didn't get a sudden urge for thick-crust Chicago-style pizza.

"It's just a delay," Terry said, trying to calm me down and pass the time. He still wouldn't tell me why we were on hold. "We'll be ready when Oleg calls again."

"What happens if he doesn't?" I asked. "What happens if this is it? What if he doesn't reach out to me? What if we've totally blown it? What if he gets spooked or called back home or— Shit, it could be anything."

Finally, Oleg did call. It was two Fridays later. He didn't sound any different than he usually did. He didn't mention the Sunday morning I'd left him waiting. He suggested we meet that Sunday at the same agreed-upon spot.

This time the agents said, "Let's do it."

CHAPTER 25

PHONY ARREST

There was no more delaying. The plan was a go.

I left the apartment a little after eleven on Sunday, October 28. I pulled the Corvette out of the parking garage and headed up the West Side Highway. The temperature had just cracked sixty. The morning was sunny and clear. I was wearing jeans, a long-sleeve blue dress shirt, and a black New York Motor Club baseball cap. I'd already punched the address for Pizzeria Uno into my GPS—West Belt Plaza, Route 23 South, Wayne, New Jersey.

Three painstaking years, a quarter-century family relationship, thousands of hours of thinking and scheming, begging and pleading, cajoling and coordinating, and it all came down to this. I was ready for the operation to be over, and I couldn't bear for it to end. I was psyched and exhausted, hopeful and depressed, as focused as I could possibly be. My emotions were all in conflict. My nerves were on edge. My adrenaline was riding high.

As I pulled onto the George Washington Bridge, I noticed my phone wasn't working. The calls were going straight to voice mail without ringing. I half thought someone might be messing with me. Were the Russians tapping into my cell phone? Was it the FBI? I'd never had reception trouble on the West Side of Manhattan. Was I imagining things? Admittedly, I was stressed.

I called Terry. "You good?" he asked me. "Everything's together on our end. Frank will be with us. He's command-and-control." There was Frank's name again. I was starting to get a sense of the larger team at work.

While I was talking to Terry, I got a message that Ava had called. What the hell was going on with my phone?

I called Ava back. I could tell she was speaking words. I knew the words were in English. I knew she was frustrated about something. But damned if I could process what she was trying to say. She was complaining, I believe, about something that had happened at work. "Ave," I said sharply, "I just can't do this right now."

I called Terry again. "I'm just getting to the strip mall," I reported. "On Route 23."

I called him again when I got to the parking spot he and Lisa had showed me. I was happy to see the space was open. No one had told me what to do if the spot was taken. I took a breath. I gulped hard. I was ready to roll.

"All right," Terry said. "Godspeed."

"Godspeed?" I said to him. "What the fuck, man? What is this? *Men in Black? Streets of Fire?* Am I gonna get shot here?" I totally went off. "Is that like 'Break a leg' or something? Don't tell me that now. I'm about to go into this. Don't be like the pilot saying 'I love you' just as the plane goes down."

I know that Terry, who'd been in this from the start, was trying to say something deep and profound. He was trying to find the right words. And I'd blown up at him. I was on the edge of losing it, but the eruption had gotten that mostly out of my system. I had one last job to do.

Taking a deep breath, I quoted my favorite line from Gary Busey's FBI agent in *Point Break*: "Take your positions. It's showtime."

Before I left the car, I checked the G-Shock watch. It said 11:55. The watch part was working, at least. I looked out the window. To the left. To the right. Then behind. I made sure no one else was around. I opened the door and climbed outside.

I crouched in the parking lot, pretending to tie my shoe. I adjusted my hat.

I blew into the watch-recorder and pulled back the band. I made sure the LED light was blinking. It was.

We were a go.

I walked across the half-empty parking lot toward the entrance of Pizzeria Uno. I was two paces away, just about to reach for the door, when I heard a voice.

"Naveed."

I turned to see Oleg over my right shoulder. He had somehow managed to sneak up on me. *Oh, fuck!* I thought. *We were supposed to meet inside.*

I tried not to look startled. I turned and smiled. I put out my hand to shake. He reached for it and didn't let go immediately. My heart was pumping hard.

"How are you?" he asked. "Of course I was worried."

"I'm fine," I said. "Nice to see you."

"What happened last time?" he asked, still holding on to my hand. I wondered if he could feel my pulse racing.

"I had a family thing. I'm sorry. I couldn't get away. It was one of those things. Sorry."

"It's okay," he said. "Everything's fine."

"It was my niece's birthday. I just had to go. Sorry to make you come for nothing."

"Listen," he said, "let's don't go here. You want to go back to

Hooters? It's right over there." He pointed across the sprawling parking lot.

Fuck, fuck, fuck!

"Sure," I said cheerily. I wasn't sure at all. Weren't some of the agents already inside Pizzeria Uno? Would they know I'd been here and now I was leaving? What would this do to all their work? Oleg had called another last-minute audible. As with the thumb drive, I couldn't think of a reason to say no. "Let's go to Hooters," I said.

It wasn't "right" there. It was at the opposite end of the parking lot and across an exit road, a good ten-minute walk away. Maybe the last-second switch shouldn't have surprised me. I already knew what a Hooters fan he was.

Oleg wasn't making any of this easy—on the FBI or on me. Inside and outside the pizza place, the agents must have already started scrambling, though I had no way of knowing for sure. Would they get to the Hooters and position themselves? Whatever they did, I understood, I had to get Oleg out of the restaurant and out to the car.

When we got to Hooters, the restaurant was packed. The TVs were blaring. The brunch Bloody Marys were giving way to the game-day beers. The Sunday crowd was already howling for a packed afternoon of NFL football. The Giants-Steelers game had a one p.m. start. It was anyone's guess what the G-Shock watch was picking up.

When the Hooters Girl came over in her sleeveless tee and short shorts—she was blond this time and as large-chested as any of them—I wasn't feeling hungry at all. But we started with an order of mild chicken wings. Oleg got the fish-and-chips. I ordered the steak quesadilla. We both had Cokes. I'd tried the salad last time, but this was Hooters. Take a page from Terry's book of nutrition: Why even think healthy or lean?

I wasn't sure what was going on around me. I was trying to assess what our last-second switch-up meant for the FBI. I assumed they were scrambling, finding new positions for themselves. I tried not to look at the door every time new patrons came in.

Over the din of the busy restaurant, Oleg leaned across the table and started asking me about DTIC. Clearly, he'd bought in to the whole database idea.

"What other kinds of searches are you capable of?" he wanted to know. "Why does it take so long to order the documents? Don't you have access to more than this?"

His words were straightforward enough. But he couldn't help himself. He was slipping back into that Russian condescension, the tone that said to me: "We are unimpressed with what you can deliver, but we want to continue to use you." That was never a good tactic for motivating me, but they must have taught it in Russian espionage school, and Oleg kept trying it on me.

For now I was thinking, *Let's see how unimpressed you are when you figure out I was using* you. However I was feeling, I had to stay focused on the business at hand. It was my job, even with the end in sight, to pretend things were moving ahead, to motivate him, and to do it in a way that wouldn't raise his suspicions. I would stoke his appetite mercilessly and squeeze him for as much as he had in his pocket. I had to be the materialistic young American traitor he had slowly gotten to know. And in this final act of ours, how hard could that be?

I wouldn't have to deliver whatever it was I was promising. The FBI would have swooped in by then. I could promise Oleg anything. My only real challenge was getting him out to the car. I assumed some of the agents were inside Hooters. Many of them lived in this part of Jersey. For all I knew, they hung out at this bar every Sunday afternoon, munching on fried mozzarella sticks and watching the game. They must have seen us turn outside Uno's and walk together across the parking lot—right? Right?

"Look," I said to Oleg, cutting off his questions, "I can get you more, a lot more. I just need to get paid."

"Did you bring the previous material?" he asked. He was talking about documents related to the navy's Future Combat Systems, the F-22 Raptor plane, and cruise missiles.

"I have a lot of stuff in the car for you," I said. "I really didn't want to bring it into the restaurant. I am happy to get you more. You can see it if you want to. I just need to protect how I do my searches, and I have to get paid."

He started asking about other categories, technical military terms I only half recognized. "Do you know what they are?" he asked me.

"It doesn't matter," I said. "Tell me what you want. I'll just search for it. You can give me more subjects. We can make it work."

I was laying it on pretty thick. He was getting excited. And I kept pushing.

"I want to discuss business first," I continued. "How much do you have on you? If I'm going to give you what I brought for you, I want everything you have."

"I think you will be pleased," he said.

It was then, as we asked the Hooters Girl to get a check for us, that Oleg told me what I already knew: His New York tour was ending, and he would soon be heading home.

"I am sorry to be leaving. But do not worry," he told me, turning more personal and warm. "I will introduce you to the new people. They will be very excited to meet you. They will work closely with you."

It all sounded nice, I told him. We would see what the future brought. But didn't we have a piece of business we had to take care of first? I kept it simple, like I always did with Oleg, like I always did with the FBI. "You will give me the money," I said. "We will go to the car. I will give you the files that I have."

"Yes," he agreed.

Oleg seemed excited about everything I'd promised. But to him, every minute we sat at the table was another minute his huge win was delayed. As far as he was concerned, he was heading home a hero. He was leaving a valuable agent behind. He seemed cocky, completely sure of himself.

He paid the bill, and we got up to leave.

It was total bullshit, my extravagant promise of valuable files in the car. I was completely bluffing. All I had in the Corvette trunk was a box filled with assorted papers that, at best, would give me about twenty seconds before Oleg realized they were nothing. The moment I unlocked the trunk for Oleg—before he could tell that he'd been duped—the agents would swoop in from all directions, and this three-year drama would be over. It wouldn't matter what was or what wasn't in the car trunk. It wouldn't matter what else Oleg was expecting. It wouldn't matter how much money he had paid.

I would unlock the trunk, and I would take off my cap as he glanced inside. It would be like a Taurus and Fusion rally in the parking lot. The agents would screech toward us in their cars. Oleg's world would change forever. My tour as a self-taught American double agent would be done.

As we stepped outside Hooters, Oleg handed me a fat white envelope. "It's fifteen thousand dollars," he said. "I told you that you would be pleased."

I nodded and said nothing.

As we began walking together across the sunny parking lot, I couldn't see the black Corvette at first. There was a busy exit road between Hooters and the Uno's parking lot. Oleg and I had a few last moments together. I took advantage of them. Almost certainly, this was my last opportunity. Fifty paces from where we were standing, I might never see Oleg again.

"I have some news for you, too," I said as we walked toward my car. "It's big." I knew Oleg never liked surprises. He looked at me, half excited, half alarmed. "The letter came from the navy. I got accepted."

"You got accepted? That's great!" he roared.

"I'll be a U.S. Navy intelligence officer."

"Congratulations! That is wonderful news! Do you have a copy of the letter?" he asked. Oleg loved paperwork.

"Not with me."

"You will show it to me later," he said.

This news, like the documents waiting in the Corvette trunk, was a bit more than exaggeration. I couldn't give him the letter even if I'd wanted to because it hadn't come yet. I did know the board would soon be meeting. I had observed some pretty good indications that the answer would be yes. But no formal decision had been made, much less sent out to me.

Still, I enjoyed saying it, and Oleg seemed to enjoy hearing it even more. "That is excellent," he said again. Given the briefness of our future together, why deny my purported partner in espionage one last thrill? For me, it was one last time to prove my prowess at lying to the enemy. I wasn't sure if I was being kind or mean. But as I always had with Oleg and the FBI, I pushed straight ahead.

The traffic coming out of the parking lot was heavy. Sunday brunch at downscale eateries was evidently popular in Wayne. As Oleg and I stood at the curb waiting for the walk light to turn, he reached into his pocket and took out a piece of paper that he handed to me. I gave it a quick glance. It contained a handwritten grid of lines and boxes with a list of government job titles—many of them, both high and low—and their levels of official secrecy: top-secret, secret, restricted, and so on.

"What is this supposed to be?" I asked Oleg.

"These are the codes for all the different levels of clearance," he said. "I thought you'd like to see them."

And he meant *all* of them. The job titles went from the lowliest "civilian" all the way up to members of Congress and the Senate and even "President of the United States."

"Here is where you are now," he said, pointing to a box on the lower third of his chart. "You have access to material that is export-controlled and everything below that. That is good. But look where you will be as a navy intelligence officer." He pointed to a spot six or eight rungs up the grid that someone had already marked with a pencil. "Big difference," he said with a giant smile.

"Big difference," I agreed.

From what I knew about government classifications, the grid was probably accurate, though I'd never seen the practical details of secret access laid out so clearly. Had he gotten this chart from the U.S. government? Or had the Russians made it up themselves? I shouldn't have been surprised. Secrecy was the business that Oleg was in.

I didn't give Oleg a chance to take the chart back. Just as the light was changing, I folded the paper in half and slipped it into my pocket. I walked as the traffic cleared. This was too good to lose.

"There is so much else I can get you," I told Oleg.

"This could be very good," he said.

"I hope," I told him.

As we talked and walked, Oleg sounded almost wistful. Like he was proud of the asset he had developed for his country, the young American he was convinced he held in his hands. For once, he spoke to me like he recognized what I was capable of and appreciated what I had done.

"We want to throw you a big party," he said. "Vodka and lobsters. Music. It will be fun. It will be a very big party."

I listened but didn't speak.

"You will get numbered bank accounts," he went on. "You will get a retirement plan. You will be treated like a true professional. They are very excited about this."

He didn't say who *they* were, exactly. I assumed he meant his superiors or his colleagues at headquarters. In Moscow? At the Mission? Maybe both. But he made clear to me that whoever they were, they were very happy with what I had been able to do for them and all the documents I had been able to retrieve.

And with my new place in Naval Intelligence, they were expecting much, much more.

Oleg and I walked a diagonal route across the parking lot. When we approached the black Corvette, I followed the script exactly as the agents and I had agreed. The time for improvising was behind us. My free-flowing promises had more than motivated Oleg to do what I wanted him to do. Now he seemed entirely clueless about what the future held.

"It's all right here," I told him as I held the car key in my hand.

He took a step closer.

I pushed a button on the fob, and the trunk popped open.

He leaned in.

I glanced across my right shoulder and saw nobody else nearby. With my left hand, I tossed the bulging envelope of cash onto the floor of the trunk, right beside the empty cardboard box.

Oleg leaned in to see what I had in there. He squinted from the bright afternoon into the darker trunk. This time I didn't slam the trunk on his head.

As he peered inside, I took a step back from the car's rear bumper. I glanced to the left, then the right, and still saw no one.

With my right hand, I removed the Motor Club cap from my head and lowered it to my side.

There was half a second of silence.

Oleg's head was in the trunk. He was staring into the cardboard box where the papers were supposed to be, giving his eyes a moment to adjust from the bright sunlight. He began to turn his head toward me as if to ask, "Where are these documents?" But he didn't get a single syllable out.

After one more half second, the calm of the parking lot flew into mayhem.

Out of nowhere, three cars raced around from the right. No lights. No sirens. Just three Ford Fusions—Terry's black one, plus a silver one and a gold one, all 2007s or 2008s. I definitely won the cool-car contest in the parking lot that day.

All the cars slammed to a stop almost simultaneously just a few short feet from us. In an instant, five car doors flew open and five FBI agents jumped out. There was Terry and Lisa, my immediate team.

Like a movie character suddenly cornered by the authorities, I lifted both my hands to shoulder height in a gesture of half surrender.

There were two young agents I didn't recognize. There was Frank, the supervisor. Terry pointed him out. A couple of other agents were standing on the periphery.

One of the young agents stood beside me as I faced Oleg. "Who is that?" the agent demanded.

I didn't answer.

"Who is that to you?" he yelled again.

"Nobody," I said.

"Who?" he yelled one more time.

He was talking, and I was staring at Oleg. The whole thing felt like an out-of-body experience, like I was standing there watching it come down.

The agent didn't let up. "What's his name?"

"Pasha," I said.

Pasha? Where did that come from?

I knew where. The night before, as I was trying to stay calm for my big adventure, Ava and I had been watching *So You Think You Can Dance* on TV. There was a contestant on the show named Pasha.

As all this was unfolding, Oleg was just standing there. Saying nothing. Doing nothing.

Terry walked back to the open Corvette trunk. "Got something, boss," he called out to Frank. He was holding the big white envelope of Oleg's cash. He turned to me. "What is this?" he demanded. Terry, the agent who'd been with me the longest and knew me best of all.

After Pasha, I said nothing else. Oleg still hadn't said anything. No one touched him. He stood there wide-eyed, his face betraying the tiniest hint of the confusion that must have been surging through his brain.

A thought entered my head. *Look at Oleg. He's the loneliest man in the world.* I understood his confusion and watched as he managed to remain disconnected. In an instant, this cheeriest of afternoons had turned into a horrible fast-paced mess for him.

The agents in their matching Ford Fusions.

Me being grabbed in front of him.

The hopeful excitement he had felt a few seconds earlier—his own impending departure, the rash of documents to come, my long-awaited navy acceptance, the eye-popping secrecy grid, the talk of a lobster-and-vodka celebration, the numbered bank accounts, the retirement plan, this triumph so close he could taste it—all snatched abruptly from his powerful grip.

He never flinched.

For their part, the agents deserved Academy Awards.

"Anything in your pockets that will poke me?" one of the agents asked as he began patting me down. "Anything sharp at all?"

Oleg, I noticed, expressed no concern for me, this young American he had been so recently flattering. He said nothing to protect me, nothing to the agents on my behalf. He said nothing to anyone.

Whatever genuine appreciation he had for me or concern for my well-being—and I'm guessing it wasn't much in the end—was clearly overwhelmed by his own fear, military training, and sense of self-protection.

Saying not a word, he turned his back on me and began walking slowly away.

No one put me in handcuffs. I'm not sure why. But I was pushed into the back of a gold Ford Fusion. The two younger agents got into the front seats. Just as quickly as they'd converged on us, the agents were driving me away.

I couldn't see Oleg's face through the rear window. He was walking out of the parking lot. All I could see was the back of his stocky frame moving silently away.

The agents didn't take me far in the gold Fusion, just far enough to be sure that Oleg had departed and could no longer see us. Then they stopped the car.

"By the way, my name is Fred," one of the agents said, turning around in his seat. "This is Sam. We're both so glad to meet you."

"Very nice work," Sam said.

"Very well done," said Fred. "We used to work with your parents."

They drove me up to the third level of a nearby parking garage. When we got up there, it was filled with agents and cops. I didn't know who most of them were. There had to be at least a dozen vehicles and twenty or twenty-five people. I'd had no idea so many people were working behind the scenes. We started with a tight, tiny group, a couple of agents and me. Look at what that had expanded into! All of them seemed fully familiar with what had gone down. Compared with the tense craziness of the parking lot, the atmosphere in the garage was celebratory and loose. A bunch of law-enforcement professionals, all congratulating each other and congratulating me.

It was surreal. I saw two guys holding doggie bags from Pizzeria Uno. I could only imagine how they'd found out about the switch and bolted out of there—but not without their food.

A couple of people were talking into radios, getting updated reports from agents assigned to follow Oleg back to the city.

"You like our RP?" Terry asked. "The rally point."

"Pretty cool," I said.

"Listen," Terry said, noticing how I was paying close attention to the radio squawks about Oleg. "He's on his way outta here. His career is over as of right now. God only knows what happens to him when he gets back home. It won't be pretty." He handed me the keys to the Corvette. They did not want me hanging around. "You gotta go now," he said.

"Are we sure he's left?" I asked Terry. I knew they were good at their jobs, but I needed to hear that Oleg wasn't watching us from behind a mailbox or hunkered down in his car seat.

"He's gone and he's not looking back," Terry assured me.

"Am I gonna run into him on the highway?"

"Highly unlikely."

"What kind of danger am I in? What about my family?"

"None."

I nodded. They seemed confident that Oleg was gone from my life, that my years of duplicity and looking over my shoulder were truly over.

I climbed into the car. I turned the key and listened to the comforting loud rumble of the engine. They'd given Oleg enough time to be way ahead of me. I agreed it was time to get out of there.

My mind was racing. Even faster than I usually drove.

What kind of turmoil had we caused for the Russian espionage apparatus inside the United States?

Were the Russians worried about my well-being? Highly unlikely. Were they worried about what I might say? For sure. What did they make now of our three-year relationship or the twenty years they had known my family?

At that moment, no one knew what would happen next. But as I took one last look at the celebration in the garage, I understood that the feeling was triumph. God only knows what the Russians thought. But to be on the safe side, I took a circuitous route back to Ninety-sixth Street.

CHAPTER 26

VICTORY LAP

I had a voice mail from Juli. Somehow, I'd missed her call. Before trying her back, I slipped out of the office and rode up to the building's fourth floor. It was empty up there, perfect for talking on the phone without anyone overhearing. Whatever news Juli had for me, I didn't want an office full of curious ears.

Juli answered immediately. She didn't stretch out the drama. "Listen," she said. "Congratulations. I just found out. You got in."

Yes!

Juli's announcement sounded almost matter-of-fact. My response did not. "Oh my God!" I shouted. "I can't believe it! Am I really in?" I was loud and excited. If I'd been in the office, everyone would have been staring at me.

This wasn't a dream. I was in, Juli assured me. "It doesn't surprise me at all," she said. "But I'm very happy to be the one to tell you. This is quite an accomplishment, Naveed. You worked so hard for this—for *six years*."

"Thank you so much for everything!" I said, finally catching my breath enough for complete declarative sentences. "I really appreciate it. Do I get a letter or something? What's next?"

Juli laughed. "Oddly," she said, "the navy doesn't normally send out letters to successful applicants. They only send something if you don't get in. If you're accepted, you just get a phone call."

Whatever. I didn't care about the communications protocol. They could sail the news to me on a paper airplane if that was what they wanted to do—as long as the answer was yes.

"There is an acceptance letter in the system," Juli said. "I can print one up for you if you like. The navy just doesn't see fit to actually mail it."

"And what about getting sworn in?" I asked.

As Juli explained, the navy didn't go overboard on commissioning ceremonies, either. "It's kinda up to the individual," she said. Some people just signed the forms and mailed them back—no ceremony at all. Others chose to organize a public swearing-in with friends, family members, coworkers, and a big presentation. Juli had another idea for me.

"How would you feel about doing something a little more personal?" she asked. "If you'd like, we could have a private commissioning for you in the office here. We've done that before. Your wife could come. You could invite your friends from the FBI. All very low-key."

I liked the sound of that. I'd certainly gotten into the navy in an unorthodox manner. Why shouldn't my swearing-in reflect the uniqueness of that path? Ava wasn't big on pomp and ceremony. This was the woman who'd skipped her own Columbia University graduation and hadn't heard her name called out as one of the stellar students in her class because she'd gone with me to adopt a kitten. Plus, I really liked the idea that a couple of the agents I had worked so closely with might be there with me. As I had learned in our years together, these guys didn't like risking any compromise of their secret work. But a small, private get-together in the navy recruiting office? Why not?

The navy wasn't the only one planning a ceremony. It turned out the FBI wanted to celebrate, too.

Terry called to say that his FBI supervisors wanted me to come down to their office and accept the Bureau's formal thanks. I told him I wasn't sure I needed official thank-yous. I hadn't gotten involved for that reason. "Oh, come on," Terry said. I didn't put up too much of a fight. I appreciated the gesture. And in my three years of working with Terry, Ted, and the New York counterintelligence agents, they had never invited me to their office. We'd always met outside.

"You mean I finally get inside?" I teased Terry.

He just laughed. "You can bring your wife," he said. "I want you to meet my supervisors. I don't know exactly who can make it, but we'll have a couple of senior people there. They're very excited about getting the chance to meet you.

"Maybe we'll go out to dinner afterward. You have to eat, right?"

Ava and I should have taken the subway to our little get-together with the FBI. I realized that five minutes after we left home. As many years as we'd spent getting around New York City, you'd think we'd be experts at avoiding rush-hour traffic. But Ava was five months pregnant. I figured we'd be coming home late. So we grabbed a cab downtown.

Bad idea. Very bad idea.

The Manhattan traffic was atrocious. We were due at 26 Federal Plaza at five p.m. I called Terry with apologetic updates as we inched down the West Side Highway. I repeated several times: "We should have ridden the train, I know."

It took us an hour and ten minutes for a ride that should have been half an hour. We arrived, tense and a little embarrassed, forty minutes late. What a smooth operator I was! I couldn't even get to my celebration on time!

Terry met us in the lobby.

"Man, I'm sorry," I said.

"Don't worry about it." He shrugged. "They'll wait." He badged us through security and ushered us into a special-access elevator.

"Pretty nice elevator," I said after the doors had closed and we began our express ride to the FBI executive suite. "Is this what you take to the office?"

"In all the years I've been at the New York office, I've never taken this elevator," he said. I think he was being serious. Ava shot me a nonverbal "That's weird." But Terry's elevator comment was just my first indication of how unique our visit would be. Green Kryptonite and his handlers, clandestine to the end.

Terry led us into a large empty conference room. There was an American flag in the corner and a large TV. There was plush blue carpeting on the floor. Lisa and a photographer were waiting when we got there.

From the conference room, I could see a large cube farm of desks and file cabinets sprawling out across the open floor. So late in the day, most of the desks were empty. Frank and Jerry joined us. Then a tall, trim bald man came in. I didn't know who he was at first, though I noticed that the other agents seemed to defer to him.

As he made small talk with the others in the room, Terry whispered to me that this was the number one FBI man in New York. He was assistant director of the FBI in charge of the New York field office, the largest FBI field office in the country. That made him responsible for some of the Bureau's highest-profile and most important cases. He had at least a thousand people working for him.

"How's it goin'?" he said to me brightly, reaching out to shake my hand. "I'm Joe Demarest. I heard you had some trouble with the traffic."

"A little bit," I said sheepishly.

Despite his elevated duties, Demarest couldn't have been more gracious or appreciative. "It's so nice to meet you," he said. "I'm so happy you could make it here today for this special occasion."

He seemed especially eager to speak with Ava. "You should be proud of your husband," he told her. "He did a very important thing for his country. He made a unique contribution. I hope you understand how important this is."

"I guess now I do," Ava said.

The two of them spoke for several minutes. I didn't hear all of it. But what I heard was extremely flattering. I appreciated his talking to my wife that way. I don't know if he thought I'd left Ava in the dark about everything I'd been up to or if he realized how much she already knew. I hadn't always gone into detail with Ted, Terry, and Lisa about what I had shared with her. But the big boss seemed eager for my wife to know that the role I'd played was highly unusual and that it mattered a lot.

Until that ceremony, I'm not sure I realized how big a deal the FBI considered what I had done. I'd always thought it was huge. But that was just me. Now, hearing it from someone with such standing in the FBI, I began to realize how uniquely huge it was.

The whole thing felt surreal, to be standing around in this conference room with the head of the FBI's New York field office, hearing what wonderful things I had done. I wasn't used to this kind of attention. I'd spent three years undercover, for God's sake. No one could know what I was up to. The fact is, I wasn't used to any attention at all.

"Okay, let's do this," Demarest finally said.

As I stood beside him and the photographer snapped away, the assistant director began to speak. "On behalf of the Federal Bureau of Investigation," he said, "we want to thank you for all your cooperation and assistance. This was truly remarkable. You did a great thing."

He handed me a framed letter that I didn't have time to read, and then he said, "And I want to give you a check." It was for fifteen thousand and change, made out to me. The amount was no coincidence. It was the amount of the last pile of money that Oleg had given me and I had turned over to the agents.

He looked at Terry and Lisa and added: "We have something else for them, right?"

Terry said they did. Smiling broadly, he announced, "A mug that says, 'The FBI Always Gets Its Man!' "

I knew that J. Edgar Hoover had said that. Tim Curry, playing the undercover FBI butler in the movie *Clue,* had said it, too. And now I had a mug that said it. I loved the message, so clear and unequivocal. This time, I thought with pride, I had helped to make it true.

I thanked Demarest for his generous comments and the others for showing up. "I would have arrived sooner if I'd known I was getting such a cool mug," I said. Then I told Demarest and the others what an honor it was to have been involved in a case as important and interesting as this one and how lucky I'd been to work alongside these agents. "As a civilian," I concluded, "I know how rare it is to be invited inside like this. Thank you all very much."

Demarest smiled and nodded. "At the very least," he said before telling us all good night, "I think you guys deserve a decent dinner out of this." He turned to Lisa, Ted, and Jerry, Frank's boss, who reported to Demarest and carried himself like a linebacker: "You gonna take Mr. Jamali and his wife somewhere good?"

"Absolutely," Lisa said.

Then Jerry, Lisa, Terry, Frank, Ava, and I headed out for dinner at a French restaurant a short walk from the office. On the way, I had a chance to read the framed letter that Demarest had given me. It was written on official letterhead, U.S. Department of Justice, Federal Bureau of Investigation stationery.

"I am pleased to join my fellow New York Agents in thanking you for your significant contribution to our Nation's national security," the letter said. "Over an extended period, you dedicated your time and resources to facilitate our efforts to protect our country. Your ideas, enthusiasm, and dedication enabled us to achieve success in this vital area of our responsibility. You can take pride in the role you played and the success achieved."

The letter was signed Joseph M. Demarest, Jr., Assistant Director in Charge of the New York Division of the United States Federal Bureau of Investigation.

We had a great meal. Ava, who'd heard so much about the agents—Terry especially—finally got to spend a little time with them. I learned some things. I found out Frank lived in Westchester, not far from where I'd grown up. He had a daughter at SUNY Purchase, he said. Lisa, who I knew was a West Point graduate, talked about her time as a captain in the army, deployed in Iraq. While serving there, she'd adopted a stray kitten, then managed to bring it home with her. That couldn't have been easy, from what I know about military bureaucracy. It was a softer side of Lisa I hadn't previously tuned in to—or maybe she'd never shown.

Jerry told us how he'd once worked in France, how he drove a BMW, and how well the car handled.

A Bimmer? I smiled politely and thought, *Buddy, you have no idea what good handling is.*

Jerry asked questions of everyone—Ava, me, and the other agents. He didn't seem to know them well. He had a lot of people working for him. Even after the years I'd spent with the agents, I felt a strange combination of awkward and thrilled to be sitting at dinner, laughing and talking, being treated as an equal by this FBI counterintelligence supervisor. I'd worked with them. I'd considered them my teammates. But I'd never really been one of them. I almost thought someone might come to the table and question me: "Sir, this table is for FBI only. What are *you* doing here?"

Terry and I had our usual banter. I told him that the restaurant bathroom was probably nicer than his living room. And though I wasn't going to give him too hard a time around his bosses, I couldn't resist sneaking in a few jabs. "You want carrots tonight?" I asked him. "You want some legumes? You'd probably prefer the steak frites. *Frites* means *french fries*. I think you're safe there."

"Nothing green, please," he said.

"Nothing healthy of any sort, you mean. You're the only person I know who drinks regular Coke. To you, Diet Coke is health food." Terry didn't have much of a comeback, but I had trouble giving it up. "It's been so long since you've eaten anything healthy, I don't think your body could take the shock to your system. The bad guys don't need to poison you with anthrax. You could be felled by a solitary pea."

At one point, Frank pulled me aside and said, "You know, every time my guys would meet with you, they'd walk back into the office with their heads hanging down. They would plop down in their chairs looking extremely frustrated and exhausted. They always felt like you were worth it, but they also knew that nothing would ever be easy with you."

Frank didn't seem to be complaining. He was just laying it out there. I understood there had been certain challenges to having me as a partner: I was learning as I went. I didn't always like the rules the FBI had to play by. I insisted on being way more involved than your typical helpful civilian would be. That was all part of my charm but also part of what made me a pain in the ass.

"Your ability to frustrate the crap out of them was unparalleled," Frank said.

Now, some people might have been insulted by that. Not me. I considered it one of the most sincere compliments I'd ever received in my life and one that I was proudest of. "Thank you, Frank," I said. "That's very kind of you."

I don't think that was the reaction he expected.

Before we headed home that night, I had something I'd been waiting to share. I'd been reluctant to mention it earlier, not certain how the agents would respond. Now the danger was behind us. The case was officially over. We had no more need for secrets.

I was ready to show them my tattoo.

"You wanna see something?" I asked Lisa and Terry before we got up from the table. I rolled up my sleeve, and they looked closely at my arm. "You know what it says?"

"Is that Morse code?" Terry asked. "Dots and dashes, right? It's been a long time since I was in the Boy Scouts. What does it say?"

"Green Kryptonite," I said. "In honor of Ted."

"Wow," Lisa said. "You tattooed 'Green Kryptonite' on your arm? You must be really committed. Gotta give you that."

Terry just shook his head. "I am so glad I didn't know about that before," he said. "We'd have been filling out forms and answering questions from the bosses for at least three months." He paused and looked more closely at me. "You tattooed 'Green Kryptonite' on your arm?"

CHAPTER 27

ENSIGN JAMALI

For years, I'd been hearing about Quantico.

Nestled on 385 wooded acres in Virginia, the Marine Corps Base Quantico is home to the FBI's main training facility, the FBI Academy. Quantico is where new recruits and experienced special agents go to learn and hone their trade. That sprawling campus in Quantico is also home to the FBI crime lab, officially known as the Forensic Science Research and Training Center, and various other programs that support federal law enforcement, including the FBI's Behavioral Analysis Unit, the Technology Services Unit, and the FBI National Academy, which trains law-enforcement leaders from around the world. I don't think anyone would argue if I said the FBI Academy is generally considered the premier law-enforcement training program in America.

I'd never been to the FBI Academy, I'd seen it in movies and read about it in dozens of thrilling action novels. I had, however, visited the marine side of the base a bunch of times for work. Marine Corps University, which is located there, was one of our Books & Research clients. It's a secure facility closed to the public. But now, it seemed, after my official blessing from Joe Demarest, the FBI Academy was eager to hear from me. The Oleg Victory Lap continued.

I was invited to lecture at Quantico.

Ava and I flew down to Washington in late April. We stayed at the elegant Mayflower Hotel, famous for many things, including being the hotel where New York governor Eliot Spitzer (code name Client No. 9) allegedly entertained call girls.

We drove from Washington out to Virginia in our rental car, to an anonymous-looking strip mall across from the base. Terry picked us up there and whisked us through a marine checkpoint to a second gate that was manned by a uniformed FBI officer. No one was supposed to know we were there. As far as I could tell, no one did—until the FBI guard insisted on seeing my identification and Terry had to walk into the Visitor Center to sort everything out.

All this secrecy, and I'd been invited!

After that minor holdup, we were back in clandestine mode. We continued walking until we got to a point where an instructor propped open a door to one of the buildings and slipped us inside.

Before I made my presentation, Lisa would speak, providing a detailed briefing about Oleg's case. I'd be invited in after she was finished, the real-life double agent at the center of the operation. "They will eat this up," Terry assured me.

While we waited, he took Ava and me on a backstage tour of the Academy. He showed us the library, the dining hall, the three dormitory buildings, the gym, the thousand-seat auditorium, the pistol and rifle ranges, and the stop that got my blood flowing, the pursuit-driving training track. We saw Hogan's Alley, a ten-acre town with building facades designed by Hollywood set designers to resemble a small American city. Don't you know some wild shoot-outs have gone down there! A sign welcomes visitors to Hogan's Alley. It says that weapons firing and arrests may occur. It also says at the bottom: HAVE A NICE DAY.

As Terry, Ava, and I walked around, recruits in khakis and polo shirts kept running past us. They carried bright orange dummy handguns in leather holsters on their belts. "It's so they'll get used to carrying a firearm without actually hurting anyone," Terry explained.

He pointed out the numerous deer that shared the base with FBI agents and marines. "They are totally desensitized to the sound of gunfire," he said. Indeed, the ones we saw were nibbling happily at the woodland underbrush, not even flinching at the target practice nearby. These deer would really take the thrill out of sport hunting.

In the gift shop, I met a French police officer looking at the "FBI Fashion" rack. He was from Marseilles and was at Quantico for training. He seemed excited to meet someone who could speak his language. "My mother is French," I told him.

Jokingly—at least I think I was joking—I asked Terry if it was okay for me to use my Amex card to buy some FBI T-shirts. "Will the Russians wonder if they see that coming up on my bill, 'What's he doing in the FBI Academy gift shop?' " Terry said he thought it was *probably* okay.

By then, Lisa was finishing her presentation, and Terry took me into the room.

The briefing was held in a secure conference room, a vault-like enclosure where the agents would discuss secret stuff without the risk of outsiders listening in. This one looked like a classroom without windows and with long rows of stadium seats. They wouldn't let Ava in to listen, which seemed kind of silly considering how much she knew. That didn't seem to matter. She had to wait in a nearby classroom.

Before I started my talk, several people came up to say hello, congratulating me and making friendly conversation. "I used to live in Irvington," one man said. Irvington is ten minutes from Hastings and Dobbs Ferry. I wondered if the people I'd been invited to speak to had been given a Naveed Jamali dossier in preparation or Lisa had given them a really detailed intro. They sure seemed to know a lot about me. "I knew your parents," said one agent in his early forties. That surprised me, though it reminded me that this journey hadn't just lasted three years. It was more like twenty-three years since my parents had been approached by members of the Russian Mission and then the FBI.

As I waited for Terry to introduce me, I glanced at the attendance sheet on one of the desks. I'd assumed the audience would be all FBI agents. But people had signed in from the Central Intelligence Agency, the Defense Intelligence Agency, and the Drug Enforcement Administration. "I didn't realize this was such a diverse group," I told Doug, the proctor, when he wandered in.

"Let me just take that," he said hurriedly, whisking the sign-in sheet off the desk. I guessed I wasn't supposed to see where the people were from. Or their names.

Terry took the podium and introduced me. "This is the guy we worked with," he said vaguely. "Over the course of three years, he spent many hours sitting in front of Kulikov. His experience and knowledge from that time is unique." He looked at me. "With that, I'll turn it over to him." It was strange how he never said my name.

Ever the young business guy, I began with a dreaded PowerPoint, explaining to the federal agents my rules for catching a spy.

"I was a proxy in the truest sense of the word," I said. "My job, in a sense, was to represent both the Russians and the Bureau in a complex negotiation, since neither could speak directly to the other. I had to find the sweet spot. The middle ground that would appeal to the Russians while also limiting the Bureau's risk.

"But first," I explained, "I had to develop a relationship with Oleg. By the time I first approached the FBI about getting more involved, my parents had known the Russians for two decades. I had to find a way to change and expand a long-standing relationship. I had to convince Oleg, who then had to convince his superiors, that I was willing and capable of delivering something valuable to them."

I never knew the full context of what I was doing, I said. The agents felt no responsibility to read me in on that. "I was just the double agent," I said. "But the whole time I was interacting with Oleg, I had hints of a larger backstory unfolding beyond my view. I kept noticing things in the paper and on the TV news—signs of escalating tensions between the U.S. and the Russians."

I said I was struck by Moscow's decision a year earlier to eject two American attachés by yanking their travel permission while they were on a trip. "And in January, the Russians ordered General Henry Nowak to leave," I said. "He was the senior American defense attaché in Moscow. Things just keep getting tenser."

The agents and their colleagues seemed to be listening. A couple of them, I noticed, were even taking notes.

"The first step is having access to the target," I said. "But having access alone is never enough. You have to make the relationship progress. How many of you take the train or ride the elevator with people you've seen for years?" Almost everyone nodded or smiled. "In most cases, you know nothing about these people, not even their first names. That relationship has to grow and change. You have to take the person from casual contact to friendly acquaintance to someone you might plausibly grab dinner with. It's a process. It's a careful dance.

"You don't see someone in the elevator and say, 'You want to have dinner tonight?' Or 'You want to do business together?' Or 'You want to join me in a conspiracy to commit espionage?' " The men and women laughed. "If you believe the person might be interested, you have to build up to things like that. You might strike up a conversation. After a few of those, it might make sense to continue the conversation over dinner or a beer. Now you're building toward something real."

Some of this was basic human relations. It applied far more

broadly than the world of counterintelligence. But the agents seemed to be listening raptly, as if this were the first they had heard any of it—or the first they'd heard it applied directly by someone in the field.

"This was my approach with Oleg," I said. "Build slowly. Let him get comfortable. Help the trust grow. Of course," I added, "it's even more difficult when the other party is totally paranoid and secrecy-obsessed. The best way to counter that, I found, was to give him the illusion that he was always in control. Our goal was to get him to start tasking me to retrieve intelligence for him—or, if you prefer, spy against my country for his."

When I looked back now, I said, I saw the progress readily enough. "As we moved from the introductory to the developmental to the operational, each new phase was marked by some key moment—meeting outside instead of inside my office, Oleg accepting the NATOPS manuals, signing on for DTIC—that one pushed our operation to the next, deeper phase."

The agents had lots of questions. To me, that was the most interesting part of this extraordinary day.

"How much prep did this take?" one of the agents wanted to know.

"A lot," I said. "For every hour I spent with Oleg, I probably spent sixty with Terry and Ted."

"What did Oleg think your motivation was?"

"The Russians, like us, know about MICE, the concept that people betray their countries for one of four reasons—money, ideology, coercion, or ego. In choosing the right motivation for me, I settled on money. That's the one that felt most natural to me. So when I was with Oleg, it was always about money. Not that I needed it but that I wanted more. Lots more. That choice—that clear choice—narrowed the things I had to focus on. It made our negotiations and discussions mostly about how much he was going to pay me. It really came down to answering a single crucial question: 'What do you charge to sell out your country?' "

"What was Oleg like personally?"

"He was a pain in the ass," I said. "He was so goddamn cheap it was almost shocking. He would overnegotiate." I told them about the free books he bagged on every visit to the office. "I almost felt he would take the paper out of the printer if he could figure out how to open the tray."

"Were you scared?"

"Only after a meeting was over. When we were set to meet, I had to get into character. I'd watch movies. I'd read books. I had all these little tricks. The guy who was meeting Oleg had the same name I did. He looked and sounded like me. But he wasn't the real Naveed. He was greedier, more materialistic, and definitely more focused. He was willing to sell out his country. That was the most diametric difference. Each time I met with Oleg, I had to become that guy who looked like me. He was never scared. He had a goal. And in that crucial moment, it was all mano a mano, just the two of us. No one else was there. All the planning and discussions—go, no go, yes, no—they had all evaporated. They were done. In that moment, there had to be total clarity of purpose and technique. Afterward, when what I had done had caught up to me, I realized the enormity of it all. But in the moment, battling wits with Oleg was all that I could focus on. It was challenging, fascinating, and immensely fun."

Another agent raised her hand. "So how did you decide how much money to charge him? Did he think you were that greedy for money?"

"My demands always had to be realistic," I said. "You can't force it. There has to be some give-and-take." I paused and took a sip of water. I had to think about the question for a moment. "There was always a strong element of theatrics with this," I went on. "I built my matrix for cost based on who Oleg thought I was. What I mean by this is that if you show up with a ten-thousand-dollar Breitling watch and then offer to work for a few hundred dollars, they'll know something is wrong. But if you place your ask too high, they just won't be able to do it. I understood that they had limited funds. They understood my motivation. It was all about money with an added dash of ego. And once they understood my motivation, it was only a matter of finding the right amount. He knew enough about what I liked to gauge the likelihood of what I'd need. Was the amount I demanded enough to get me motivated, and could they afford to pay? In the end, whatever motivation you choose has to be something you're comfortable with. You'll have to defend it time and time again."

"Are you going to write a book?"

"That isn't something I've thought about," I said, and I hadn't at the time.

Really.

It was clear to me from the questions—and how many I got— that these investigators rarely got the chance to hear from someone who'd spent so much personal time with a real-life American-based Russian spy. These agents might devote their careers—two or three decades or more—to fighting foreign espionage. But they rarely have the chance to do what I had done, sit for hours with someone committing the crime. I'd had that chance, and they seemed fascinated to know what I had learned. I'll bet I had racked up more hours with a Russian spy than all of the law-enforcement people in that room combined.

Once the questions ended, I closed with a nod to the agents I worked with. They deserved it. "One of the major reasons that this worked is that I was given a tremendous amount of freedom to answer all of these questions for myself. Ted, Terry, and Lisa shielded me from the administrative and bureaucratic hurdles they faced every day. They deferred to me on many operational and tactical decisions. This allowed me to develop methods and processes that I felt comfortable using, that felt natural, ones the Russians were less likely to detect as duplicitous.

"I know how risk-adverse federal law enforcement can be, and this was a huge gamble. I hope all of you leave here with the impression that taking that risk paid dividends. Also, remember the other reason this worked: The operation was nontraditional, and so was I. We departed from the usual playbook. We didn't follow a script, at least most of the time. If we had, the Russians surely would've recognized the FBI's fingerprints. Then instead of me standing here with you and Oleg cooling his heels in Vladivostok, things would've been very, very, very different."

I paused for dramatic effect. "Remember," I said, "take the risk. Don't shy away from it. If we want to beat these bastards, we have to be creative, and we have to avoid the path they expect to find us on."

With that, the room broke into loud applause, and I tried not to blush.

My reflections didn't end at Quantico. I spent many hours asking myself questions and rethinking the answers I thought I knew. For a long time after my phony arrest, I was convinced the FBI had made a mistake by moving when they did. But I came to understand that, as upset as I'd been with the way we abruptly ended the operation, the timing did make a certain amount of sense. Ted, Terry, and I weren't working in a vacuum. There had been, I learned, other investigations that intersected with ours. From the inside, I saw one important piece of America's relationship with the Russians. But mine wasn't the only one.

I kept thinking about what those three years had meant. How important was Oleg to the Russians and to the security concerns of the United States? How much damage did we do to Russian intelligence? What I had seen—was it the full extent of Moscow's corruption of the diplomatic process or just the tip of the Russian-espionage iceberg? How closely had the Russians been following me? How badly had we fooled them? What inkling did they have that the young American they trusted was a double agent working with the FBI?

For some of these questions, I would never know the answers. In casual conversations, background briefings, and whispered hints, I began to deepen my understanding. Some of my conclusions I grew confident of. Others, I am afraid, remain only guesses.

For instance, I grew certain that I was not alone as an active source of information for the Russians in New York. I became convinced that Oleg had other Naveeds and the Russians had other Olegs. The Anna Chapman arrests that followed my operation would prove that, with or without official confirmation. Chapman was a glamorous Russian national arrested in New York City in 2010 with nine others and accused of spying for Russia. She quickly became an international celebrity and a hero back home. After pleading guilty to a conspiracy charge, she was deported back to Russia in a prison swap and singled out by Vladimir Putin for her brave patriotism.

Terry told me he was convinced that the Russian Federation is as committed to learning American secrets as their Soviet predecessors ever were. They dedicate as many resources and personnel. The labels have changed, of course. The superpower balance isn't what it was. But the passion and the commitment, the focus and the dedication, are all equal to anything from the past.

How much did our efforts set back the Russians? Quite a bit, I came to believe. We tied them up. We pinned them down. We learned what they were missing and wanted from us. We didn't wait for them to stir. We took the fight to them. We followed Terry's dictum from the day we got the NATOPS manuals. We caught a spy by spying. The agents and I, working together, showed how proactive can be successful when it's done right. Across our three-year operation, we exposed the techniques, methods, assets, and networks that the Russians employ against a country that is supposedly their ally.

Never again can anyone complacently believe that Russia's so-called diplomats are practicing mere diplomacy. They are spies—some of them, at least. The only question is how many, how often, and where. Whether open-source or closed, the intelligence they are gathering is of value to them and a threat to us.

Ava and I learned a lesson from our FBI rush-hour-traffic fiasco. I didn't want to be late for my own intelligence swearing-in. So on the morning of June 5, 2009, Ava and I rode the subway downtown. By now, she was eight and a half months pregnant with our first son. Honestly, it was amazing she could get up and down the subway steps in her Old Navy maternity jeans and stretchy white top. I carried the camera bag and wore my light gray suit: We were headed downtown for serious business, and I thought I should dress the part, even though I was always more comfortable in knock-around jeans, a loose-fitting sweatshirt, and a pair of beat-up Nikes.

We walked slowly from the Chambers Street subway station to 26 Federal Plaza. After clearing security, we rode the elevator—the regular elevator—then walked down the hall to the navy recruiting office, the same one where I'd taken the Aviation entry test and been regaled by the stories of Commander Jeff Jones.

"Come on in," Juli said brightly when Ava and I got there. Juli was wearing her usual khakis, and her dark hair was pinned up tightly, like it always was. But there was a genuine warmth coming from her that I had seen only glimpses of before.

"You showed a lot of patience," she said. "I don't know too many people who worked for this as hard as you did. You waited a long time for the navy."

I smiled at that but said nothing. *If only you knew what I had to do,* I thought.

Before we got started, Juli handed me some paperwork. As I

have learned since, almost everything in the military starts with paperwork. She sat me down and began handing me forms to fill out. Medical benefits. Life insurance. A full list of my dependents. I'd have another name to add to that one soon. I'll admit, even the mundane act of signing navy paperwork felt important—especially when I came to the block that asked for "Rank/grade."

"Ensign/O1," I wrote proudly.

Terry arrived after I finished signing, though his trip was a whole lot shorter than ours was: He came down by elevator. He was wearing one of his standard-issue dark FBI suits.

"So they decided to take you, huh?" he said. "They said you had to get some experience, and you did. So what? They had to let you in? Is that about it?"

If strangers had wandered in off the street and overheard any of this, they'd have been certain Terry was a total asshole. I knew it was his way of saying how proud he was.

"I think I'm starting to understand," he said. "To get into the navy, you have to catch a Russian spy."

"At least one," I answered.

"I don't remember seeing that in the regs," he said. "But it must be in there somewhere."

"Thanks, Terry," I said.

Juli looked up at the mention of "Russian spy," but she never asked for a fuller explanation. Frank arrived, and everyone was there.

"You ready?" Juli asked me.

"Let's do it," I said, "before someone changes their mind."

Nothing is ever entirely a joke. I really did have the feeling that at any moment, this could all be snatched away. I certainly didn't want to risk that.

Juli showed me where to stand, next to a large navy seal on the bright blue carpet. An American flag stood in the corner to my right.

She asked me to raise my right hand. Without referring to notes, she led me through the U.S. Navy Oath of Office, speaking clearly and firmly the whole way.

"I, Naveed Jamali," she began.

"I, Naveed Jamali," I repeated.

"Having been appointed an ensign in the United States Navy . . . "

"Having been appointed an ensign in the United States Navy . . . "

And I repeated everything else she said: "Do solemnly swear that I will support and defend the Constitution of the United States against all enemies, foreign and domestic . . . that I will bear true faith and allegiance to the same . . . that I take this obligation freely, without any mental reservations or purpose of evasion . . . and that I will well and faithfully discharge the duties of the office upon which I am about to enter—so help me God."

Then Juli turned to the other three and said: "Ladies and gentlemen, I present to you the newest ensign in the United States Navy, Naveed Jamali."

There were only three of them, but they all flashed giant smiles and applauded furiously. I smiled so hard I thought my teeth might crack.

Juli went to her desk and retrieved a framed copy of the commissioning letter that she'd pulled off her computer, the one she'd told me the navy doesn't usually bother sending anymore. "Here," she said.

I told Juli how impressed I was that she knew the Oath of Office by heart. She laughed. She was clearly proud of that.

"I want you to promise me something," she said. "When you get assigned to a unit and you start to issue the oath for reenlistment, please don't read off a paper. The oath isn't that long. Memorize it! Reading takes the seriousness and majesty away."

She had a point, I thought. I liked that she understood the deep importance of joining the military, even if she couldn't possibly know every recruit's inspiration, what monumental steps were taken, and what dreams led each individual to this place. I promised her I would never read an enlistment oath as long as I was in uniform.

Ava had taken out the camera and was taking pictures. A picture of me with the framed letter. A picture of me in front of the flag. "I need a shot of Naveed and Juli," she said.

As Juli and I posed together, I noticed Terry scampering away, making sure he wasn't in the shot. "I don't want to ruin the pictures," he said. Even in the safety of the navy office, the agents didn't like being photographed.

I don't know how I could have been more grateful or more thrilled. I had set a goal, and I had achieved it. I had picked up where my parents left off—they are real heroes for serving their adopted country— and built on what their twenty years of patience had achieved. I had helped my country and was beginning the next chapter of my life. I was celebrating all of it my way with some of the people who had helped make it happen. This day, this appointment, was what I'd been aiming for.

Now, I was convinced, I could do for the navy what I had been doing for the FBI. Going undercover. Fighting espionage. Officially attached to a program this time. Serving as a full-fledged team member, not someone hanging out there on his own.

"This is gonna be awesome," I told Juli. "I know it is."

Anything was possible. Maybe I'd end up in Singapore or Brussels or some coastal nation in Africa like Commander Jones had suggested, or maybe I'd be assigned to Oleg's old turf, the United Nations.

I had always heard people say, "Try to turn your passion into a career." I was doing that. And going forward, I wouldn't be an affiliate with no official connection. I'd be doing it for the U.S. Navy. The double agent, retired, was truly coming in from the cold.

Ava gave me a giant hug. Terry and Frank shook my hand and patted me on the back.

"I really want to thank both of you for everything . . ." I said, trailing off.

"Listen, Naveed," Terry said sternly. "You did this. This is your accomplishment. We helped make some introductions. But this is all you."

He was being nice, but I was certainly proud. I had done something for my country that no one could have expected me to do. I had looked inside myself and found talents I never knew were there. I had stayed strong, stuck with it, and put myself on the line. I had beaten the Russians, helped America, and made some lifelong friends. Now I was heading off on an amazing new adventure. There was only one thing missing. Too bad, I thought, Lino wasn't here to share what he had launched.

As all those thoughts were rushing through my head and everyone was standing around, Frank gently pulled me aside. "You know that oath you just took?" he asked me.

"Yeah?" I said.

"We take an oath very similar to that one," he said. "Welcome to the team, man."

God, I'd been waiting a long time to hear somebody say that.

Acknowledgments

It turns out that running a counterintelligence operation and writing a book have a lot in common: They both require a team of dedicated professionals. First and foremost, thanks to my brilliant coauthor, Ellis Henican, who helped me tell my story right. As a first-time author, I am extremely grateful to the team at Foundry Literary + Media, who helped shape the project from the start: my agent, Hannah Brown Gordon; foreign rights agent, Kirsten Neuhaus; and agency partner, Peter McGuigan. I am just as fortunate to have been paired with a wonderful crew at Scribner—two excellent editors in Paul Whitlatch and Brant Rumble and a driven publicity posse headed by Brian Belfiglio and supported by Kyle Radler. For smart insights and generous help, I also owe three publishing pros on the rise, John Glynn, Jane Callahan Dornemann, and Roberta Teer. Many thanks to Creative Artists Agency, especially to Michelle Weiner and Zach Nadler, for giving the story a life far beyond the printed page. Lastly, thanks to my lawyer, Loan Dang, for her tireless efforts on my behalf.

While I can't use their real names, I am forever indebted to the FBI agents who watched over me: Ted, Terry, and Lisa. They are true professionals whose daily duty is nothing short of keeping our country safe. I feel honored to have known them and lucky to have worked with them.

Transitioning from amateur double agent to uniformed member of the military was a huge culture shock for me. Luckily, I had excellent mentors and friends to help me through. This project would never have come to life if my good friend and shipmate Jake L. hadn't encouraged me to write about my experiences and introduced me to my agent. Deep thanks also to navy recruiters Lino Covarrubias and Juli Schmidt, who helped me achieve my dream, and to my navy mentors John B., Tony A., and Mark W., who showed me that being a great leader is synonymous with being a great teacher. One of the unintended benefits of joining the navy was meeting some friends whose humor and support have cemented lifelong bonds: John W., Charles A., Dan M., Chris F., and Kris C., among a blessedly long list of others. There is also Doug K., a man who describes himself as "the Hispanic George Clooney" and I call a friend, mainly because the alternative is far, far worse.

The book was helped immensely by two extraordinary technical advisers: Frank Figliuzzi, former FBI assistant director for counterintelligence, and Captain Gary Barron, reserve naval intelligence community lead. Those two know everything.

Thanks to Alice and Stuart Brent for all their thoughts and suggestions, and to Nancy, Mark, Alice, and Adam for their friendship. Finally, thanks to my parents, Claude and Naseem Jamali, for launching this long adventure by bringing the Russian into our lives in the first place.